The Best of

Reminisce

WE FIND IT HARD TO BELIEVE, but *Reminisce* has been "bringing back the good times" for over a decade now, since 1991! With so many years behind us, it seemed time for this memories magazine to do some reminiscing of its own.

This big volume brings together a variety of popular stories and photos from the first 10 years of *Reminisce* and *Reminisce EXTRA*. Choosing from thousands of great memories published wasn't easy, either, because all of them are special.

At *Reminisce*, we get a kick out of being different from most magazines. The true-life stories found on our pages are mostly "written by the readers", not professional writers. These folks took time out of a busy day to put heartfelt memories on paper and send in precious family photos. Pretty incredible, when you think about it.

We'd like to thank every contributor who has shared a little piece of their past with us through the years. And we thank those loyal subscribers who make up the *"Reminisce* family". With support from readers like you, we'll keep bringing back the good times...and plenty of smiles.

Bettina Miller
Editor

The Best of
Reminisce

Editor: Bettina Miller
Assistant Editors: John Schroeder, Lee Aschoff
Copy Editor: Kristine Krueger
Editorial Assistants: Blanche Comiskey, Melody Trick
Photo Coordinator: Trudi Bellin
Art Director: Kristin Bork
Production: Ellen Lloyd, Catherine Fletcher
Photo Set Designer: Sue Myers
Photography: Rob Hagen, Dan Roberts
Photography Studio Manager: Anne Schimmel

The Magazine That Brings Back the Good Times

Editor: Bettina Miller
Managing Editor: Lee Aschoff
Associate Editor: John Schroeder
Copy Editor: Kristine Krueger
Editorial Assistants: Blanche Comiskey, Melody Trick,
    Jack Kertzman, Mary Ann Koebernik, Kris Lehman
Photo Coordinator: Trudi Bellin
Contributing Editors: Clancy Strock, Hal Prey
Food Editor: Janaan Cunningham
Recipe Editor: Janet Briggs
Test Kitchen Home Economist: Sue Draheim
Design Director: Jim Sibilski
Art Director: Sue Myers
Photography: Rob Hagen, Dan Roberts
Food Photography Artists: Stephanie Marchese,
    Vicky Marie Moseley
Photography Studio Manager: Anne Schimmel
Production: Ellen Lloyd, Catherine Fletcher
Publisher: Roy J. Reiman

© 2002 Reiman Media Group, Inc.
5400 S. 60th St., Greendale WI 53129
Reprinted, 2009

Reminisce Books
International Standard Book Number: 0-89821-345-2
Library of Congress Control Number: 2002107256
All rights reserved. Printed in USA.
Cover Photo: Harold M. Lambert
Back Cover: RP Photo

For additional copies of this book or information
on other books, write: Reminisce Books,
P.O. Box 26810, Lehigh Valley, PA 18002-6810
or visit CountryStoreCatalog.com. Credit Card
orders call toll-free 1.800.558.1013.

In This Memorable Book

4

By Clancy Strock
Contributing Editor

HERE IT IS, a warm and sunny Sunday. Church services are over and the brunch dishes are cleaned up…now what?

Let's check the TV listings in the paper—there's a baseball game on one channel and a pro golf tournament on another. The local movie houses are offering a wide choice of films, but none holds much appeal. There's a book I haven't finished, but it's not due back at the library for a while.

Years ago, families never faced such indecision on Sundays. The unanimous choice was always the same: Let's go for a drive!

For my family in Sterling, Illinois, Sunday just wasn't Sunday without a long meandering drive to nowhere in particular. The main idea was to get out of the house and see what was going on in the world.

"Where shall we go?" Dad would ask. We'd all chip in with ideas—the airport…Castle Rock Park…Aunt Martha's house…wherever.

Whose Crops Were Tops?

Living on a farm as we did, our summer drives always began with Dad checking out the neighbors' crops. Who had the tallest corn? Had the drought burned up their pastures as much as it had ours? Were the oats far enough along for the threshing ring to swing into action?

Many a Saturday morning, Dad sent me out with a scythe to cut down the weeds along our roadside fence. He figured it would make his corn look taller to the neighbors who'd be taking their Sunday drives!

Sometimes we'd set out for a nearby town to "drop in" on friends or relatives if they happened to be home and not taking their own Sunday drive.

If we did catch them at home, we'd be warmly welcomed. Little Jimmy would be sent scooting to the neighborhood grocery for a few pints of ice cream (there were no refrigerators with freezer compartments back then) while the hostess made iced tea or lemonade.

The kids from both families would scurry upstairs, where the girls would

H. Armstrong Roberts

Whatever Happened to Sunday Drives?

talk about new doll clothes, and the boys would inspect a balsa wood model airplane under construction or haggle over baseball card swaps.

Meanwhile, the adults sat in the living room or on the porch talking about weather, politics, local events and when —if ever—the Depression would end.

One Sunday each month, we visited my dad's Uncle Otto and Aunt Mary. When we arrived at the older couple's home, my sister, Mary, and I would be shooed into the front parlor, where we were allowed to inspect Uncle Otto's remarkable collection of coins from all over the world.

When we became bored with that, we'd open the latest copy of *National Geographic* and catch up on tiger hunting in India and boomerang throwing in Australia.

That got boring, too…but what came next was worse. Mary and I felt like convicts doing time on death row, knowing that when the adults had finished gossip-

ing, they'd expect a "concert". Mary would get out her violin, and I'd uncase my cornet. Even in the best of hands, violins and cornets are not ideal instruments for duets. Somehow we labored through a hymn or two and perhaps *Whispering Hope* or *The End of a Perfect Day*. We were awful.

Picnics Were Pleasant

My favorite Sunday drives were in summer when Mom packed a picnic lunch. There were lots of nice parks within 40 miles of home, many of them alongside the Rock River.

We'd find a peaceful spot and feast on cold fried chicken, potato salad, coleslaw, fresh rolls, pickles and olives, washed down with lemonade from the big green thermos jug. A thick chunk of chocolate cake topped things off.

Then we'd just sit on the grass under a big old elm tree and watch boats scoot up and down the river past fishermen who never seemed to catch a fish.

Another favorite destination was

White Pines Forest State Park. A swift shallow stream wound through the park, and the main road crossed that stream four times.

There was a narrow footbridge across each ford, but most cars simply plunged right through the hub-deep water, to the accompaniment of happy shrieks from passengers. The footbridges were lined with whooping kids hoping to be splashed with a refreshing spray of the cool clear water.

That park was heavily wooded with a magnificent stand of towering trees. Trails padded with pine needles meandered through them, uphill and then down into dark glens heavy with ferns. No man-made cathedral I've ever seen comes close to the beauty of that forest.

At least once each summer, we'd take a Sunday drive to a nearby gristmill. It was owned by an ancient gentleman who claimed the Indian chief Black Hawk used to make regular visits to have corn ground for his band of warriors.

Looking back, I think it's unlikely the old fellow ever actually met Black Hawk, but his stories were spellbinding.

The real purpose of our visit was to gather watercress that grew near the mill, where springs bubbled up out of limestone rock. The watercress was crunchy-crisp and sweet as candy. Trust me, it was worth the long journey.

In the fall, Dad knew a fine woods where hickory and walnut trees dropped an abundant crop. Gunnysacks in hand, we gathered our winter nut supply while squirrels protested above.

Another good day trip was to the northwestern corner of Illinois, magnificent rolling country you'd never

"*It was good to get out and see what was going on in the world...*"

expect to find in our pancake-flat state.

We'd walk around Galena, where Ulysses Grant lived for many years. Then we'd stand on the banks of the Mississippi and try to envision how things looked back when the steamboats brought great log rafts downriver from Minnesota and Wisconsin.

Not too far away was the state's vest-pocket version of the Grand Canyon, the Apple River Canyon. Trails went down into the deep gorges, where your shouts were rewarded with echoes that bounced around like a Ping-Pong ball.

As fine as my memories of Sunday drives remain, I do recall some down sides. Roads weren't terribly good back then, and tires were prone to blowouts.

Dad carried a patching kit and pump so he could repair a flat tire on the spot. While he was sweating and grumbling, Mom sat in the car fanning herself and we kids explored the roadside ditches, practiced our cow-calling skills or petted a horse that came up to the fence.

After World War II, when I had a family of my own, a favorite Sunday diversion was a drive to model homes. It wasn't that we were in the market for a new house...it was just fun to see how "the other half" lived. Some of those homes even had *two* bathrooms!

I've since learned that real estate agents everywhere call folks like us "Sunday gawkers".

Enjoyed Ups and Downs

A perpetual Sunday drive request from our kids was for a trip on "the roller-coaster road". That was a hilly blacktop stretch a few miles outside of town that featured a long series of abrupt ups and downs.

Traveling briskly along this road, everyone in the car came close to weightlessness as we topped each hill and were then mashed into our seats at the next dip. It wasn't exactly NASA training for life in outer space, but it came close.

And speaking of flight, it was always fun to drive to the nearest airport, park near a runway and watch airplanes take off and land. Where had they been? Where were they going? That's a Sunday diversion some families still enjoy.

No matter where you lived, there were plenty of interesting Sunday drives. You could take another look at homes where your ancestors once lived ...check the progress on the new barn a neighbor was building...visit "shirttail" relatives...or take in a nearby town's Watermelon Festival or Sauerkraut Day or Fourth of July parade.

Wherever you ended up, it was good to get out of the house and see what was going on in the world.

What to do, what to do? What could be better than another Sunday drive?

I know...I was there.

Clancy Strock's recollections have appeared in Reminisce and Reminisce EXTRA magazines since their early days. His looks back at unforgettable times bring a flood of shared memories from readers. ☏

SUNDAY SUPPLIES. Loading the family car for a drive meant filling the trunk with all the necessary supplies, including, of course, the picnic lunch Mom packed.

H. Armstrong Roberts

Our Brand-New Bel Air Was a Real Beauty

By David Brondel, Centertown, Missouri

NORMALLY I'd have been depressed on that August day in 1958. After all, in only 3 short weeks, I'd face what all 10-year-old boys dreaded—the nightmarish return to school.

But back in July, Dad had made August much more bearable by ordering a brand-new 1958 Chevrolet from Bommel Brothers Chevrolet in Westphalia, Missouri. The delivery date was the first week of August, so Mom, my sister, Kay, and I waited eagerly for that day when Dad would come home from work to announce our new arrival.

In 1958, anyone getting a new car was the envy of our small hometown of St. Martins. So Dad had a little spring in his step as he opened our front door after work. "Well," he said with a grin, "let's go get it!"

By the time Mom came out of the kitchen, Kay and I were already headed out the door toward our soon-to-be-traded '52 Chevy Deluxe.

The 25 miles to Westphalia was like a trek to the moon. I counted every fence post and found over 100 different positions a 10-year-old could assume in the backseat. When Dad finally announced that we were there, Kay and I left that old Deluxe like it was on fire!

I raced to the back of the building. "Dad," I yelled, "I can't find it—it's not here!"

I was about to have one of those fits the old people talked about—one of those terrible kinds that they called a "conniption".

"Just hold on, boy," Dad said with a bit of frustration. "We're not in the building yet. Keep your shirt on."

Once inside the showroom, a salesman shook Dad's hand and explained the car was in the service area receiving its final mechanical check. As the two men kept talking, I felt those conniption feelings welling up again.

Just Like Dinah's

Just when I thought my end was near, I heard the salesman tell Dad, "Well, let's go take a look, Mr. Brondel."

As we stepped through the double doors to the service area, my eyes locked on the most beautiful car I'd ever seen. Two-toned paint, chrome trim and chrome hubcaps accentuated the magnificent machine.

The colors, lavender and white, were new for 1958, we were told. (The car on *The Dinah Shore Chevy Show* was said to be this color, although there was no way to be sure, as our Philco television was black and white.)

Kay was first to sit behind the wheel. She'd be 16 in only 4 months and able to drive this wheeled wonder. Oh, how I hated the thought I'd have to wait more than 5 years!

Then Dad got in, depressed the clutch and turned the key in the ignition, waking the powerful engine from its sleep.

Finally, I slid in behind the wheel, dreaming of the day I'd be able to operate this thing on my own. I was inhaling the new-car fragrance when my eyes fell on the odometer. I couldn't believe what I saw—the mileage read 000015.

Who Drove Our Car?

"What's the matter, boy?" Dad asked.

"Look here," I said, pointing to the numbers. "Somebody's been driving our car. It ain't new!"

Carefully, Dad explained how new cars had to have a few miles on them. Otherwise, how could they test them at the factory for defects?

Well, I admitted to myself, I suppose that's why he's the dad and I'm just the kid.

Soon after, we took a trip to Little Rock. Several more trips followed as the years went by. That old '58 Chevy saw me through my first date and a few more besides. In fact, it stayed in the family until 1972 as the odometer piled up a whopping 128,000 miles.

Dad's gone now, and so is that '58 Chevy. But my boyhood memories of a time when worries were few and summers were heaven will never fade. ☎

SEE THE USA. David Brondel, left at age 10 in the spring of 1958, was really smiling that summer when his dad traded in this 1952 Chevrolet for a brand-spanking-new 1958 model (shown at top left). The family drove the '58 for 14 years.

How I Loved Making Ice Cream at Gramma's

By Yvonne Leslie, Mt. Clemens, Michigan

ON HOT SUMMER Sunday afternoons, my family joined aunts, uncles and cousins at Grampa and Gramma's farm to make ice cream.

"Hurry now," Gramma would say to us kids after giving us hugs. "Go get some milk and cream."

Down to the springhouse we'd run. Built from stone, that springhouse had the cool feeling of a cave. How we loved to walk inside and feel the cold floor against our bare feet. A 5-gallon metal can was waiting there, filled with rich cream and fresh milk from Grampa's black-and-white Holsteins.

When we returned, Gramma would say, "Now, go get some eggs."

Off we'd dash to the chicken coop, where brown and red hens fiercely protected their freckled eggs. While my brothers distracted the furious little birds, my sister and I collected the eggs we'd need.

Using the eggs and milk we brought her, Gramma cooked the custard. Meanwhile, Grampa crushed ice in a clean feed sack with a mallet. Then he filled a metal canister with the custard and placed it in the center of the wooden ice cream bucket.

As he layered ice and salt around the bucket, Grampa solemnly explained, "You've got to have the right proportion of salt to ice. Too little, and the cream won't freeze…too much, and it'll freeze too fast and be lumpy."

Cranking Was a Contest

Grampa, Dad and an uncle took turns cranking the freezer while sitting on the steps of Gramma's shady back porch. As they cranked, they joked about their strength, seeing who could turn the handle longest.

"Turning's easy until the ice cream starts to freeze," Grampa reminded. "Just see how strong you are then!"

While the men worked and the women visited, we kids and our cousins stole slivers of ice to put down each other's shirts and chased one another around the house and under Gramma's weeping willow. We'd regularly stop to ask the men, "Is it ready yet?"

After about an hour of cranking and questions, the ice cream was finally firm enough, and Grampa would announce, "Get your spoons!"

With great ceremony, he slowly pulled the wooden dasher from the middle of the hardened ice cream and placed it in a large bowl. All the children gathered 'round to help scrape the pale yellow treat from the dasher and taste the icy confection inside the canister.

That was the only taste we'd have for a while, because Grampa would cover the ice cream container with more ice in order to allow it to "set". But we'd group around that freezer and look at it so longingly that Gramma soon took pity on us and pronounced the mixture ready.

Time to Dig in!

She served sliced peaches to top the frozen treat—for the adults, that is. We children, purists all, ate our ice cream plain.

The rich, eggy-flavored concoction tasted absolutely wonderful. The texture was smooth with just a hint of graininess, and the temperature was tongue-numbingly cold!

Minutes after starting to eat, we kids would slowly set our bowls down and grab our foreheads, softly moaning. The dreaded "ice cream headaches" had struck!

As the dull, cold ache gripped our foreheads, our mothers would scold, "You ate too fast! Now slow down—there's plenty for everybody!"

The only cure was to dance around the yard holding our heads. As soon as the pain diminished, we'd pick up our bowls again.

When we were stuffed, we'd lie down on the lawn until our parents were ready to leave.

The ice cream had been great, and the visiting was so much fun. That's why we never failed to ask our parents on the way home, "Can we come back and make ice cream with Grampa and Gramma next Sunday?"

Musical Memories

These folks will never forget the sweet sounds of yesteryear.

Take That, Benny

WE NEEDED a band for our senior ball at Towanda (Pennsylvania) High School in 1936. So I wrote to Benny Goodman and asked him what he could send for $500.

His answer? A piccolo player.

Then I contacted Hal Ritter and his local "Red and Black Pennsylvanians". We got a 10-man band for 4 hours for $45.

—*Albert Remsnyder*
Towanda, Pennsylvania

Dropped from The Charts

MY FIRST JOB was in 1951 at The Lunch Box, a little truck stop in Skokie, Illinois. The place was too small for tables, so it had just a counter with about 30 stools.

There were those little jukeboxes on the counter, too. For a dime, you could play current hit records.

Each day my friend Grace and I would play *Because of You* on the jukebox, over and over. Then one day we found the song was no longer listed.

We asked the owner, Carl Reed, what had happened. He said his mother, who also worked there, couldn't stand to hear the song once more and had taken it off.

—*Joan Smith Bicknase*
Cary, Illinois

BASS MAKERS. When Roland Washburn (right) kept asking for a string bass, his father, Jesse, suggested they make one. The two studied violin making and, after a few months and many hours of hard work, they succeeded. Roland played the bass in high school, then went to Brigham Young University—but he quit school to go back to making basses. In a year, he finished five. BYU bought four, and one went to a bass player at the Coconut Grove Ballroom in Salt Lake City. Roland, now of Mesa, Arizona, kept the first one and played it for many years at dances in Utah, Wyoming, Montana, Idaho, Oregon and Washington.

VOILA, THE VIOLA! "In 1926, I was a 12-year-old budding musician with the junior orchestra at Mark Twain School in Webster Groves, Missouri," writes Ione Pinsker of Fortuna, California (second row, right of the triangle). "By the time they got to me, the only remaining instrument was the viola, which I disliked, but I had promised to finish the semester on any available instrument. My real education was learning to appreciate music and recognize and enjoy accomplished musicians."

Still Spinning Her Musical Memories

WHEN THE 45-rpm records came out in the 1950s, we bought a portable player, not because it was portable, but because it was cheap. Closed, it looked more like a suitcase rather than a record player.

We had Sun Records by Elvis and Jerry Lee Lewis, and records by Pat Boone and Perry Como among others. Eventually we had to buy a stand that had room for the player on top and the records on the bottom.

We bought most of our records at the five-and-dime store in Sonora, California. Once or twice a year, we'd go shopping in Modesto, where there was a "real" record shop.

Eventually, 33-1/3 records came out, then cassette tapes. But many of my favorite songs were on the 45s, so I taped them and can listen to them in the car.

Now I can still enjoy the music, and the memories.

—*Delores Jones Dennis*
Lexington, Kentucky

NO, NOT *THAT* NBC. "When I was a student at the National Business College in Roanoke, Virginia in 1936 and 1937, I sang with our college orchestra, the Ambassadors," writes Mary Davis Cruise of Paradise, California. "The only name I remember is Lewis Shropshire, the serious-looking fellow in the middle of the back row. He instructed the band and kept it together."

SHOCKED SOUSA. Les Tobiason (far left) and his fellow bugle players surprised the great bandleader.

Bandleader Beamed

IT WAS intermission at a 1928 Sunday-afternoon concert in the Milwaukee Auditorium, and John Philip Sousa's famous band had left the stage. This was the cue for our South Division High School band to take the stage.

We were to play under Sousa's direction as a reward for winning the city band tournament that year.

Sousa, who was 74 at the time, stepped up to the podium to direct us in his own composition, *The Thunderer*. When we reached the part where he'd included a bugle call, Sousa went to the cornets and trumpets, which usu-ally played it, only to be shocked to see them rest their instruments.

That's when five of us, standing near the band, played the part on our bugles, which were long "show trumpets" without valves.

Smiling, Sousa directed the band to the end of the number. After bowing to the applause, he walked over to ask about this change in the piece.

Our director explained that the five of us wore white uniforms, in contrast to the band's blue ones. We marched in the front row to play a fanfare before each number, including the bugle call for *The Thunderer*. Sousa liked the idea and shook hands with each of us.

Now I tell my grandchildren and great-grandchildren that although I couldn't play a regular instrument, except the Boy Scout bugle by rote, I played under the direction of the great John Philip Sousa! —*Les Tobiason Eugene, Oregon*

MUSICAL ROOTS. "A few years after this picture was taken at the Corinth, Montana schoolhouse in 1933, my brothers and I formed the 'Montana Hot Shots'," relates Arnold Almer (third from left) of Vancouver, Washington. "Calvin (third from right) played accordion; Gordon (second from right) played drums. I played the banjo. For dances at War Man School on the Crow Indian Reservation at St. Xavier we got $1 each, which was considered good wages."

The End of a Perfect Day

By Albert V. Burns, Spanish Fork, Utah

I WAS my mom's first child, born late in the afternoon one day in March 1924.

That evening, my father brought our family radio to the hospital in Elizabeth, New Jersey. It was equipped with headphones; Dad figured it would provide Mom some entertainment without disturbing other patients.

After an hour of getting nothing much but static, he finally found some music. He listened through one headphone, my mother through the other.

A tenor was singing the Carrie Jacobs Bond classic *A Perfect Day*:

"When you come to the end of a perfect day,
And you sit all alone with your thought,
While the chimes ring out with a carol gay,
For the joy that the day has brought..."

It was the only music they could pick up that evening, so it became the lullaby with which Mother sang me to sleep when I was an infant. Later on, in childhood, when I'd come to her with some hurt, she hummed "our song" as she treated whatever pain the sharp edges of the world had inflicted, whether physical or emotional.

On summer evenings while I played outdoors, I could hear Mother playing the piano in the living room. Whenever I heard *A Perfect Day*, I knew it was time to gather up my younger brother and sister, go in the house and get ready for bed.

Later, I joined the Boy Scouts and was allowed to stay out until the unheard-of hour of 9:30 p.m. As I walked home and neared our house, I started whistling the song.

Whistled Their Song

"For memory has painted this perfect day,
In colors that never fade,
And we find at the end of a perfect day,
The soul of a friend we've made."

Years later, when I returned home from World War II with a medical discharge, I asked the cab driver to let me off a block from home. Once again, I walked down the street whistling our song. Mother came running out the front door, apron flying, to greet me with tears in her eyes.

A few days later, my aunt asked if I knew that, before I went into the Air Corps, Mother never went to sleep at night until she could hear me coming down the street whistling and knew that I was safely home.

The years passed and my career took me and my family to Peru, Mexico, Los Angeles and finally, Honolulu, Hawaii. Those were long years, with only short, too-infrequent visits home. Then, in 1964, a cable arrived from Tucson, Arizona: "Mother in hospital. Serious stroke. Come ASAP. Dad."

When I arrived at the hospital, Dad and my sister and brother were at Mother's bedside. Since her stroke, they had been trying vainly to communicate with her.

There Wasn't Much Hope

The doctor said the damage was so severe that there was no hope that she would recover consciousness. In fact, he said, he couldn't figure out how she had held on to life for as long as she had.

I tried talking to her, to no avail. As the doctor had warned me when I arrived, she didn't even know we were there beside her:

Suddenly a thought struck: If words couldn't reach her, was it possible that music might?

With tears on my cheeks and with trembling lips, I tried to whistle. I found it was difficult, if not almost impossible, to whistle and cry at the same time. But finally, I was able to control my emotions enough to whistle for her:

"Do you think what the end of a perfect day,
Can mean to a tired heart,
When the sun goes down with a flaming ray,
And dear friends have to part?"

When I finished the stanza, there was an almost imperceptible movement of one of Mother's hands. Dad asked her, "Jessie! Jessie! Do you know who that is?"

Almost miraculously, her lips formed a weak smile. She said, softly but clearly, and with great love and pride, "My boy."

Her mind might have been beyond reach, but her heart had heard. Two words—just five letters—but their memory has bolstered my spirit through good times and bad for almost 4 decades since she whispered them.

A short time later, she gave a deep sigh, almost of contentment, and was gone. "Her boy" was once more safely at her side and Mother, at last, could allow herself to sleep. ☏

By Jay Lucas
Solway, Minnesota

I WAS 6 years old, in 1948, when I got my first "paid-for" haircut at the West Side Barbershop in Little Falls, Minnesota.

Normally, of course, Mom cut my hair at home for free. I couldn't see why she was making such a big deal about the fact that I'd gone to bed the night before and forgotten to take the chewing gum out of my mouth!

Having a big wad of gum stuck to my head really did not bother me. But it sure seemed to bother Mom. She'd tried her best to get the gum out using ice, combs, brushes and scissors—all to no avail.

Finally, in desperation, she'd phoned my dad at his grocery store and told him he had to take me to the barber. Neither of them were happy at the prospect of spending 25¢ on a store-bought haircut, but Mom was beside herself.

Dad dutifully left the store in the care of his clerk and walked me to the barbershop. I sensed some underlying tension—and I didn't think it was about the 25¢!

Dan, the kindly barber, was nearing retirement. His gray hair was trimmed short and neat. Mom had phoned ahead and explained the situation, so Dan greeted my dad with a friendly handshake.

Promised a Penny

Dan knew that this would be my first real haircut, and he seemed bent on making me a customer for life. He even promised me a shiny penny if I was a good boy.

I looked at Dad for his interpretation of our "never-accept-money-from-strangers" rule. Dad nodded his approval, then buried his face in *Field & Stream*.

Dan pumped up the barber chair and fiddled with it much like the dentist had on my first visit to him. Suddenly I began to get the picture—I was in trouble!

My entire body became rigid as Dan turned on his electric shears and began to mow. Not since the schoolyard bully had grabbed me by the hair had my head smarted so

much. Getting rid of that gum was not going to be pleasant!

Dan kept a firm hand on my shoulder and mowed away until the motor of his clipper began to melt from overheating. As the metal grew hot against my skull, I had visions of toasted hair.

Job Wasn't Done

Thankfully, the barber soon set the clippers aside and picked up his scissors. Apparently, though, he felt the "big job" was done and trimming up didn't require his full attention. He began talking with Dad about the Yankees and the Dodgers.

The old barber's hate for the Yankees was obvious as he punctured the air with his scissors each time he said. "Those blasted Yankees!"

Unfortunately, when he returned his scissors to my head, he'd do so without looking, often nicking me in the process. Each time I flinched, he passed along these words of encouragement, "Be tough like a man."

Mercifully, all things do pass. A few minutes later, I was able to make my escape from the West Side Barbershop—with nicked-up ears, a shiny penny and the shortest haircut in town.

At last, I was "a man"…and one, I might add, who never chewed gum in bed again! ☏

Ewing Galloway

My First Haircut Was
Shear
Terror

DIDN'T LIKE 'DO. The author thinks his hair is "geeky" in this photo of him and Mom on his first day of kindergarten. When he got his first real haircut from a barber, he reacted much like the young boy above.

I Became a 'Bromo Bomb'!

By Gerald Julian, Murray, Utah

BACK WHEN Harry Truman was whistle-stopping his way to an upset over Thomas Dewey, and television sets stood 4 feet high with a picture tube the size of a greeting card, our small town's high school basketball team was in the finals of the Utah State Tournament.

Two friends and I had traveled from American Fork, a rural town on the Wasatch Front mountain range, to the big city of Salt Lake to cheer on our team. We 16-year-olds checked into the 12-story Newhouse Hotel.

Went to His Head

It was my first stay in a hotel, away from the watchful eyes of my parents, and the excitement went to my head—in the form of a throbbing headache. I told my companions that I didn't know whether I'd be able to attend the big game.

My friend Kenny (whose dark penny loafers, yellow pegged pants and red hair made him resemble a pencil complete with eraser), suggested we stop at

a nearby drugstore on the way to the game and get something to make me feel better.

This big-city drugstore was unlike any I'd ever seen before. Out front, bold gold letters proclaimed the establishment "The Heinz Apothecary".

Pulling open the door, we felt as if we were stepping into a cathedral. Even the soda fountain, with its walnut-paneled bar, white marble top and dark stools, seemed more like an altar than a place to shoot the breeze with friends.

So This Is Bromo?

Gingerly the three of us sat down at the ornate soda fountain near a set of gleaming curved spouts sporting black handles that looked like jaunty top hats.

The soda jerk, dressed in a crisp white jacket and black trousers, put down the glass he was drying and asked, "May I help you?"

Chuck, my other friend, sensed my hesitation. With a nod in my direction, he said, "He'd like a Bromo-Seltzer."

The soda jerk tipped the hat of one of the spouts and partly filled a tall glass with water. Then, using one of those long ice cream soda spoons, he reached down the throat of a tall brown bottle and ladled out some white powder into another glass. Setting both glasses in front of me, he turned away to talk to Chuck and Kenny about the basketball tournament.

Although I'd often heard the musical jingles for Bromo-Seltzer on the radio, I'd never actually seen the stuff before. It seemed peculiar to me that it didn't come in tablets like aspirin, but I assumed that it was taken in the same manner.

So, picking up the glass with the powder, I dumped it into my mouth, then followed it quickly with the water chaser. As it turned out, that wasn't the smartest thing I've ever done.

Instantly it felt like a thousand ants were biting my tongue. Millions of mini explosions burst inside my mouth. The pressure bulged out my cheeks, and

my throat slammed shut to protect my windpipe.

Meanwhile, Chuck and Kenny were talking to the soda jerk, unaware of the twin balloons painfully distorting my

> ### *"Chuck and Kenny turned and stared at me in disbelief..."*

face...until white froth began shooting from the corners of my mouth in a fine spray.

Their conversation interrupted, they turned and stared in disbelief at my desperate hand-to-mouth combat. Just then, my cheeks reached their elastic limit

and my nose became a double-barreled seltzer dispenser!

Chuck, Kenny and the soda jerk all jumped back to avoid the Bromo blast. Afterward, as I bent over gasping for air, my friends and the soda jerk suddenly realized how this whole drama must have begun. They started laughing, slapping the countertop and each other and pointing at me.

"I'll help clean up the mess," I gasped when I could finally talk again.

"Forget it," the soda jerk said, wiping his eyes. "I owe you for a good laugh."

As the three of us headed for the door, Chuck asked, "Well, do you still have a headache?"

I looked at him in surprise. "No, it's gone."   ☎

Scrappy Youngsters Took Charge

By Robert Tessmer, Dearborn, Michigan

THIS PHOTO from 1942 shows a scrap drive for aluminum to be used in the war effort for building planes. My Boy Scout Troop 1111 in Dearborn, Michigan mobilized the effort. I'm the Scout on the far left with city officials standing behind me.

It was only 15 months later that I was drafted into the

100th Infantry Division and saw 6 months of combat service in the mountains of southern France during the winter of 1944-45.

I received the Bronze Star and Purple Heart medals for wounds in action, as well as the Combat Infantryman Badge, and I earned the rank of Staff Sergeant and Squad Leader.

Grandpa And I Made the Funnies Fly

By Brendan Sloan, Sioux Falls, South Dakota

WINDY SPRING DAYS always take me back to when my grandfather and I made kites out of lilac twigs, string and the Sunday funnies in Mitchell, South Dakota.

I remember how Grandpa came home quietly through the back door, with the newspaper under his arm, after tucking the old Mercury in the garage.

I knew his careful way of closing the door so it wouldn't slam, his soft shuffling tread and the gentle whisper of his twill trouser cuffs rubbing against each other as he walked into the kitchen.

Grandpa was a gas station attendant, and he proudly wore a green military-type cap with a big red star. I liked to wear that cap after he came home. It smelled of Brylcreem, Camels and the gas station.

Seated at the kitchen table, we'd plan our first kite of the season. Waving his hands toward the ceiling, Grandpa would lean back in his chair and explain the laws of aerodynamics. "That kite'll go higher than the water tower—higher than an airplane!"

After discussing our plans, we'd rush outside and cut some long lilac twigs before Grandma called us in to dinner.

That evening, construction began in the basement. The cut twigs—barely green on the inside—were bound with string to form a resilient cross. Notches were cut onto the outside edges, and more string was run around the perimeter to create the kite's skeleton.

Working there in the basement, just Grandpa and me, we could talk about Indian lore and a world of wondrous things. We'd kneel on the cold concrete floor near the stoker that rumbled coal into the furnace to keep away the chill of the evening.

Two dangling bulbs burned shiny reflections on the rows of jarred fruit regimented last fall and cast light on our tools— a stained coffee cup full of flour-and-water paste, a fat ball of string, lilac twigs and a stack of neatly folded Sunday funny papers. No gray newsprint kite would do for us!

After the paper was smoothed over the stick framework, the edges were pasted down tight and the whole thing was weighted down with a few pieces of scrap lumber to dry overnight.

Then it was time for me to go up to bed while Grandpa listened to the ball game on the radio.

When a good flying day finally came, the best rags were chosen from the scrap basket to make the tail. Grandpa always said, "When you're launching a kite for the whole town to see, you make it right from head to tail!" Ours was gorgeous.

We took it out together—he held the kite while I kept the tail and string out of the puddles.

From the top of our favorite hill, the spring wind took the kite from our hands and bore it up. No running for us; we offered the kite to the wind. If accepted, it flew…if not, we waited.

Up so high at the end of a long string, our funny-paper kite made a brave pink splotch against the blue prairie sky. For a long time, Grandpa made me believe he could still read *Terry and the Pirates* from the ground. I finally got wise to that one.

As our kite soared ever higher, we took turns holding the string and pulling the kite through its tricks.

A skinny little boy, a smiling old man and yesterday's newspapers…memories of those simple spring days still make me soar. ☎

>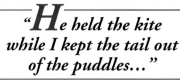
> "*H*e held the kite while I kept the tail out of the puddles…"

Would That Special Boy Bid for My Box Supper?

By Carol Conner, Colorado Springs, Colorado

"THERE," I said as I pasted on the last little window box filled with flowers. All the construction-paper windows were on the box now, along with a blue front door with a bead for a doorknob. There was even a tiny mailbox with a sign next to it that read, "Cottage for Sale."

"It really does look like a cottage!" I exclaimed.

It was my offering for the box supper at my country school in southeast Iowa. Mother and I had made mine different from the others by basing it on the popular song *Cottage for Sale*. It would be filled with goodies for whoever bought it at the auction.

I hoped it would attract a bid from curly haired, brown-eyed Paul. Up till then, we'd only exchanged glances at a distance. What if he bought my "cottage" and we got to sit together and share supper? My daydreams soared.

The Wait Was Endless

On the evening of the box supper, we kids participated in a program with recitations, songs and folk dances. I remember peeking through a hole in the stage curtain at our classroom, so unfamiliar a sight with all the grown-ups sitting there.

Finally, it was time for the auction.

Suspense built until I thought I'd burst! If only I could give Paul a clue. I looked at him, looked hard at my box and then back at him. He smiled, but his eyes didn't follow mine.

When my box was brought out, the tension grew worse. The bidding started slowly, and the price steadily went up. But Paul wasn't bidding! He hadn't yet bid on any of the boxes.

I became uncomfortably aware that one person seemed to be topping each bid made by any of the boys. It was a grown-up, every bit as old as the teacher!

Then a horrible thought hit me: Mother and I had done *too well* decorating the box—that man thought it was the teacher's!

I wanted to yell out, "No, it's not Miss Larsen's box, it's mine! Don't buy it! *Please*, don't buy it!"

Of course, I remained silent. Eventually the stranger outbid the bunch. Later, Paul bid on and won a box that looked like a covered wagon.

When the auction was over, the stranger worked his way through the crowd carrying my little "Cottage for Sale".

Dinner for Two

"I'm Augustus Troxel," he said. I told him my name and took the lid off the box. On top, Mother had put a special treat—stuffed olives in two little waxed paper packages.

Mr. Troxel picked one up, turned the package over and stared at it through the waxed paper.

"What's this?" he asked.

"Olives," I answered.

"Never ate those things," he said, putting it back in the box.

People around us were already eating, but Augustus kept glancing around the room.

Paul, looking embarrassed, stood with Miss Larsen—the covered wagon had been hers. Tears felt close. After all my work making that cottage, Paul hadn't even bid on it. I set out the sandwiches and celery sticks, thinking Mr. Troxel probably never ate those, either.

I dug deeper into the box, aware that the man had gotten to his feet. I took out the bananas and cake before I looked up.

I couldn't believe it—there stood Paul and the teacher! "Honey," Miss Larsen said to me, "these two men got things a little mixed up. Would you mind trading partners with me?"

Would I mind? She was offering me the greatest gift of my young life!

"No, Miss Larsen," I said as Paul smiled and sat down beside me. "I wouldn't mind at all."

MEMORABLE MEAL MAKER. In the early '30s, Carol Conner (above) made a box supper in the hopes that one fellow would buy it and they'd share. At the auction, things didn't look good!

We Battled 'Black Blizzards'

By Vendla Walton, Tucson, Arizona

I WILL NEVER forget my first "black blizzard". Rising above the western horizon like billowing smoke from a world afire, it rolled toward our little town of Garden City, Kansas at incredible speed.

Dashing to my car, I drove home and raced inside seconds ahead of an all-engulfing darkness that plunged a sunny day into midnight.

Gray powder sifted into the house, hung in the air and seeped into drawers, cupboards and closets. It invaded my ears, gritted between my teeth and turned my hair stiff and dingy gray.

We'd had dust storms before, but nothing like this monster. I don't remember how long that first black blizzard lasted—maybe 24 hours, maybe longer. One choking "duster" raged for 3 dirt-saturated days and nights!

After a while, it got so we could tell which state the dust came from by the color of the light that filtered through. A reddish tinge was Oklahoma...gray-black was Colorado...a yellowish hue meant Nebraska...dark brown was Texas. We didn't like the taste of any of them.

It was the mid-1930s. My school-teacher husband and I were newlyweds and, with the Depression in full swing, very thankful for his $88-a-month salary. I was happy to be cooking for two, but my bride-like dreams of a clean, cozy home had blown away on dirt-laden winds.

Hints for "Dust Busters"

Survival techniques were common topics of conversation among friends. We taped windows, rolled up rugs, took down curtains and packed away anything we could do without. Dishes were rinsed before each use, chairs and beds were shrouded in sheets and small rugs pushed against doors.

Inevitably, housekeeping standards plunged. If the color of the furniture showed through, why dust? If dirt wasn't thick enough to scoop, why bother?

One couple we knew was caught in a furious black blizzard on their way home from work. Their house was a couple of miles and two turns away, and they easily could have missed it in the darkness. But by following the curb (the only thing they could see), they eventually made it home.

Reasonably clear days were cleanup days—clothes were washed, furniture scooped off and floors cleaned. With an eye on the horizon, I'd hurry to get the clothes washed and dried and back inside before the next storm hit.

Life inside was bad enough, but outside there was often no life at all! The milkmen and mailmen didn't make deliveries, schools were closed and businesses had no business.

More Dirt Than Money

On not-so-bad days, milkmen and mailmen wore caps, raincoats or slickers and handkerchief dust masks. Dirt shoveled from the streets and sidewalks was trucked away, along with the dirt shoveled from inside buildings.

Buried lawns died. One man built a lawn vacuum cleaner on a cart but got discouraged at having to use it so often. Another disgruntled neighbor covered his yard in concrete and painted it green!

On surrounding farms, dust drifts buried machinery and fences. It was so deep, it sloped to the eaves of buildings. Roads were buried or blocked, and stock tanks that held water filled with mud.

It might seem that our married life had a grim, grimy beginning. Grimy? Yes. Grim? Not really.

Sure, it was difficult, but we were happily married and had great friends—young couples like ourselves, all with too much dirt and not enough money!

With the resiliency of youth and a we're-all-in-the-same-boat attitude, we laughed and griped together and had parties, fun and many happy times.

And...there was always the hope that some wonderful day, it would rain and the dust would settle for good. ☎

DUST BOWL DAYS. Top to bottom: Author's husband, H.L. Walton (on the left), and a friend prepared to brave the storm...special measures were needed for sleeping...local janitors dug out after a black blizzard in '35...and a farm wife shoveled mud from a water tank.

What'll We Get Dad for Father's Day?

By Eileen Ehnert, Kiel, Wisconsin

WHEN I WAS about 5 years old, back in the late 1930s, Father's Day wasn't the booming business it is now.

We didn't go to the nearest department store to our home in Germantown, Wisconsin to buy presents. We simply didn't have the money. But that didn't stop us from giving Dad something. Lacking the nickel to buy a greeting card, we made our own "wish card" after searching the seed catalogs and old Sears catalogs for appropriate "gift ideas".

We'd carefully cut out pictures of a rod and reel, a flashy red jacket, a battery for the car and a watch or diamond ring for good measure, then paste them on the cardboard from an old writing pad.

The edges were decorated with the most mouth-watering pictures of fruit and the prettiest flowers we could find.

When the big day finally arrived, we presented Dad with our wish card. This meant that we *wished* he would receive everything pictured on the card. Then we'd tell him about the present we *were* giving him—we were taking him fishing!

What About Bait?

Dad would be allowed to help us dig worms. The first couple of years when we presented Dad with our "fishing gift", it was a struggle to find enough worms. But after that, it seemed one corner of the garden was always miraculously damp and the worms much easier to find.

My oldest brother and Dad did the digging. The rest of us had to put the worms in the pail and would argue over who got to use the little shovel from the sandbox. We weren't about to touch those dirty wiggly things!

By the time enough worms were found, Mom had a picnic lunch packed. We thought we were ready to leave, but we always forgot to check the fishing poles first—after a winter of storage, some of them needed new line or sinkers and hooks.

Again, after our first few outings, things subtly changed. Around the middle of May, Dad would suddenly find he had "nothing to do" one Saturday afternoon and decide to get the poles ready. His explanation was that he wanted to be all set for our July vacation.

We always believed this and giggled in anticipation of his surprise when the fishing poles would be used in June.

Lots of Duties for Dad

Finally we'd be on our way. Dad fought the holiday traffic with four impatient, hungry, wiggling kids demanding that he hurry so all the good fishing spots wouldn't be taken.

Arriving at the fishing hole caused a lot of confusion. Everyone wanted their hooks baited first. But we wouldn't think of hooking on a worm ourselves—they squirmed too much. That was Dad's job.

Now came the best part of the day. We'd eat Mom's lunch while we jiggled our poles, hoping to attract the attention of some fat fish wandering past.

When the fish were biting, Dad was kept busy running from one kid to the other, removing our trophies and re-baiting the hooks. These duties were also his, along with untangling line and freeing snags.

By the end of the day, we were worn out from an exciting adventure in the fresh air. But it was worth it, because we had given Dad the best possible Father's Day.

He always told us so while we tumbled into bed…and he got ready to clean the fish! ☎

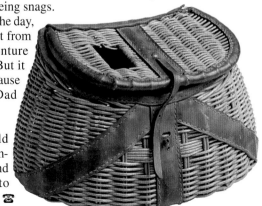

My Most Embarrassing Moment

Dad's Stroke of Genius

DURING the Depression, there was barely enough money for essentials, let alone the white shoes I was told I'd need if I were to perform in the school play.

Knowing there was no way I'd get a pair, I went to bed brokenhearted. So, imagine my surprise when I woke the next morning to find white shoes sitting by my bed!

My father, an interior decorator, had taken my old brown shoes and painted them white. I was so happy I thought I'd burst with joy. In fact, I was so proud that when I went onstage to say my piece for the school play, I told the whole audience about how my daddy had painted my shoes white.

The audience became deadly quiet. Then, suddenly, everyone started laughing and clapping. I never *did* get to read my poem.

I'm sure my parents were mortified, but I loved those shoes and wore them for a long, long time. —*Egypt Burden Lancaster, California*

Last One in the Pool...

DURING the 1928 football season at high school in Kearny, New Jersey, our coach, "Red" Fogarty, ordered us to stay out of the school swimming pool. "Swimming will soften muscles," he said.

But one late afternoon, following practice, a 190-pound guard said, "Hey, guys. The coach is still out on the field. Whaddaya say we take a quick swim?"

The varsity center and I said, "Let's go!" So the guard jerked open the shower room door that led to the pool, and we three *completely undressed* football players burst through—to the screams of a pool filled with girls!

The guard's momentum carried him right into the water. The center tried to stop but skidded on the wet tile, teetered on the edge of the pool and fell in.

I was able to sit down to stop my forward progress, turn and crawl back to the locker room.

News of the incident spread through the school like a Hollywood scandal. Every time I came near a group of girls, there were stares, whispers and a chorus of giggles. And I turned as red as a traffic light.

The coach never disciplined us. He must have figured our embarrassment was sufficient punishment.

—*Clavin Fisher West Simsbury, Connecticut*

Now What Did You Say?

WHEN I was a bashful 16-year-old, I went to a drugstore that was new to our area to buy the latest deodorant product, called "Fresh".

I picked up a few other items I needed while looking for the new product. When I couldn't find it, I went up to a male clerk at one of the cash registers and asked, "Can I get Fresh here?"

The clerk looked at me solemnly for a few seconds, then clarified, "The deodorant?"

It wasn't until I left that I realized how my question could've been misinterpreted. I was so embarrassed I never went into that store again.

—*Peg Shand, Brooks, Oregon*

And If Elected...

I RAN FOR seventh-grade representative at my junior high school in Downey, California in 1949. There was an assembly for the entire junior high body, and at the end we were supposed to give our names and tell what office we were running for.

I was scared to death and my knees were shaking. I got out my short statement and went back to my seat on the stage.

I was still a little shaky, so I put my hand on the chair before I sat down. Unfortunately, I put my hand on the seat portion of the folding chair, and it folded.

My arm went straight through, and I fell headfirst into the stage curtain. To make matters worse, I instinctively reached out for some support and grabbed the boy next to me, Bobby Waldren, around the neck. There I was, face down with my legs sticking out from

Do Not Read This Note

I BEGAN TEACHING biology at Elkhart High School in 1960. I had many embarrassing moments during those days, but one stands out.

I was giving a test, so the classroom was very quiet while my students were answering the written questions. I began writing the next assignment on the chalkboard when I happened to turn around in time to see a student passing a note to the kid next to him.

Quietly, I walked down the row to his seat and took the note, then went back to the board to finish writing the assignment. As soon as I was done and glanced down to read the note, the class burst into laughter. *I had been set up.*

I turned around with a red face. The note said, "Smile if you don't have any underwear on."

After class, word of the incident about "Mr. D" and the note was quickly passed around the school. Even the students in my next class were laughing.

I learned a lesson that day: Never read an intercepted note until class is over and the students are gone.

—*Ron Dannheiser, Elkhart, Indiana*

under the curtain, and the rest of me behind the curtain with Bobby in a headlock.

But I won the election. Everyone thought I'd done that on purpose and congratulated me on the best campaign skit of the assembly. —*Ronn Couillard Visalia, California*

Won by the Seat of His Pants

IN 1932, at the age of 8, I was a contestant in a horse-riding contest at a small circus sponsored by the local Masonic order in Brockton, Massachusetts. The prize was a pony and saddle.

I was to stand on a broad-backed circus horse as he cantered around the ring. Each contestant was supported by a pulley and rope attached to a very wide belt around the waist.

Just as I got the hang of it, the man at the other end of the rope gave it a little pull, so I was now standing on tippytoes. I struggled to keep my balance, then noticed my pants were slipping down!

I was quite a sight for the audience—a boy holding up his trousers with one hand, while trying to keep his balance with the other.

The crowd responded with laughter and wild applause. And guess who won the pony? I did! (See the photo below.) —*Robert Sperry Bonita Springs, Florida*

Would You Like Coffee with That?

YEARS AGO, my husband and I took my sister and her husband on a 1-day sightseeing trip to Niagara Falls, which is about 90 miles from our home in Erie, Pennsylvania.

After a lovely day, we stopped for

Uncle Lampooned Messy Apartment

THE WORLD was my oyster. In 1961, I'd just landed my first job and rented my first apartment in a converted Victorian house in Pittsburgh.

I loved socializing, so my apartment didn't get much attention. One day that hit home, literally, when I came in and found a "present" from my Uncle Nick (right).

Nick was an illustrator with a local advertising firm and did cartooning as part of his job. He called my attention to the mess the best way he knew how—with a cartoon.

The cartoon (above) shows me in the kitchen with the sink piled high with dishes. There are various kinds of vegetation growing from the stove, oven, windowsill and refrigerator. The floor is more like a lawn, complete with groundhog, rabbit and a robin pulling out a worm.

You can bet I got out the mop and bucket pretty quick.

I later moved to a newer apartment, and good ol' Uncle Nick was there to help me clean it. —*Joan Zekas, Pittsburgh, Pennsylvania*

dinner at a well-known restaurant. The restaurant was noted for its food, and its darkened atmosphere was considered "chic" at the time.

We had a number of appetizers and a delicious entree. After the entree, we were given another dish. Dessert, I figured, and dove in with my knife and fork. But the dessert was tough, and no matter how hard I sawed with the

knife, I couldn't cut it. That's when I noticed the others looking on in amusement, which soon turned to laughter.

In the dark restaurant, I had been trying to eat the hot napkin brought after the meal!

To this day, I don't know whether to laugh or blush when I see a hot napkin. —*Donna McCarthy Erie, Pennsylvania*

Our Small-Town Drugstore Was 'The Place to Be'

By Jerrold Anderson, Bonita, California

YOU WON'T HEAR modern teens ever saying, "Meet ya at the drugstore!" But when I was growing up in Frederick, South Dakota in the '40s and '50s, our drugstore, like similar institutions all across the country, was a haven for young people.

Norm Glarum and his wife, Mel, purchased the K&S Drugstore in 1945 and operated it for more than 30 years. We kids all respected Mr. Glarum, but none of us *ever* thought to call him anything other than "Norm".

With his ever-smoldering pipe, he looked a lot like a college professor. He had horn-rimmed glasses, a head of barely managed thick brown hair and a mischievous smile that seemed to say, "I know you did it...now, just tell me what and where!"

Passing out praise and criticism in equal measure, Norm was as likely to recognize an accomplishment as to offer an admonition to "spend a little more time with the books".

Norm the Coach

For an athlete, a Saturday morning visit to the drugstore was compulsory after Friday night's game. A critique from Norm was as valued as the same words from the coach.

Norm's arrival into the drugstore from the rear was usually accompanied by his rendition of a favorite old Dakota song in his best Scandinavian accent, "Oh the Johnson (pronounced 'Yonson') boys they owned a mill, they owned a mill way up on the hill..."

Summer days in South Dakota were often torrid. Most businesses were cooled by aging overhead fans, so the air-conditioning at K&S was a draw.

Entering the drugstore, you saw a candy counter on the right, behind which was a wondrous world of comic books (where a couple of kids could usually be found "browsing"). On the left was a magnificent soda fountain with a marble counter.

Just beyond the soda fountain were two booths facing a spectacular gazebo built right in the middle of the store. Inside were four more booths and a jukebox.

Said Good Night to Irene

For 5¢, we heard hits of the day. *Goodnight Irene* was played so often that one night a clerk took the record out to the alley and permanently "put it to sleep"!

Those interior booths were the most popular places in Frederick. As soon as school let out, kids sprinted to the drugstore to get one. Often, popularity depended on being fleet of foot.

Kids flocked to the drugstore for all reasons...if they were bored, when they were happy, to share the glory of a big victory or celebrate a successful school play. They came to see and be seen.

There was no doctor in Frederick, not even a school counselor—but Norm dispensed medications and admonitions in a non-judgmental manner. A young person was assured of an open mind and sympathetic ear, accompanied by a healthy dose of advice.

Today when I visit Frederick, I usually find myself standing in front of the old K&S Drug building, which now houses the public library.

Norm passed away in 1979, but I expect that he would heartily approve of the new tenants. After all, the building is still a storeroom of memories—memories of youthful laughter, mindless chatter, the clinking of glasses, shuffling of cards and a little South Dakota ditty, "Oh the Johnson boys..." ☎

THIS IS IT. K&S Drugstore was the place to be seen as a teen in Frederick, South Dakota in the '50s.

COUNSELOR. Owner Norm Glarum (left) and Mike Kroll, a friend of the author, posed outside the drugstore.

FOUNTAIN OF YOUTH. Norm dispensed both ice cream sodas and friendly advice to teenage customers at K&S Drugstore.

DRUGSTORE COWBOY. Jerrold Anderson, at 18 (left), strides the streets of Frederick, perhaps with a package from Norm's.

An Angel in the Back Row

By Helen Gage DeSoto, Apple Valley, California

I HAD ALWAYS BEEN SHY in large groups and was terrified of "getting up in front". But somehow, deep down, I felt that teaching would be different.

So I planned on a career in the classroom, and in my senior year of college, it came time for me to do practice teaching with real high school students.

I intended to teach English, but I ended up in a Spanish class. Spanish was my second major. Young for a college senior—not yet 20—I felt nervous about trying to control a roomful of students so close to my own age.

After graduation in the spring of 1941, my first teaching job was in Shorewood, Wisconsin, a suburb of Milwaukee. The real teacher did everything possible to help me adjust, starting me with small matters like taking attendance, grading and returning papers, dictating tests and working one-on-one when extra help was needed.

Gradually the students got used to me, and I got to know some of their strengths and weaknesses. I *should* have been in great shape to take over the running of a classroom.

Butterflies Attacked

When the day finally came for me to take full charge, the butterflies had charge of *me*. I tried to compensate for my nervousness by spending hours on lesson preparation. That way, so I hoped, nothing could surprise or rattle me. It didn't work that way.

After starting the lesson, I couldn't evoke a single

TEACHER AND AN ANGEL.
Helen Gage (top) feared looking young to her students, but she found respect from Jack Schmidt (above). Jack sent his photo after a *Reminisce* staffer found him listed in the phone book, still living near where the story took place. Jack, now of Whitefish Bay, Wisconsin, was happily surprised upon hearing of his former teacher's "thank you"…and Helen's wish is now complete.

response from my students. Not only were there no hands raised to answer my "stimulating" questions, but even the boys and girls I knew to be the smartest shook their heads or mumbled, "I don't know."

This was worse than butterflies. This was pillory. This was failure.

A cold realization flooded over me that what the skeptics had said was true—I might have the knowledge but would never have the temperament for this kind of work.

Would She Quit?

As I stared out at the class, my knees shaking and stomach in turmoil, I vowed that if I could just live through the hour, I would never return. I'd become a librarian or a researcher…anything but a teacher.

Suddenly, toward the back of the room, a boy raised his hand. "Would you repeat the question?" he asked.

Although my mouth was dry, I managed to speak and he answered…correctly!

He then asked me to explain something else, and the class began to stir out of its apathy. As the whole room miraculously came alive, so did I. The hour flew by in the most exciting way I had ever experienced.

To the Rescue

From then on, I found only delight in working with that class— and if things ever seemed to be getting slow, that boy came to my rescue. Because of him, I discovered I truly was a teacher—and a good one.

I'm retired now after more than 30 rewarding years in the classroom. I often think of that boy and what he did. He actually saved my career!

I don't remember the names of very many of the thousands of students I've taught, but I will never forget him.

After all these years, I still wish I could say, "Thank you, Jack Schmidt, Shorewood High School, Class of 1942. Your raised hand that day is the nicest thing anyone's ever done for me. It made a huge difference in my life." ☎

23

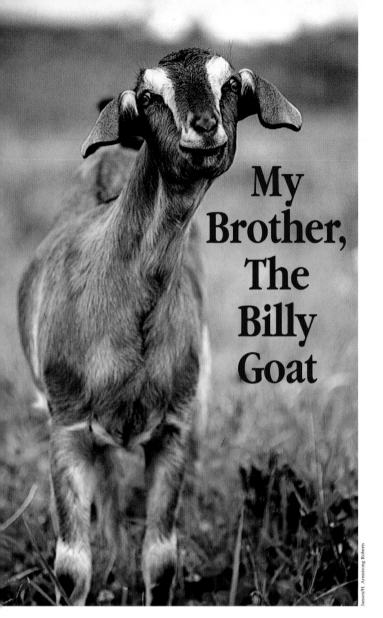

My Brother, The Billy Goat

By Libby Walsh, Eagle, Wisconsin
as told to Susan Sizemore-LaPorte

ONE CHILLY NIGHT in 1927, Dad sent us kids to bed much earlier than usual, promising us candy the next day if we retired without a fuss.

I was 6 years old at the time, the middle child of seven siblings. We all knew something was up, but we did what we were asked. Back then, you didn't question Dad—you just did what you were told.

Our house in Union, Illinois was big, but it didn't have the conveniences of running water, electricity or central heat. The kitchen had a pump where water was drawn for cooking, washing and baths...and there was an outhouse out back.

Since the only sources of heat were the potbellied stove in the living room and the cookstove in the dining room, little heat actually made it upstairs. But we were far too excited that night to notice the cold anyway.

What *Were* Those Noises?

Strange sounds were coming from downstairs. Curiosity finally got the best of me, and I started down the stairs to investigate. But Dad caught me halfway down and sent me back to my room.

Later, I heard the voice of a neighbor, Mrs. Helwig, downstairs. Then I heard a faint "putt, putt, putt" noise outside that grew louder by the second 'til it sounded as if it stopped right outside our bedroom window.

There was a knock at the front door, followed by Dad yelling, "I'm on my way!" This was odd, because nobody ever came calling this late at night. Hearing all those noises downstairs kept us children from sleeping.

Where's the Goat?

We were so excited that Dad had to come upstairs a few more times to try and calm us down. On his last trip, he told me that we had a new billy goat and that I could see it in the morning if I would just go to sleep. I was so delighted that I crawled into bed and squeezed my eyes closed so morning would come quicker.

Early the next day, my sister Bea woke me and we quickly ran downstairs looking for the new billy goat. Dad led us to a blanket-covered basket sitting next to the potbellied stove. He pulled back the blanket to reveal a little red, wrinkled baby...*boy*.

None of us children had known Mom was expecting, so the new baby was quite a surprise. To be honest, though, I remember feeling a little cheated because I'd gotten a new brother rather than a billy goat.

Dad later explained that the "putt, putt" noise was the town doctor's Model T pulling up to the house. We also learned that Mrs. Helwig was a midwife who helped deliver many babies in the area.

Two years later, we were in the middle of doing our chores one Saturday morning when Mom announced it was time for everyone to go outside to play. We were amazed since we hadn't finished our chores, although we were happy to comply! Mom even sent out a tray of peanut butter sandwiches with my eldest sister.

About an hour later, old Mrs. Helwig came hurrying down our walkway, not even stopping to say hello. At that point, Bea turned to me and said, "I think we're getting another billy goat!"

She was right. Later that afternoon, our sister Barbara was born. ☎

JUST KIDDING. No goats, but lots of kids, including the author, Libby (wearing long dress), and the "goat-boy" (in shorts).

24

My First Garden Party Was No Picnic

By Marie Hinkle
Granbury, Texas

PAIR OF PARTY-GOERS. With a fancy dress just like Grandma's, Marie Hinkle was all set for her first garden party.

THE INVITATION came in a small pink envelope scented with lavender. As Grandmother opened it, I leaned on the back of the chair, peering over her shoulder. I sensed it was something very special as she read:

Mrs. Eula G. Bates
requests your presence at
a garden party
on Saturday, the sixth of May
at three o'clock in the afternoon
in the rose garden
3516 Townsend Drive

The year was 1939, and we lived in Forth Worth, Texas. Grandmother was a member of the "Macabees", a ladies-only branch of the "Odd Fellows" lodge that met regularly for business and social activities.

The garden parties Grandmother attended always called for long dresses, gloves and freshly permed hair. Visions of tiny sandwiches and lemonade served in the garden filled me with a burning desire to be grown up enough to join her.

I pictured myself in a long satin gown, acting very proper as I nibbled on cookies and sipped punch. I wanted to experience the fragrance of the roses mixed with the ladies' perfume and smile smugly at the neighborhood kids peeking through the fence with envy.

I especially wanted to forget I was a skinny, freckled 8-year-old not likely to be included in any grown-up party.

When the big day arrived, Grandmother surprised me by calling me into her room. "We must hurry if you are to be ready to join me at the party," she said.

"But I'm not a grown-up lady, and I have no long dress," I replied tearfully.

Grandmother gently assured me I was her little lady and that she had just the dress for me. She slipped a long silky nightgown over my head and tied it at the waist with a blue ribbon.

It took some pulling and draping to make the "gown" short enough, but soon I felt like a princess. As a crowning touch, Grandmother tied a blue ribbon in my hair. I sat proudly in the front seat of her old Dodge as we drove through Fort Worth to the party.

The garden, as I recall, was in a small side yard surrounded by a white board fence. An arch over the garden gate was covered with roses, and honeysuckle grew on the fence.

It was fun looking at the ladies all decked out in their fancy long dresses and wide-brimmed hats. Most of the ladies were pleasingly plump, and I could tell their corsets were uncomfortable on that warm afternoon. Lavender perfume drifted across the garden and mixed with the scent of blooming flowers.

At first, I enjoyed listening to adult conversations while stuffing myself with cookies and trying not to spill my punch. But soon I became bored. Then my gown loosened at the waist and dragged on the ground, causing me to stumble and spill my punch.

I found myself wishing I were dressed in my old clothes and playing with the neighborhood kids peering in from the other side of the fence.

At last, the afternoon ended and we were on our way home. Curled up in the backseat, my gown stained with punch and my stomach aching from too many cookies, I drifted off to sleep.

My last conscious thought was, "Gosh, it's good to be a kid again!"

With Just a Box Top And a Dime...

By George McIntyre, Redlands, California

REMEMBER the roaring engine of Captain Midnight's plane above the somber tolling of a tower bell...or the chilling Comanche war cry of Straight Arrow galloping from a secret cave astride his golden palomino?

How about the hollow drone of a control tower operator transmitting landing instructions to Hop Harrigan, America's Ace of the Airways? If you do, it's a pretty safe bet you grew up during the '30s and '40s.

Yes, those were the opening themes for three of the more popular radio afternoon adventure series. During radio's "Golden Age", those day-to-day cliffhangers were serious business for millions of kids like me, when I was growing up in Garden Grove, California.

The most rewarding feature of being a steady afternoon listener was the opportunity to send away for all kinds of special secret equipment used by our heroes.

What Kid Could Resist?

No doubt the best remembered are the code-o-graphs from Orphan Annie and Captain Midnight. A new model came out every year—usually in the shape of a badge with a small rotating dial. Twenty-six different code combinations could be made for ciphering and deciphering messages, which were usually clues to the next day's story.

It was a "once-in-a-lifetime" opportunity to have the same item as our radio heroes, and it *didn't cost a single pen-*

ny...just a box top, pour spout or label, and a dime "to cover the cost of postage and handling".

After the announcer's buildup, often performed in a fevered frenzy, who of us could ever again venture outside the safety of our homes without the protection of a Jack Armstrong Egyptian Whistle Ring...a brass ring with a small siren-like whistle mounted in the center.

Hadn't the same ring saved Jack, Billy, Betty and Uncle Jim from disaster in the "Cave of the Mummies"? I vividly recall Jack himself telling us how we could mystify our friends by blowing on the ring while it was being worn, and no one would ever suspect the sound came from a ring.

Apparently, Jack's adventures had never pitted him against the likes of Miss Garrigan, my third-grade teacher. One short blast on the ring during history class brought her straight to my desk and the rather harsh removal of the ring from my finger.

How had she *known*?

The formula for obtaining these premiums was an action-packed adventure in itself. The first step was to convince my mother just how much my growing body needed the program's product.

Next came the Supreme Court Oath that I would single-handedly consume the entire contents of the package. This was frequently done while a half-empty box from the last premium offer was being shaken under my nose.

How I choked down some of that stuff, supposedly "chock-full of goodness", with a relishing smile between gulps is still one of the great unexplained mysteries in my life.

Finally the container was empty enough and the box top was mine. The box top and dime were then ceremoniously merged into an envelope crudely addressed to some far-off utopia called Battle Creek or Minneapolis.

Years later, my dad still teased me about how I would mail in my box top, then run into the house from school the next day asking, "Did it come yet?"

Alas, corduroy knickers were replaced with brand-new long pants, and it came time to enter high school. I brashly tuned those faithful radio companions out of my life, and the busy years of college, Army, family and career didn't allow much time for looking back.

Then, on a visit home, I wound up in the summer kitchen with my mother, rummaging through my old toy box…just as I'd left it more than 50 years ago. I found my prized Captain Midnight code-o-graph but realized the rest of the collections of rings, pins and badges had long been lost.

When I returned to California, I started my search. I contacted relatives and friends, begging permission to look through their attics and basements. No one was immune to my forage.

Antique shops, swap meets and garage sales became my homes away from home. The first year was far from promising, but the hunt went on. I began making contacts with other collectors across the country as we bought, sold and traded our treasures through the mail.

Once again came the wait, only this time, it was not nearly as long…and the prize not nearly as shiny and perfect as I'd remembered. Still, it held the same excitement, and more importantly, it was mine again.

Prized Premiums

I recently met a prominent Los Angeles attorney who told me his family was so poor when he was a kid, they could not even afford the dime, let alone the luxury of an 89-cent can of Ovaltine for its precious inner seal. To him, each premium Radio Orphan Annie offered was just another heartbreak.

Today, his collection of Orphan Annie premiums rivals

that of the Ovaltine Company archives in Chicago.

As you can see, I've had a wonderful time collecting old radio premiums. But I've also come to the sad realization that the kids of today will never experience the fun of radio heroes, box tops and little brown packages from Battle Creek.

For somewhere, while generations were busy changing hands, the flickering glow of television screens silently slipped into our living rooms and began to take away the creative imaginations of its unsuspecting viewers. When we listened to our radios, we created with the mind's eye. We could *see* Superman leap tall buildings in a single bound and bend steel with his bare hands.

God bless Jack Armstrong, Tom Mix, Buck Rogers, Captain Midnight, Hop Harrigan, Orphan Annie, Bobby Benson, Straight Arrow, Chick Carter, Don Winslow, Dick Tracy and the rest of the gang…wherever they may be.

They're still as much a part of me today as they were when I was a chubby little boy staring into the depths of our stately floor-model Philco, marveling at their daring deeds so very long ago. ☎

HEROES of the airwaves included Jack Armstrong, the All-American Boy (right), and Captain Midnight (far right).

JACK ARMSTRONG'S SECRET WHISTLE CODE

JACK ARMSTRONG

UNCLE JIM

INSTRUCTIONS

One Whistle . . . . (Short) Attention

Two Whistles . . . . (Short) Be on guard for trouble

Three Whistles . . . . . . (One long, two short) In danger, come at once

Four Whistles . . . . (Short) We're being watched

Two Whistles . . . . (Two Long) Important news — meet me at once

BETTY

BILLY

27

The Great Pantry Raid of 1949

By Sylvia Alden Roberts, Sonora, California

SUGAR 'N' SPICE. Author (inset) thought she was fooling her grandma (above), but when it comes to stealing sugar, the best advice is to come clean.

RATION STAMPS and even the Great Depression were still fresh in the mind of my grandmother in 1949, and we lived accordingly.

I was raised solely by my grandparents, whom I called Mama Lady and Papa Man, in their home in San Antonio, Texas. Though we were by no means wealthy, we were not nearly as bad off as I was led to believe.

To hear Mama Lady tell it, we were "going over the hill to the poorhouse" at just about any moment. She was always pointing out that things were "hard to come by". She often hinted that my new crayons may have been just the purchase that would send us to our financial doom.

By the age of 5, I had come to equate quality with quantity. So when Papa Man brought home an entire bushel basket of grapefruit he received as payment for a favor, I was very nearly overwhelmed by the extravagance.

I was allowed to share this bounty with Ginny Haines, my friend next door. Ginny was unfamiliar with the tartness of grapefruit and convinced me the flavor could be improved with sugar.

I knew sugar was a precious commodity to my grandmother and that she would never allow us to use any. So, without asking the permission I knew we wouldn't get, I took a cup from my toy tea set, and Ginny and I tiptoed into the dark cool pantry.

The sugar sack sat on a high shelf, along with the jars of beets, tomatoes and peaches that Mama Lady had pickled, canned and preserved. It was out of the reach of two 5-year-olds, so we dragged in a heavy wooden chair from the kitchen.

I climbed onto the chair, and with one knee on a shelf, reached over my head and scooped out a cup of sugar. I handed the cup down to my waiting partner in crime and climbed off my precarious perch.

We slid the chair back to its place, then giggled our way back to the porch steps and our waiting grapefruit.

Success Was Sweet

The success of our adventure was exhilarating as well as tasty. So much so that after the grapefruit was gone, we raided the pantry again, this time wetting our fingers, sticking them in the teacup, then licking the sugar off our hands.

We managed to avoid Mama Lady all that afternoon as we sneaked in and out of the pantry. We were almost caught once when she came out to take her wash off the line. After that we began to hide—under my bed, in a wardrobe and even in the bathroom.

It never occurred to us that the sugar sack had been full when we began our raids. Nor did we realize the trails of evidence the overloaded cup had been leaving to our hiding places.

Didn't Think Ahead

Most unfortunately of all, I never stopped to think that at the end of the day, Ginny would go home, and I'd be left—with an almost empty sugar sack —to face Mama Lady.

Mama Lady knew what had happened as soon as she walked into the pantry, crunching with every step, and saw the ants, the sugar all over the shelves and the nearly empty sack. She knew when she followed the trails to our hideouts, and when I came moaning to her side, begging for something for my tummyache.

And as if my miserable tummy weren't punishment enough, I had to suffer the added indignity of going out to the backyard and cutting my own switch from a peach tree.

The use of the switch was followed by a blistering lecture and a massive dose of castor oil.

Believe me, the taste of that medicine would not have been improved even with a spoonful of sugar. ☎

REEL LIFE. When John Forrest, a school principal, shared this tale with his students, one of them related it to his dad, Rob Bennett, who was inspired to paint this picture.

First Fishing Trip Ended with a Splash

By John Forrest, Orillia, Ontario

THE SUN ROSE over the sparkling waters of Lake Simcoe in Ontario on the final day of my first big fishing trip with Dad. So far, it had been nothing but a disaster.

I had snagged the outboard propeller, tangled my tackle, lost lures and even punctured a hole in our war-surplus raft. It had teemed rain and been miserably cold…and chipmunks had raided our rations.

Worst of all, I hadn't caught a single fish. That was tough for a kid in a family of fishermen!

In our family, a long line of fathers had taken their sons on fishing trips to mark their coming of age and to give the next generation a tale to tell. My trip had been delayed by Dad's tour of duty in World War II, but now, in the summer of '46, my time had come.

As we set out on the final day of our trip, I was one determined young fisherman. The weather had cleared, the leaky raft was patched, my reel was repaired. I was ready!

Dad pull-started our ancient Viking half-horsepower outboard and we set out, fishing every likely spot on the lake. I plopped plugs, spun spinners, cast and cranked. I baited and waited. Nothing.

That Sinking Feeling

In the meantime, Dad landed his limit of smallmouth bass. But as the sun dipped toward the horizon, time ran out for me. When Dad turned the boat back to camp, my shoulders slumped in disappointment. I was a fishing failure.

As our raft approached the dock and Dad shut down the motor, I reluctantly began to retrieve my lure. Suddenly the line went tight. I pulled back and a huge largemouth bass exploded from the lake! The fight was on!

The bass twisted, turned, leaped and dived—using every trick it knew in its fight for freedom. But I was reeling furiously and gaining ground. Then, suddenly, catastrophe struck! In the midst of this titanic struggle, the patch on our raft popped loose. We were sinking!

Dad scrambled for the pump, shouting instructions all the while. But I stayed calm, ignored our predicament and played my fish. That mighty bass broke water time and time again as our craft crumpled and sank slowly to the bottom.

The struggle continued. My heart pounded in my throat as Dad and I stood side by side, knee-deep in water, working together to land that battling bass. Then my line went slack.

Did He Get Away?

I reeled furiously to take up the slack. Was he still hooked? My question was answered when the bass made one last leap in a green and gold spray of water on scales and landed beside us.

Dad triumphantly netted him!

Shaking with excitement, we abandoned ship and waded ashore, bearing our prize on high. My chest swelled with pride as fellow campers, who'd gathered on the dock, cried, "Way to go, kid!" and "Great fish!"

Brownie cameras clicked, and measurements were taken before I gently placed that monarch of the lake in the dockside holding tank. Dad and I then rescued the raft and began packing our soggy gear. Although he didn't say much, I could hear a new respect in his voice.

When it was time to go, I knew there was one more thing to do. I walked alone to the dock, paused for a moment, then carefully tipped the tank, returning my fish to the lake.

The bass' fins flashed a final time as he swam from sight —a weary warrior headed home. I said a silent "thank-you" to speed him on his way.

We would both have our tales to tell. ☎

Welcome to America, Papa!

By Fred R. Vreeken, Layton, Utah

MY PAPA came to America from Holland in 1914. Only 17 at the time, he was absolutely awed at the sight of New York City. Never had he seen such tall buildings and so many people.

"I think I will like America!" Papa said in Dutch to his 18-year-old brother, Carl. "It's wonderful!"

The two immigrants couldn't understand English, but somehow they found their way to the train station to begin a 3-day journey to Salt Lake City.

Boarding the train, the brothers were amazed at the clean, roomy coach. The seats were covered in beautiful blue velour, with white linen headrests. The two young Dutchmen had never seen such luxury before.

A "Guardian Angel"

Soon after the train chugged out of the station, a porter came down the aisle with popcorn, candy and soft drinks.

The amazed Dutchmen just stared at the porter, who smiled and offered them bags of popcorn.

"What's in that bag he is holding?" Papa asked Carl in Dutch.

"I don't know," Carl answered. "It looks like little white flowers!"

Having dealt often with immigrants, the kindly porter took it on himself to "look after" the Dutchmen. He came closer to the suspicious pair, popped a handful of kernels in his mouth and began to chew.

"Mmmmmm!" he said.

Papa and Carl understood that popcorn was something to eat! More importantly, they had just made their first American friend.

That popcorn was the brothers' first morsel of food all day. As the hours passed, they grew hungrier…unaware that hot meals were being served right on board in the dining car.

DAPPER DUTCHMAN Martin Vreeken emigrated from Europe in 1914. Photo above was taken in 1915, when he was 18 and living in Salt Lake City, Utah.

Finally, when the train pulled to a stop at a depot, Carl spotted a small store and cafe in the distance.

"Look, Martin, a store!" Carl exclaimed in Dutch. "Here is a dollar. Run as fast as you can and buy a loaf of bread. But hurry right back—if you miss the train, we'll probably never see each other again!"

What Did He Say?

Papa snatched the dollar from his brother's hand and nearly flew over the tracks. Bounding breathlessly into the little cafe, he shouted, "Brad! Brad!" Startled patrons almost fell off their stools when the wild-eyed young man burst through the door.

At first, the frightened fellow behind the counter, who didn't understand what the noisy intruder wanted, thought it was a holdup!

Papa threw the dollar on the counter and pointed impatiently at a loaf of bread he had spotted. No one moved, so once again he barked, "Brad!"

The proprietor cautiously handed the loaf to Papa, who tucked it under his arm like a football and fled out the door.

Bread cost a nickel a loaf in those days, and a dollar was an awful lot of money. But Papa wasn't interested in change…the cost of missing that train would have been far greater!

Hurdling the tracks, he dashed back to the coach, where Carl extended a hand to pull him aboard.

Triumph!

Papa returned to his seat and wiped his brow. As his hammering heart slowed, he loosened his collar and gave his brother a big smile. The two gloated over their little victory, devouring the entire loaf of bread.

Then they sat there for over an hour before the train finally chugged out of the station!

The porter had evidently watched the whole show, because hours later, at the next stop, he awakened the two dozing Dutchmen and took them to a depot restaurant for their first hot meal in days.

"It was such a treat because we were so hungry," Papa would later say in fond remembrance.

And as long as he and Carl lived, they never forgot the kindness of that porter—the first friend they made in America. ☎

It was mid-morning, and I was a hungry 5-year-old.

Never mind the fact I'd earlier put away a farm breakfast of one country ham biscuit and one plum jam biscuit (each as big as a pancake), washed down with a foamy glass of fresh milk from "Bessie", Grandma's gentle cow.

Since lunch would not be served for a long time, I knew what I had to do—visit Grandma's garden for a taste of her wonderful red ripe "maters"!

Homegrown tomatoes were a favorite part of summertime visits to my grandparents' Kinston, North Carolina farm during the 1930s. I was also enthralled with the space, the animals, the peace, Grandpa's dedication to the land and Grandma's contentment with her home.

Grandpa had built me a tree house in an old oak just outside the house, and that's where I was when my mid-morning hunger pangs hit.

In Search of Salt

I clambered down and scampered to the house. Bounding up the steps, I glanced beneath them to spy "Queenie" and her litter of kittens relaxing in the shade.

The screen door squeaked as I pulled it open. Grandma was standing at the sink, humming as she cleaned a chicken to fry for our lunch.

"Can I have some salt, please?" I innocently asked.

"Sure, honey. But don't go filling up on tomatoes before lunch," Grandma said in her best "you-don't-fool-me" tone. I took a handful of salt and dashed out the door. I was so happy, I skipped down the path to the garden, my bare feet slapping the warm earth and sending up little puffs of dust.

I sang to myself as I skipped, "To the garden hippy-hop, to the garden ready or not, to the garden for maters so red, I don't care what Grandma said!"

The garden was laid out in perfect rows, and the tomato plants were neatly tied to wooden stakes. Their crimson fruit decorated the lush green vines like red ornaments at Christmas.

Took Her Pick

Grandma's tomatoes grew in all sizes, but I preferred only the tiniest ones, not much bigger than my brother's marble shooter. I picked six of these tasty morsels, put them in the pocket of my feed sack dress and set off for the barn to feast in privacy.

Once inside, I flopped atop a pile of

I Recall Grandma's Red Ripe 'Maters'

By Jane Wood, Wilson, North Carolina

plant bed sheeting and took a tomato out of my pocket. I carefully wiped the tantalizing treat on my skirt to remove any dirt or dust.

Then, holding the tomato by the stem with my little finger extended like a lady holding a teacup, I took a small bite out of the bottom to make the juice flow. Quickly I dipped the dripping tomato into the salt in my left hand and popped

it into my mouth. I closed my eyes to savor the flavor as the red juice, still warm from the August sun, bathed my taste buds with garden goodness.

One gulp and it was gone!

Dusting off tomato number two, I again sang my happy little tomato rhyme to myself…and wondered how long it would be before Grandma would call me and Grandpa inside for lunch!

When Wheaties Gave Us Wings...

By Robert Fudold, Casco, Michigan

WE OFTEN had to "make do" when I was growing up during World War II in Detroit, Michigan.

But one thing never in short supply was the fun we had listening to our favorite late-afternoon radio programs. Shows like *Little Orphan Annie* and *I Love a Mystery* were most popular on our block.

Then there was *Jack Armstrong, the All-American Boy*. To be honest, my buddies and I weren't all that fond of Jack. But we had to listen in order to learn what Wheaties, the show's sponsor, would send us in exchange for box tops.

I could barely wait for the mailman to deliver my "Genuine Imitation Norden Bombsight", for example...or "Authentic Aviator's Wings" to pin on my favorite heavy red wool "lumber jacket".

But the biggest box-top promotion of all came in the summer of 1944, when Wheaties offered a series of model airplanes that really flew.

For a nickel and two box tops, you got a pair of warplanes printed on heavy cardboard, ready to cut, fold and then glue into three-dimensional model planes.

Built a Squadron

During assembly, you glued a penny in the nose cowling for weight. With a good toss, your completed fighter plane flew like a son-of-a-gun!

Fourteen different models were offered in the series, including a Japanese Zero, British Spitfire, German Focke-Wulf and a whole squadron of assorted American planes including the Mustang, Thunderbolt and Hellcat.

Each week, my pack of friends and

I rushed to the market to rummage through the Wheaties boxes on the cereal shelves after hearing that a new model fighter plane was being offered.

Who could blame us? With each commercial, announcer Frank McCormack warned, "When they are gone, they'll be gone forever."

Another Bowl, Please

Our folks wondered if we'd ever tire of eating "The Breakfast of Champions". On market day, Mom would ask, "Why don't we get Cheerios or Rice Krispies this time?"

"We can't," I'd bleat shamelessly. "I promise I'll eat my Wheaties...I'll eat 'em all!"

Of course, I was already putting away bushels of the stuff. But I seemed to be enjoying it, so my mom always bought more.

After the war, the model airplane mania was finally grounded. Wheaties began offering baseball cards and other premiums...and I started eating other cereals. But I never got over those model airplanes.

Winged Back in Time

Nowadays I'm still nuts about those great old war birds. That's why I attended a model airplane convention recently. Passing one of the booths, I couldn't believe my eyes—there for sale were the same model planes of my youth!

Most of the other men crowded around that display were as excited as I was. The wives in attendance simply shook their heads in disbelief.

I headed home that day clutching four precious planes to my chest. That very night I assembled the Focke-Wulf, just as I had nearly 60 years before.

There was one major difference, though. I had to run out to an all-night convenience store and exchange five pennies for a nickel. Today's pennies, made with lighter alloys, are no longer quite heavy enough to give maximum performance.

The salesclerk looked at me a little strangely, but I was too excited to care. A few minutes later, nickel in place, I sailed that little model plane out into the moonlight.

And you know what? It still flew like a son-of-a-gun. ☏

Bring Back the Layaway Plan!

By June Stahl, Canfield, Ohio

MOST YOUNG PEOPLE today have never heard of the layaway plan. Well, I think it would do us all good to bring back that time-payment program once offered by most every large department store.

Before the days of credit cards, folks purchased clothing, furniture and all manner of household items "on layaway".

It was wonderfully simple: You made a down payment on the article you wished to purchase, and the friendly clerk took it off the shelf, "laying it away" for you.

Then you paid regular installments, working your way toward the momentous day when you could finally take that wonderful new item home!

I began using the layaway plan back in 1944. I was living at home in Youngstown, Ohio at the time and had just taken my first job.

From my first $15 paycheck, I gave my mother a few dollars for room and board, which was a token gesture, since that didn't begin to cover my support.

Small Shopping Spree

After paying Mother, I raced downtown to go shopping with a friend who'd also just received her first paycheck. The money seemed to smolder in our purses, just begging to be spent!

My friend and I each found the "perfect" winter coat, and with $2 down, we had them laid away.

Every 2 weeks thereafter, I eagerly made another $2 payment. Some weeks it was really a struggle, but the excitement and anticipation of having my new coat kept me going.

With each payment I made, I dreamed of the day I'd get to wear that pretty camel-colored coat. I could almost feel the warmth it would give me, and I pictured how proud I'd feel when I wore it.

After what seemed like endless weeks of dreaming, the big day arrived. I still remember the thrill I felt when I marched into that store to make my final payment! All the waiting and sacrifice were worth it.

My friend felt the same way I did, though she had a little unsolicited help...her boyfriend secretly made her last two payments and surprised her one evening with her new coat! They were married the following year.

Garments Were Goals

I think it's sad that today's young people don't know the thrill of buying something on layaway...and the satisfaction of wearing a garment that you struggled to pay for. Nowadays, it's just too easy to whip out a credit card. You buy an article, wear it for a while, then forget about it. By the time the bill finally comes in the mail, you barely remember buying that item.

In society today, we expect too much and buy too much. We charge articles we don't really need. We're in a hurry, wanting too much too soon...and I admit I'm as guilty as the next person.

The layaway plan was slow but oh, so satisfying. I can't help but think it was good for our economy—and that if we'd bring back the layaway plan, we just might bring back some basic values that seem to be lacking today.

One thing is certain—the good old layaway plan would put a little old-fashioned anticipation and fun back into shopping.

CLASS PHOTO. The 1930 graduates of Holy Family Hospital School of Nursing in Manitowoc, Wisconsin wore caps and heels.

Hospital Headgear 'Capped' a Career

By Cynthia Frozena, Manitowoc, Wisconsin

WHEN I WAS a little girl in the 1950s, Dad took me to visit his uncle at the V.A. Hospital in Milwaukee, Wisconsin. It was a huge place with long halls and highly polished floors.

Children weren't allowed in patients' rooms, so he left me at the nurses' station. All the nurses wore crisp, highly starched uniforms that rustled softly when they walked. But the best part of the uniforms were their caps.

Each nurse wore a white cap. Many were similar, but some were unique. The nurses took time to talk to me, oohing and aahing over my dress and manners. When they asked me what I wanted to be when I grew up, I exclaimed, "A nurse!"

They nodded their approval and assured me I'd be a welcome addition to the profession. Many years later, I fulfilled that vow and became an RN.

Slowly, over the years, my fellow nurses and I gave up wearing our caps. And those crisp white uniforms evolved into pastel tops and colorful jackets with white slacks and jogging shoes. Our profession was changing.

A Team Approach

We wanted to look less clinical and authoritarian. Doctors, nurses and technicians became a health care team. In some hospitals, everyone from housekeepers to nurses started wearing "scrubs".

One day while working at our local community hospital, I entered a patient's room just as she was asking the housekeeper for a pain pill. When the housekeeper explained she wasn't a nurse, the patient complained that everyone in the hospital looked the same to her.

As I neared her bed, she asked, "Why don't you wear white uniforms anymore? And what happened to your caps? I used to love seeing nurses in their caps."

I gave my patient her medication and helped her get comfortable, reflecting on her words. Many of my patients over the years (especially older ones) lamented the demise of nurses caps.

When we wore them, there was no mistaking a nurse for anything but a nurse.

Those caps had an interesting history, too. No one knows for sure exactly where the tradition began, but the custom of caregivers wearing caps probably started with the first women to care for the sick. They were often nuns who wore the distinctive habits and veils of their religious orders.

Large Caps Covered Hair

In the mid-1800s, when modern nursing began, nurses wore large dust caps to cover their long hair. Nursing schools started around this time, and each school designed a distinctive uniform and cap.

Over the years, as women's hairstyles changed, so did the caps. When student nurses finished their first year of study, many schools held capping ceremonies. Each student was called to center stage, and her cap was solemnly placed on her head.

Class pictures of newly capped students depict the young women wearing the symbol of their profession, filled with pride at their accomplishment.

But those days are gone. Nurses no longer wear caps for many reasons. Caps often became dirty and were difficult to launder.

Sometimes they got caught on new kinds of medical equipment.

Like most nurses today, I don't wear my cap anymore. But I still have it. It rests in a box far back on a shelf in my closet, a reminder of my connection to a group of dedicated nurses who wore their caps with pride…and inspired a little girl to follow in their footsteps. ☎

HEADING BACK. Nurses caps were moving to the back of the head when this LPN had her portrait taken. Author Cynthia Frozena laments she has no pictures of herself wearing a nurses cap. Colleagues gladly shared theirs.

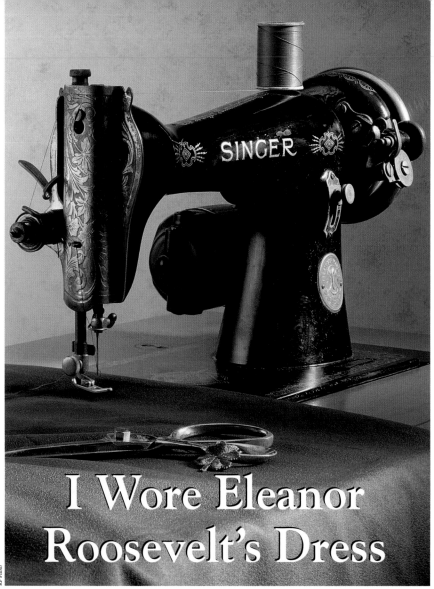

I Wore Eleanor Roosevelt's Dress

By Dorothy Stanaitis, Gloucester City, New Jersey

EVERY CHILD in 4B at James Rhoades School in Philadelphia knew that Eleanor Roosevelt was the President's wife. We were all intensely patriotic during World War II.

When the newsreel at the Saturday matinee showed the President or his wife or the American flag, we clapped, stamped our feet and whistled.

That was just one of our patriotic rituals. We also collected newspapers by the bundle, crushed tin cans and gathered all kinds of scrap metal.

We even painstakingly peeled the tinfoil from our chewing gum wrappers and rolled them into large balls. We intended to donate these balls to the war effort, but most kids just took them to school and showed them off.

Every Monday morning, we brought a dime to school so we could buy a 10-cent stamp. We'd lick and stick those stamps into a booklet that earned us a war bond when it was full. Then we vigorously sang *Remember Pearl Harbor* before opening our *Elson Grey Reader* to begin our daily lesson.

We were so busy with our patriotic activities that we didn't spend the usual amount of time on the regular celebra-

> ## "*How* could this have happened?"

tions such as Washington's and Lincoln's birthdays. This particular year, we didn't even make the chain of green construction paper shamrocks for St. Patrick's Day.

I wasn't thinking much about St. Patrick's Day either, until one morning I was awakened by my mother, who was Scottish-Irish, singing *MacNamara's Band*. It was March 17.

We never made too much of our Irish heritage. Most of our neighbors on Ogden Street were more concerned about being Americans than with their ethnic backgrounds.

But on St. Patrick's Day, my mother sang along with the radio all day. In the morning they played lively tunes, then by evening, more melancholy pieces like *Danny Boy* and *I'll Take You Home Again, Kathleen* were played.

So it was on that St. Patrick's Day that I went off to school humming a happy tune. My happiness didn't last long, however.

No Anguish Like a Kid's

When we got to our cloakroom and began taking off our coats and hats, my heart sank. Every girl and almost every boy in my class was wearing green, and I wasn't!

How could this have happened? If my mother was Irish, that meant *I* was Irish. Yet I had on not one item of green clothing.

The morning crept by. My misery had grown so great that by the time I went home for lunch, I began to cry as I told my mother of my disappointment.

She looked worried but didn't say anything. After she put out my chicken noodle soup and glass of milk, Mother went upstairs.

I figured she was tending to my little brother, until I heard the whir of her old Singer sewing machine. Mother made all of our clothes and many of the neighborhood children's, too.

Just Her Size

I thought no more of it until I had finished eating and was ready to leave for school. That's when Mother reappeared, and my eyes opened wide. She was carrying a dark green crepe dress—and it was just my size!

In a raffle to raise money for the war effort, my father had won a dress donated by Eleanor Roosevelt. Now Mother had cut it down so I could join in the celebration of our day of Irish heritage.

Although she realized the value and historic significance of the dress, showing her daughter how much she loved her was more important.

I was in bed when my father came home from work, so I don't know what his initial reaction was to the altered dress. I do know he'd been proud to have won it, but he was always supportive of my mother.

His attitude the next day was one of pride in the fact that our mother had put love of family before love of history.

The Sweet Smell of Excess

By Earl Weirich, Chesapeake, Virginia

THE HEADY AROMA of chocolate swirled all about us, making it difficult to concentrate on what was being said by the woman standing before us.

"Keep in mind that you may eat all the candy you want, as many different kinds as you see, as long as you are employed here at the Hershey Chocolate Factory," she instructed. "But you are not allowed to take any home with you."

Wow! Was this going to be great. My four 16-year-old buddies and I had just landed in chocolate heaven!

We exchanged sideways glances and smiled; Bucky nudged me in the ribs, and I passed it down the line.

Turning five teenagers loose to work here for an entire summer could mark the end of the chocolate industry as everyone knew it.

The year was 1944, and good help was hard to come by because so many able-bodied men and women had gone off to fight the war. But my friends and I were available.

We jumped at the chance to work at the Hershey Chocolate Factory, just a 15-minute ride from our homes in Middletown, Pennsylvania.

Did Patriotic Duty

Despite the obvious benefits of working in a candy factory, we still thought of ourselves as patriots. Tough as it was, we'd do our bit to help win the war.

Not only were we contributing to the effort, we'd finally be able to afford to take our girlfriends dancing on Saturday nights—with a hot dog and a Coke afterward.

Adding to the appeal of that first paycheck was the knowledge we'd be working in a place that would make us the envy of every kid in school, if not *the world*.

The woman giving us our orientation was standing in front of a conveyor bringing an endless line of candy bars to workers who packaged them.

Hand trucks rolled by stacked high with chocolate bars dark and light, with almonds and without almonds. It was all there within reaching distance—and we were ready to start reaching!

As our orientation continued, we grew more eager to start. Behind our greeter, we saw huge metal vats of molten chocolate, wafting its delightful fragrance into every inch of the enormous production facility. With a deep sense of appreciation, I noticed that if I held my mouth open and breathed deeply, I could almost taste the chocolate. Looking at my buddies—their heads tilted back and their mouths opened slightly—I knew they were experiencing a similar sensation.

Finally we were assigned to our new supervisor. Noticing the expressions on our faces, she grimaced as if she knew exactly what we were thinking: *Bring on the chocolate!*

For some reason, she told us she had other business to attend to and would return in 15 minutes to explain our jobs to us. We were off in separate directions the instant she was out of sight.

I headed for a pallet piled high with open cartons of Hershey Kisses. Scott had found the almond bars and had already devoured one by the time I unwrapped my first double handful of Kisses.

A Dangerous Discovery

Our supervisor was away longer than planned, affording us the opportunity to enjoy a wide variety of Hershey candies before she returned. After all, we felt it was only reasonable to learn everything we could about the products we'd be working with.

Bucky was particularly conscientious in that regard. He'd wandered off and found stacks of unusually thick chocolate bars, each with six squares that could be broken off and eaten separately.

We learned later that they were D-ration bars for our fighting forces and that just one square contained enough nutrition to take the place of an entire meal. Bucky ate two whole bars—enough for 4 days nourishment!

He didn't know that at the time, of course. But later that afternoon, he didn't look so good. The next day, he couldn't eat *anything*—candy or otherwise.

The rest of us fared a little better on our second day, although our chocolate intake went from gobbling to nibbling. When I got home that afternoon, I wasn't the slightest bit hungry…not for dinner, dessert or anything else. To make matters worse, my mother wouldn't let me in the house!

Back-Porch Quarantine

My shoes were caked with chocolate—it was all over my clothes, and my hair was beginning to harden into a permanent chocolate wave.

Mother insisted I undress down to my underwear on the back porch. Then, as soon as I got inside, I had to wash my hair and take a bath. Later, I learned my co-workers had endured similar humiliations.

Somehow, we stuck it out the rest of the summer. The weeks passed quickly, but not as quickly as our fascination for chocolate had! When we returned to school that fall, our classmates were properly envious when hearing about the sweet deal we'd had.

The most common reaction we got after explaining how we could eat *all* the chocolate we wanted was, "Gosh!" spoken with wide-eyed wonder. We never mentioned that after our third day on the job, not a single piece of chocolate passed our lips! ☎

Mom's 'Fried Tea' Was A Tuesday Tradition

By Dick Hassall, Fowler, California

JUST AS the Japanese have a lovely traditional ceremony for the preparation, serving and drinking of tea, so did my mother. It was a one-woman ceremony of sorts, purely Western and perhaps part Polish.

Back in the '30s, Mother's ritual required a functioning radio. First she'd put the teakettle on the "hot" burner of the kerosene stove in our South Trenton, New Jersey kitchen.

Then she'd bring in a basket of damp laundry from the back porch and set up the ironing board. Plugging her iron into the overhead socket, she'd make sure the radio was tuned to the first of a seemingly endless series of soap operas.

The next step in the ritual was opening the lead foil cube of Golden Key tea. Mother would spoon some into a dime store tea "egg", which she placed in a large cup that said "Greetings From Asbury Park".

While waiting for the kettle to boil, Mother began unfolding our damp laundry, all the while keeping an ear open for the triumphs and travails of *Our Gal Sunday* or *Helen Trent* or the verbal lunacies of *Vic and Sade*.

With the iron hot, the tea steeping and the radio properly tuned, Mother's daylong Tuesday ritual began. As neat stacks

---

"*I* was confined at home with a cold and observed the daylong ritual..."

---

of freshly pressed clothes began filling up our kitchen, her ironing remained unhurried, purposeful and productive.

About the time the third 15-minute program signed off, Mother would stop ironing for a moment.

Tasting her tea and finding it cold, she'd take out a skillet, pour her tea into it and set the skillet on the hot burner, which stayed lit all day since it provided the only heat in the kitchen. When the tea boiled, Mother poured it back into her cup, took a sip and realized it was now too hot to drink. So she'd set the cup back on the table, shake out the next piece of clothing and go back to her ironing.

Thus, the whole day proceeded—45 minutes of ironing, a sip of cold tea, a quick reheat in the little skillet, one searing sip...then back to the ironing board.

In the '30s, there were three sources of soap operas available on our radio: New York, Philadelphia and Chicago. This ensured Mother an uninterrupted flow of 15-minute serials from the time she finished the breakfast dishes until it was time to make supper, which was signaled by either *The Gospel Hour* or *Singing Sam, the Barbasol Man.* At that time,

the same Asbury cup of multiply reheated tea still stood on the table, reduced in volume by less than half an inch.

One winter day when I was confined at home with a cold, I observed the whole daylong ritual. When Mother finally busied herself with the pork chops and potatoes, I bravely took a sip from her cup.

At that age, I'd recently been cured of nail biting by having my fingertips painted with asafetida, an awful liquid with the power to sicken the strongest stomach.

So, too, I'm afraid, would Mother's all-day cup of fried tea...if she had ever taken the time to sit down and actually drink it!

Cliches like "it would eat the design off the linoleum" or "it'd take the enamel off your teeth" are far too weak to describe the powerful residue left in my mother's cup at 4:30 on a Tuesday afternoon.

Come to think of it, maybe I was wrong to compare my mother's ritual to a tradition. After all, a tradition seems to require some sort of enjoyable interaction, such as actually *drinking* the tea.

But I'm afraid no one in their right mind would ever have gone beyond one sip of Mother's infamous fried tea. ☎

STRONG BREW. Dick Hassall (at left in the '30s) recalls when his mother's ironing days involved a strong cup of tea.

J.C. Allen and Son

37

Remedies We'd Rather Forget

Eulogy for Eucalyptus

AS A CHILD, I lived on a ranch near a small town in California. Whenever my three sisters or I caught a cold, Mother would bundle us up and take us out to the eucalyptus tree grove.

We'd rake the leaves into a large pile, which Mother would then set on fire. When the leaves were smoldering, we had to stand in the smoke and "take the cure".

It must have worked. I haven't had a cold in over 50 years.

—*Verna McIntyre*
Modesto, California

A Remedy from Bait

MY GRANDPARENTS made an oil to rub on someone crippled by bad joints. They'd fill a small bag with earthworms, hang it in a warm spot and place a pan underneath to catch the "oil".

—*Jeanette Edwards*
Round Lake, Illinois

Baked Potato with That?

ON AN apple-picking trip to Long Island, everyone in the family but me got poison ivy. Convinced I was immune, I later rolled in a large patch of the stuff to impress a friend.

Well, in short order, the only thing on me that looked "normal" were my eyes. Mother used calamine lotion, oil of eucalyptus and other remedies suggested by the doctor and druggist, but nothing seemed to work.

In desperation, Mother coated my entire body with sour cream. She'd let it dry, then coat it again and again. Finally, in my first act of rebellion against authority, I cried, "Enough!"

To this day, I start itching when I smell sour cream.   —*Rhoda Vestuto*
Thousand Oaks, California

Remedy Bugged Him

WHEN MY BROTHER got the croup, Mom would take about eight or nine of those little mold bugs you find under rocks, sew them into a piece of cloth and tie the cloth around my brother's neck.

When the bugs died in a day or two, the croup was gone.   —*Patricia Wood*
Indianapolis, Indiana

Dad's Wart (Re)Mover

DAD was a great kidder and had an unusual remedy for every problem—like the wart I got on my ring finger a month before my wedding in 1946.

Dad got out a penny, clutched it between his finger and thumb, then spit on one side. Next he made three circles with the penny around my finger, repeated some gibberish each time, then placed the yucky side of the penny on the wart. He finished the procedure with a confident "Kazam!"

Imagine our surprise when the wart disappeared a week before the wedding! But maybe Dad just transferred the wart, because one appeared on the end of his nose!

Instead of trying his own remedy, Dad went to a doctor to have it removed, but as you can see in this picture (below), it left behind a white spot that Dad sported to my wedding.

—*Patricia Collins, Bend, Oregon*

ALL IN WHITE. Patricia Collins (right, with her father) was worried about a wart on her ring finger just before her wedding, but Dad worked some magic and it disappeared...sort of. Read her story above.

Smoke Gets in Your Ears

WHEN I was a little girl and got an earache, my dad would cup his hand around my ear and blow smoke in. I don't know if it was the smoke or the heat, but it gave instant relief.

Later, when I was a secretary, I got such an earache that I asked my boss, a smoker, to blow smoke in my ear as my dad had.

He'd never heard of such a thing and looked at me rather oddly. But he finally did it, and again, I had instant relief!
—*Barbara Sims*
Springfield, Illinois

At Least It Smelled Good

AT THE FIRST sign of congestion when we were little, back in the '20s and '30s, Mom had a special remedy.

She would cut out a bib from a brown paper bag, smear it with lard and sprinkle it generously with nutmeg. She applied this to our chests, covered with an undershirt to keep it in place.

I remember how the bag crinkled and scratched all night, and all the scrubbing it took in the morning to get off that greasy grime, but it worked.
—*Christine Nelson*
Woodville, Massachusetts

It's All in Your Head

IF I SAID I was too sick to go to school, my mother made me get up, wash, dress and eat breakfast. If after all that I was still too sick, I was allowed to stay home. I didn't miss much school.
—*Monna McConnell*
Beaver Falls, Pennsylvania

She'll Take Tonsillitis

MY MOTHER'S favorite medicine for tonsillitis was Tonsilline. The box had a picture of a giraffe from the neck up. The medicine was orange and tasted like persimmons. It was worse than the tonsillitis. I haven't seen it in years, thank goodness.
—*Lynn Dunlap*
Cleveland, Tennessee

Earache Bugged Her

WHEN I WAS a child back in the '30s in Oklahoma, I had a terrific earache. My mother was devastated because I was in such pain.

A neighbor told my mother to find a "bessy bug", break it in half and pour the blood into my ear. It sounded strange, and horrible. But when the

neighbor found the bug and poured the blood into my ear, the pain stopped almost immediately.
—*Anita Frick*
Oak Grove, Missouri

Who Needed Surgery?

I HAD a severe attack of appendicitis when I was 9. It was so bad, I had to crawl most of the way home from school on my hands and knees.

When I got home, my mother applied hot lard and turpentine over the area. I'm now 77, and I still have my appendix.
—*Violet McDonald*
Berkeley Springs, West Virginia

Frog on, Not in, Throat

MY MOTHER used a remedy for quinsy, a throat infection, that she learned from her parents, who came to Kansas by covered wagon.

A live frog was bandaged, belly-in, to the throat. When the frog "died from the infection", another was used until the infection was gone.

My mother used the remedy on me one time in the '30s. I remember being startled to look up and see a frog looking at me after it had escaped from the bandage! I'm grateful we use antibiotics for infections today.
—*Norma Gibson*
La Grande, Oregon

Internal Medicine

TO CURE the symptoms of a cold, my mother made me eat a spoonful of Vicks VapoRub dipped in sugar. I notice the label now states, "Do not eat!"
—*Cherry Jordan*
Granville, New York

Grandma Nose the Cure

WE WERE VISITING my grandmother when I was 6, and I developed a severe nosebleed the first night. Grandmother went out to the barn, collected a small wad of cobwebs, spit some "snuff juice" on them and stuffed it up my nose. The bleeding stopped immediately.
—*Edith Parker*
Saraland, Alabama

WHAT A RELIEF! Baby Pam's grin is a sure sign Grandma's home remedy worked. See Dorothy Rothrock's story below right.

Pass the Baby, Please

MY MOTHER-IN-LAW was a very "take-charge" lady who found a reason to stop by the house daily when I had my first child, Pam.

Pam (above) was a very colicky baby. The more she was held and cuddled, as my mother-in-law loved to do, the more the gas would build up, and the more Pam cried.

Finally, my mother-in-law decreed that she would cure Pam's problem. At sunrise the next day, she marched in with a bottle of oil, which she rubbed on Pam's tummy. Then she knelt down and passed the baby three times around a leg of the kitchen table!

Well, Pam let out a burp and gave us a big toothless grin. My mother-in-law, before departing, instructed me to practice the procedure daily.

My doctor later explained that when Pam was bent over as she was passed around the table leg, the gas was forced from her.

In later years, if Pam had stomach problems, she refused to get out of bed for the sunrise and oil treatment.
—*Dorothy Rothrock*
Quakertown, Pennsylvania

Raw Remedy

AFTER a kidney infection, I was given a glass of port wine with a raw egg in it. That was horrible to swallow and would be considered unsafe today.
—*Ruth Smalley*
Kenilworth, New Jersey

I'll Never Forget the Debit Man

By Marshall Holtz Jr., Vero Beach, Florida

NOWADAYS you might see your insurance man just once, when you purchase a policy from him. After that, a bill comes regularly in the mail reminding you to send your premium payments to some faceless clerk in a far-off city.

But insurance policies weren't always so impersonal. I know, because I remember our friendly neighborhood "Debit Man".

Back in the '30s, these door-to-door premium collectors commonly made the rounds to policyholders every week in order to collect the odd nickels, dimes and quarters required to pay off 52 individual installments each year.

Those household insurance agents made their calls carrying an enormous ledger book, into which they noted the receipt of every penny.

Metropolitan Life made great inroads into the life insurance business across the United States thanks to the legwork of dependable debit men—welcome visitors who plied the streets of our towns until their profession passed into oblivion sometime during the '50s.

WELCOME VISITOR. The Debit Man was a weekly collector of insurance premiums—but more than that, he was a family friend.

Debit men, who knew their customers better than any traveling businessperson, often became a friend and family confidant for their clients.

Coffee at the Kitchen Table

Besides being willing to walk and talk, they must have had an enormous capacity for coffee, consuming at least one cup at every policyholder's kitchen table. This was the official meeting place for the weekly insurance transactions, summer and winter, year after year.

In 1936, my mother took out a policy with "The Met", which she paid off over the next 30 years. I'm sorry I don't recall our debit man's name, but I can still picture him walking the streets of my hometown of Carlstadt, New Jersey.

What I recall most about this friendly gentleman is that he was always impeccably dressed in a white shirt, tie and jacket. He wore a derby hat in the winter and a straw "boater" in the summer.

Both the derby and boater have now gone the way of spats, detachable collars and collar buttons.

But back then, men's haberdasheries had hundreds of little drawers behind the counters. They accommodated the various-sized collars put out by Manhattan, Van Heusen and Arrow, which, you may recall, were the "collar companies" of the day.

End of an Era

Mom outlived her insurance policy by 20 years, so the accrued interest almost doubled the policy's face value.

When I telephoned The Met to inform them she had passed away, the agent was astonished to hear there was still an outstanding policy of that vintage.

The actual piece of paper on which the policy was written was huge, decorated with gilt edges, eagles and Old English script. The cost for this beauty had been less than 25¢ a week.

When I cashed in the policy, I couldn't help but feel that a special era had finally come to a close— an era when the friendly, dependable debit man was welcomed each week into homes all across the land. ☎

If It Was Sunday, We Were in Church

By Bill Lacey, Grafton, New Hampshire

THERE WAS never any question where our family would spend Sunday mornings. My parents made that decision long before we kids were born, and we never questioned the fact that we were going to church.

The First Congregational Church in Melrose, Massachusetts was over a mile away, but we always walked. Who had money for a car during the middle of the Depression?

I can still see that old church with its stained glass windows and tall vaulted ceiling supported by huge oak pillars. The pews were carved from the same oak, and each family had its own pew—not through any formal arrangement, but by a sort of unwritten mutual agreement.

Ours was the sixth pew from the front. Dad always sat on the aisle so he could keep an eye on my brother, Bud, and me. It was hard for us to sit still for a whole hour. Our older sister, Priscilla, did much better.

Across the aisle was where old Deacon Shumway sat. His spot was next to one of those oak pillars, where he could rest his head and take little catnaps during the service.

One Sunday, Bud, 2 years older than me and full of mischief, asked Dad if he could sit in Deacon Shumway's pew. Much to my surprise, Dad agreed! Naturally, everyone saw what was going on and waited to see what would happen next.

When Deacon Shumway arrived, he was clearly startled. "Harrumph!" he growled, plunking his considerable bulk almost on top of poor Bud. Then followed a series of nudges and bumps that crowded Bud into, and eventually *around*, the pillar to the empty seat on the other side.

It was a wordless exchange, completely effective. Within 5 minutes, Deacon Shumway was snug up against his beloved pillar, snoring softly.

Bud and I were resourceful at finding ways to amuse ourselves without disturbing other churchgoers. From bitter ex-

---

"Bud and I were resourceful at finding ways to amuse ourselves..."

---

perience we knew that if we really misbehaved, we wouldn't be allowed to read the Sunday funnies when we got home.

One day something wonderful happened—Mr. and Mrs. Pinda, the plumber and his wife, took over the pew directly behind us. Mrs. Pinda was not a woman to hide her light under a bushel! Her soaring soprano could be heard throughout the church when we all joined in singing hymns. What her vocal technique lacked in accuracy, it more than made up for with volume and enthusiasm.

She loved to linger on the high notes long after everyone else had let them go. Then she would swoop down to catch up with the rest of us, hitting every note on the way down in

THREE ANGELS, except in church, where Bud (center, at left) and Bill often engaged in activities unlike the sort extolled from the pulpit.

one triumphant avalanche of sound.

From then on, Bud and I could not wait to get to church. Diving for the hymnal, we'd look up the day's selections and gleefully point out the high notes where we knew Mrs. Pinda would "rise to the occasion".

Nearly always rewarded with a tour de force performance, we'd practically burst holding in our laughter. Mom and Dad were in no position to put a damper on our merriment since they, too, were struggling to maintain their composure.

After church, it was time to greet everyone. That took only 15 minutes but required lots of patience from us kids …those funny papers were waiting at home!

It wasn't until 10 years later, after I'd graduated from high school and become an infantry foot soldier in France and Germany, that I came to realize just how much that church and our old friends meant to me.

Those dark days would surely have been a whole lot darker if I hadn't felt all that love and support reaching out across the miles. It was then that I was glad Mom and Dad had made the decision, long before we were born, about where we'd be every Sunday morning. ☎

I Remember My First Perm— Boy, Do I Ever!

By Olga Krossick, Gettysburg, Pennsylvania

NOT LONG AGO, I purchased a home-permanent kit and stopped in at the home of my daughter, Joan, to have her help me with the rollers.

As Joan rolled my hair, I sat in her kitchen with a cup of coffee, browsing through her latest copy of *Reminisce*. All at once, I laughed out loud as memories of my first perm came flooding back....

The year was 1937, and I was 11 years old. My mother had taken ill and was in the hospital, so my two grown sisters, Helen and Jenny, came back home to McAdoo, Pennsylvania to take care of me.

They spruced up the house because they knew that would please Mom. Then they hit on an idea—why not spruce me up, too? A new head of curls would be just the thing, they decided. I thought it was a great idea!

Six Blocks to Beauty

I was blessed with a beautiful head of long, straight hair, blond and baby-fine. I knew my mother loved it—she spent hours gently combing it and commenting on its silkiness. But I didn't mention that to my sisters.

Hand in hand, we walked six blocks to the local beauty parlor. The place was garishly bright, with pink tile walls stained from caustic chemicals. The air was so thick with fumes that I could actually feel it on my face. My eyes began to burn. The beautician seemed annoyed, as if she were wasting her time on a little kid. I didn't trust her from the start, and I don't think she liked me much either.

First, she separated my hair into strips by yanking it hard and straight. She placed the strips in felt pads, then rolled them in huge, steel rollers. My neck ached with all that heavy hardware up there, and it was hard to keep my head from flopping side to side.

Sat in "Electric Chair"

Next, the woman led me to a room where a huge, padded chair awaited. Electrical wires hung in a tangle off that chair, and I froze in my tracks, imagining it to be the infamous electric chair on death row, where many a gangster of those days got "fried".

The beautician sat me in this big terrifying chair and started hooking wires onto those steel rollers on my head. Then, with an evil glare, she stood back and threw the switch!

At first, nothing seemed to be happening. Then the rollers began to get warm...and as they got hotter and hotter, I became more and more terrified.

Finally, just as I thought my hair would catch fire, she turned off the juice. Then, as the rollers were removed one by one, my head seemed to grow and grow! My very curly hair went every which way, sticking out in all directions around my head. I felt like the Bride of Frankenstein!

My sisters oohed and aahed about the way I looked, though. They said Mother would love the "new" me. We left the beauty shop and walked straight to the hospital.

Awaited Mother's Approval

Because of my age, I was not allowed into Mom's room. My sisters went inside, and I stayed out in the hall, looking in through the thick glass of the door. My smiling sisters kissed Mother and talked to her with animated gestures. Then all three of them looked up at me in the window.

Mother's eyes widened in complete astonishment, and she didn't look too pleased. My sisters' beaming faces instantly fell. I stood there with my frizzled hair, feeling—and likely looking—ridiculous! I vowed never ever to get a perm again.

Mother glanced away for a moment, composed herself, then looked back up at me with a big smile. She winked and nodded approvingly.

Looking back at that day, I now realize how much my mother disliked the "new" me. But she realized I'd feel bad without her approval. Nothing can work as much magic as a mother's reassuring smile and nod.

It was many years before I got up the nerve to have another perm. That was just after I finished 2 years of school ...to become, of all things, a beautician.

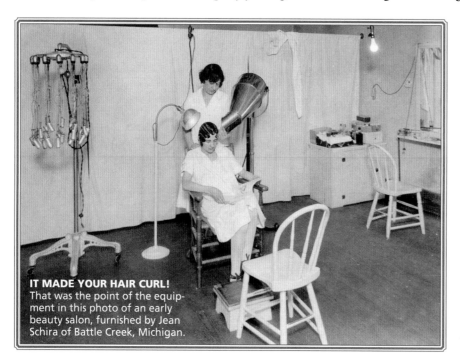

IT MADE YOUR HAIR CURL!
That was the point of the equipment in this photo of an early beauty salon, furnished by Jean Schira of Battle Creek, Michigan.

Winter Washdays Were Really Something!

By Maxine Holder, Rusk, Texas

AS I PUSHED OPEN the door to our kitchen, I was met by a wave of moist warm air. The sweet scents of Fels Naptha and Oxydol filled the room and tickled my nose. Mom was dipping steaming water from the shiny copper boiler on the stove and pouring it into the washing machine. That boiler was her pride and joy, ordered special from the Spiegel catalog.

Mounds of clothes, the Easy Washer and a No. 3 washtub crowded the floor of the tiny kitchen of our Milwaukee, Wisconsin home. "Get in here and close the door!" Mom said. "It's below zero and the stove's not even hot yet!"

She pushed up her sleeves and returned to her work. Turning to me she said, "Sit down on your chair, Maxine. You and your brother are going to have to wait a minute for breakfast—I gotta get this wash started."

Saturday was often washday at our house during winter. Clotheslines zigzagged throughout every room, since clothes dryers were unheard of in the '40s. And hanging laundry outdoors wasn't feasible in winter, because freezing clothes stiffened like cardboard and tore like paper when the wind blew hard.

Toast and Tunes

"Chummy", my little brother, padded into the kitchen and scrambled up into his chair. He reached for the box of "Corporal Stripes", a crunchy cinnamon toast we loved to eat during the war years. He passed me a slice, and we giggled when Mom called us "The Katzenjammer Kids".

The Motorola radio crooned a Frank Sinatra tune as Mom sorted clothes and started the agitator sloshing. She checked whether the wringer was safe by pounding its top. It made a loud *ker-pop* sound.

Jack Westhead

"Good, the safety works!" said Mom with relief. "Did you know Mrs. Anderson caught her apron in her wringer once 'cause the safety wouldn't work? Don't want that happening to me!"

Slowly she dumped steamy whites into the churning tub. Then she reached for her wash stick, punched down the first load and slid on the saucer-like lid.

Ate While Whites Washed

"I guess it's time to get something to eat," Mom said. Our mouths watered as she dished out hot Quaker Oats, dabbed on the butter, then reached for the blue tin of brown sugar.

While we were eating, our big sister, Jeannie, backed through the door, arms full of white sheets, quilts and Indian blankets.

Just then, the door opened and a blast of chilly air caused our toes to curl. Our older brother, Gordy, stepped inside, shut the door and rubbed his hands together briskly. "The pump's still working, Mom. It hasn't frozen up yet," he said. "But Mr.

FROM BOILER TO WRINGER, washday was a chore during the good old days. But winter had a way of complicating matters by keeping the entire operation, including the clotheslines, indoors. Author (above) and her brother Gordon did get outside to share a winter day with their dog "Pepper" in 1947.

Anderson came by for water—their pipes are frozen solid!"

While Gordy and Mom talked, I stared at a pot of Argo starch bubbling away on the stove. I knew nearly everything, including the pillowcases, would be soaked in that gluey mixture and wrung out by hand today.

When the laundry was *finally* finished and Mom's long day was nearly done, she refilled the "old No. 3" tub for our Saturday night baths. The eldest kid went first and the youngest would go last—and *boy* was that water sudsy!

Kids Were Squeaky Clean

We got scrubbed hard, too. She also washed our hair and then wrapped our heads in a towel. By the time Mom finished with Chummy and me, we were *squeaky* clean. Then, while Mom and Jeannie remade the beds with the clean sheets and pillowcases, we kids enjoyed the *Jack Benny Show*.

"Last one in the sack gets a whack!" chided Mom as Chummy and I scrambled under the covers. She snuggled us in, unwrapped the towels from our heads, then gave us each a big bear hug and a kiss.

"Don't let the bedbugs bite!" she'd tease as we rolled our eyes giddily. Nestled into my feather pillow, I sighed contentedly, feeling snug, warm and *very clean* on a deep-winter Saturday night. ☎

Family Life Around The Cozy Cookstove

By Gladys Peters, Berwick, Pennsylvania

I WAS ONE of 12 kids and enjoyed a wonderful childhood, growing up in the late '40s and early '50s.

The center of activity in our old farmhouse was the kitchen, where a grand old cookstove stood. It was a 1927 Welcome Globe, tan with nickel trim, made by March and Brownback of Pottstown, Pennsylvania.

The fancy curved legs held it up off the floor, leaving a space where our big old tomcat, "Chubby", loved to sleep.

Television hadn't yet reached our holler, so people visited a lot then…and always sat in the kitchen.

One man who'd come to see my father smoked a large cigar. Mother loved the aroma of a "good" cigar, so he would give her one to light and place on the top shelf of the stove, where it gave off its fine scent.

That stove was the heat source for our kitchen in winter. After ice skating, my brothers and sisters and I would prop up our numb feet on its bottom skirt until they were toasty again.

Mother kept a small pan on the back of the stove with water, sugar and onions that she made into a syrup to give us in case we ever got the urge to play hooky from school. And if we had a toothache or earache, we'd take off a nickel-plated corner piece of the stove, wrap it in a towel and put it next to the place that hurt.

Remember the air raid drills during World War II? Our whole family would sit in the kitchen, the only light an orange glow coming from around the draft holes in the stove. Except for the fire snapping and crackling, it was quiet. We never knew whether it was a drill or an actual attack, so that soft orange light made things a little less scary.

The stovetop had six lids. Two in front were hot, the next two were a little cooler and those in back kept things warm. Mother kept the top polished and shiny with beeswax from a tiny tin box.

A shelf on one end provided the perfect place for bread to rise. For baking, the temperature had to be just right. You had to set the draft and make sure there was plenty of fuel.

Not everyone could keep a fire going in that stove, but my father knew just when to rake it. Many times, when he and Mother were on the verge of an argument, he'd get up and rake the stove with a vengeance. After he sat back down, all was forgotten.

Sometimes, Mother let me roast a potato on top of the stove. Another treat was the yolk of an egg left over from baking. Mother would leave it in the eggshell and cook it in the hole that was made for the lifter to take the lid off. Try that on an electric stove!

After my parents passed away, it took my brother a while to get the hang of that stove, but he's still using it in the old farmhouse today—although there's also a shiny new electric stove.

The new stoves are easier, faster and cheaper, but they don't have the character of the old ones. And can you imagine still using your electric stove 70 years from now? I think not! ☎

A WELCOMING SCENE. "This photo of our beloved stove shows my brother Ernest Seely, my sister Cora Hummel and her grandchildren, Sue and Rick DeFrain," relates Gladys Peters.

Snowman Melted the Principal's Heart

By Robert Stein, Osseo, Minnesota

IT WAS one of those events that started out small, then gradually grew larger and larger as the spirit of the participants rose to a fever pitch.

When it was finished, everyone at the McKinley Elementary Grade School in Aberdeen, South Dakota—faculty and students alike—stood back and admired what they'd done!

My twin sister and I were in the fourth grade that year in the late 1930s. The first snowfall of the season had blanketed everything in snow perfect for making great snowballs and forts. That's how it started.

At recess, the boys eagerly scooped up snow by the handful and pressed it into a hard, shiny ball, which they hurled with the accuracy of professional baseball pitchers. Their targets were usually the girls, who screamed and dodged.

They Had a Mission

Others busied themselves by rolling the moisture-laden chunks into huge balls, leaving deep pathways that uncovered the ground beneath.

Soon the idea caught on, and everybody began rolling their own, competing with others to see who could roll the biggest snowballs.

Then someone suggested that *all* the snowballs be rolled together in a large circle to form the base of a gigantic snowman.

As soon as that was done, some of the bigger and stronger boys formed a line similar to a "bucket brigade" and began passing the snow-boulders hand-to-hand up to the top, where they were plopped down with a heavy thud and patted into place.

Even the school janitor got into the act and brought a ladder to ease the lifting process.

The whole scene reminded me of a bunch of ants feverishly building a mound of dirt to make their home.

Frosty Was Half-Baked

Yet all this efficiency didn't allow us to finish the job—just then, the school bell rang to signify the end of recess. Groans of protest greeted that bell, because it meant we had to return to the world of books, blackboards and schoolwork.

Even worse was the combined realization that our "snow monster" was not going to get finished. What a pity!

All that hard work and our task had not been completed. Then some-

thing unprecedented happened. The school principal came out of the building and took an admiring look at the unfinished snowman, then at the eager, sweaty faces looking up at him.

Smiling from ear to ear, he announced, "Considering how everyone is having such a good time, all classes are dismissed for the day. Carry on!"

At that point, there arose such a racket that even a hibernating bear would have been awakened.

We all returned to the task of completing the snow monstrosity, and because classes had been dismissed, even the teachers came out to help.

Strangely enough, although school was over for the day, nobody went home until the head was crowned with a knit cap, coal for the eyes and mouth, and a stick for the nose.

It's a day I'll never forget—the day a snowman came to school.

Bob Stein

Backtrackin'

"Climb aboard" as readers recall the golden age of rail transportation.

The Pied Piper Of Vera, Oklahoma?

WHILE I was growing up in the '30s and '40s in Vera, Oklahoma, we lived near the railroad tracks.

Every time a train came along, I'd run out and wave to the engineer while jumping up and down.

Sometimes he'd imitate me by bouncing up and down in his seat! Other times, a freight train might stop on a side track waiting for a passenger, and I got to talk with the engineer for a while.

A passenger train came through our town every day shortly after school got out. The man who took the outgoing mail to the train and picked up the incoming mail usually had a group of kids following him like he was the Pied Piper.

If no one was getting on or off, the train didn't stop—the outgoing mail was tossed in through a door while the incoming mail was tossed out.

Later, when streamliners came into use, the mailbag was put on a pole. As the train whizzed by, the bag was snatched off the pole and onto

One for the Railroad

THE SMALL TOWN of Phelps, New York was the only one our train passed through where the kids didn't throw stones at the train. The kids were so nice, our engineer bought candy, and all summer he tossed it out to the kids who stood by the tracks.

In that same town, a little girl set up a lemonade stand in front of her house, which was on the other side of the road from the tracks.

One day I said to the engineer, "Let's stop for a lemonade."

We did, and you should have seen the look on the little girl's face.

—Paul Keysor, Cato, New York

Home, Home on the Rails

MY DAD, along with us four boys, built two homes for ourselves out of railroad boxcars, one in Port Huron, Michigan in 1915, when I was 7, and the other in Flint in 1920, when I was 12. The first thing we did was get two big wagon wheels and some lumber to build a pushcart. That didn't take very long.

Then we walked over to the railroad yard, paid the man in charge $1 and he said, "Help yourself."

With hammer, sledge and crowbar, we dismantled a boxcar, nail by nail. The nails were straightened so we could use them to build the house.

The boards were removed, and we were careful not to damage them. They were oak.

The lumber was then loaded onto the pushcart and hauled off to our lot, where we had already put in a concrete block foundation.

The finished house was 24 x 26 feet, with one large bedroom for all of us, and a big kitchen with a stove that burned the scraps of wood left over from the construction.

—Walter Wasielewski
as told to his daughter
Natalie Becker, Vero Beach, Florida

the train. What a thrill I felt as the train went rushing past!

We were always told never to get too close because we could be sucked under the train. I wonder if that was true. —*Starr Bell Graham*
Bartlesville, Oklahoma

"SLOW DOWN!" That's what Francis Coupens says his boss would often yell at him when Francis was running this section car in 1932. "I'd slow down for a little while, then speed it up as fast as it would go," recalls Francis, of Murray, Utah. Later, he traded the fast life for one underground. "I owned a coal mine in Rock Springs, Wyoming for about 3 years, until the war broke out."

Two Bits for a Train Ride

IN MY high school days, 1946-'50, I lived in Olden, Missouri. The Frisco Railroad went by my house, and the depot was just across the tracks.

When I could scrape up a quarter, I'd stand in front of the depot, flag down the morning passenger train and ride the 8 miles to West Plains to school.

If by some miracle I had another quarter, I'd ride back home in the afternoon. Most times I had to hitch-hike, but what fun it was to ride the old steams. —*Richard Blair*
Peru, Indiana

STOP, LOOK AND WAVE. Starr Graham (on the right in photo at left) loved to wave to the engineer.

'Good-Bye Game' Was Good Fun

By Bill Beecher, Waukesha, Wisconsin

BACK IN 1939, I was a high schooler in Norman, Oklahoma. We kids really looked forward to Friday nights—that was when we headed to the local train station to play "bye-bye". Never heard of that game? Well, read on!

On a typical Friday night, we'd take our dates to the Sooner Theater at 7 to enjoy about 2-1/4 hours of entertainment, including the newsreel, Travel Talks and Bugs Bunny.

When the movie let out at about 9:15, we'd run across the street to the Lindsey Drugstore, slurp down a quick Coke and be out of there by 9:30.

What was the rush? Well, we didn't want to be late for the 9:42 arrival of "No. 6". The Santa Fe station was only a block and a half away. Arriving there in groups of four or six, the first thing we'd do is check the green chalkboard up on the wall to see if No. 6, a southbound passenger train, was on time.

If the board under the clock said "OT", we knew we had about 7 minutes to start playing "good-bye".

Public displays of affection were not quite as common back then as they are today, but "saying good-bye" at the train station platform was a perfectly acceptable thing.

Until the train arrived, some innocent hugging, a little hand-holding and maybe a little light nuzzling went on between the couples in our group. But when the train steamed into the station, it was okay to clutch and kiss!

As the train squealed to a halt and stopped hissing and belching steam, we'd run out onto the red-brick platform near the passenger car, where the conductor had put down the portable step and called, "All aboard!"

After letting those with tickets and luggage get on the train, we'd gather 'round two-by-two to "say our bye-byes" in earnest. Kissing right on the lips, tight embraces and prolonged hugs were allowed at this time...although among the "rookies" there was usually more giggling and yelling "Bye-Bye!" than anything else.

The poor conductor never knew how many passengers he was taking aboard. Sometimes only one or two legitimate ticket holders would make their way through the cluster of high school kids playing "bye-bye". Sometimes *no one* got on the train, and the conductor would just laugh and call out "All aboard!" one last time.

When the last car of the train followed the engine out of town, some "bye-bye" players dispersed to Lindsey's for a nightcap Coke and a couple of hit parade tunes on the jukebox.

Others would walk home, then give their dates a peck on the cheek, sealing a memory of the innocent fun we had back in those happy high school days of 1939. ☏

Jelly Pan Preserves Jolly Memories

By Vivian Harris, North Logan, Utah

AS THE only girl in the family, I inherited a real prize—Mama's jelly pan. It's just a heavy pot with a long curved handle, but I can't make good jelly without it.

It weighs about a ton and takes two hands to lift onto the stove. The narrowed top and bottom discourage boil-overs, and the bottom is so thick that the jelly seldom scorches.

I was born in 1931, during the Depression. Daddy died when I was 6, leaving Mama in debt and with four small children. She was a remarkable woman who went back to teaching school and provided for our every need. She also provided some luxuries, and her jelly was so good it could be considered one.

As a very young girl, I had only a couple of jobs on jelly-making day, but I watched and learned.

First Mama built a fire in the old wood range, saying she could never control the heat just right on her new electric stove.

Washing Jars Was Her Job

Since my slim hands fit inside the jelly glasses, it was my job to wash them. They were then placed upside down in a shallow pan of boiling water to be scalded. I was fascinated watching the water being sucked out of the pan and up into the glasses.

Next, the jelly pan was filled with the clear juice that had dripped through a jelly sack all night long. Mama never measured according to "directions"—she used the extra juice because it was plentiful, while sugar and pectin had to be purchased.

She didn't time the cooking, either—she knew just how the jelly should "sheet" off the spoon to set up perfectly. Her jelly could have won a blue ribbon at the fair, but she never entered it there.

Mama was so fussy, skimming the foam two or three times to make sure her jelly was perfectly clear before pouring it into the waiting jars. That part of the process was okay with me because I got to sample the skimmings on a slice of home-made bread!

The next step—melting the paraffin in a little pan kept just for that purpose—was dangerous. Too much heat and it would catch fire; too little and it didn't cover the tops of the jelly jars evenly. Mama melted and poured as I watched.

The glasses were set aside to cool before receiving labels prepared in Mama's beautiful handwriting.

The Downside of Jelly Day

It was my job to take the jars down to the spidery, dank, dirt-floored cellar in back of our house. Lifting up the door, I let my eyes adjust before venturing down the stairs. With only one bare globe to illuminate the frightening expanse, my speed in putting away those glasses was astounding!

At last, came the best part of jelly day—Mama's "roy groy" pudding, which she'd learned to make from her own frugal Danish mother.

There was always a bit more jelly than would fit into the last jar. This was left in the pot, to which Mama added the water used to rinse the cup and spoons. Tapioca was added and cooked to thicken, then the pudding was served warm with thick cream from our Jersey cow.

To this day, raspberry roy groy remains a favorite food memory for my brothers and me.

Recalling the heat of that summer kitchen, I've wondered why Mama went to such pains. I think it was yet another way to show how much she loved us. We were poor but never lived poorly. My memories of home are all sweet because of her.

Here's how to make "Roy Groy" (even if it's not jelly day): Combine 1/2 cup jam or jelly (most any tart flavor will do), 3 tablespoons of quick-cooking tapioca and 2 cups of water. Cook over medium heat, stirring to prevent sticking, until thick and tapioca is clear. Serve warm with cream topping or plain. ☎

STILL SIMMERS. Vivian Harris (at left in 1940) inherited the old metal jelly pot (below) but still can't make jelly as good as her mother, Irma Nichols (at right in 1933), did.

My Pop Invented the Popsicle...by Accident!

By George Epperson, San Rafael, California

MY FATHER, Frank Epperson, grew up in San Francisco in the early 1900s. As was true for many kids back then, one of his favorite "treats" was a sweet fruit-flavored punch made with a powdered mix. And that's just what he was enjoying one night in 1906 when he accidentally invented the Popsicle.

On that particular night, Pop was called to dinner before he'd finished his fruit punch. He left the glass and spoon out on the unheated front porch and forgot all about them.

It was a rare cold night in San Francisco, and next morning Pop found his drink frozen hard. Using the spoon as a handle, he pried the frozen drink from the glass and was delighted to eat it like a lollipop!

Pop didn't have the means to do anything about his "invention" just then, but he never forgot the concept or the potential of those frozen treats.

Years later, after he'd grown up and married, he began producing the treats at an old ice plant in Oakland...and trying out new flavors on us nine kids!

Sales Slow at First

Pop introduced his treats—which he called "Ep-sicles"—at a Firemen's Ball at the Neptune Beach Ballroom in Alameda, California. Nobody seemed interested at first, so Mom and Pop took turns walking around the ballroom floor, conspicuously eating one Ep-sicle after another.

Finally a man came up to Pop and said, "If I've seen you eat one, I've seen you eat a thousand. They sure must be good!"

Pop gave him an Ep-sicle, and the man called out to his girlfriend, "Come and try one of these things—it's really good and it's not a lollipop!"

After that, Mom and Pop couldn't work fast enough, and their Ep-sicles sold out.

In fact, Ep-sicles proved so popular that evening that my parents were offered a concessions tent at Neptune Beach, beginning the following day.

EVERYBODY LIKES **Popsicle** REFRESHING · EASY TO EAT

POP WAS TOPS! Author's father, Frank Epperson, in white coat above, invented the Popsicle. Kids lined up for his treats at this fair in Salinas, California on July 4, 1923. This is the first photo ever taken of a Popsicle!

Mom worked all night to make purple-and-orange clown costumes for Pop, herself, and my older brother and sister, who were very excited about being old enough to help out.

That summer, Pop's refreshing frozen treats were a big hit. But as Ep-sicles became more and more popular, my brothers, sisters and I continued to use our family's name for them. We called them "Pop's sicles".

One night, Pop brought home a new flavor for us to taste—orange and chunky pineapple. It was the best Ep-sicle I've ever tasted, before or since.

My twin brother and I eagerly looked forward to more of the same the next evening, but Pop showed up empty-handed. Tugging at his leg and crying, I blurted out, "I want a Popsicle like we had yesterday!"

Gently picking me up, he explained that the latest batch had been too sugary and wouldn't stay frozen. Then he added, "But, you know, that's a pretty good name—I'm going to change the name to Popsicle!"

Here to Stay

The first picture of a Popsicle was taken on July 4, 1923 at a fair in Salinas, California (above). Pop made his treats there and slept in a tent.

During Pop's lifetime, Popsicles spread all around the world. I'll never forget how excited he was the day he learned his treats were selling well in Egypt!

That's when he knew for sure that—although Ep-sicles were a thing of the past—Popsicles were here to stay. ☎

If It's Fish...It Must Be Friday

IN THIS ERA of take-out, hurry-up fast food, kids must have an awfully tough time keeping track of the days of the week.

I say this because when I was a youngster in the 1930s and Mother brought leftover roast to the table, there was no doubt in anyone's mind that it was *Monday*.

Back in the good old days, we enjoyed good, solid, substantial meals... but they were pretty plain. And they were as predictable as, well, the days of the week!

The aroma of liver, bacon and onions frying announced to the family—and to the neighbors up to a block away!—that Tuesday had arrived.

We kids came to understand at a very young age that a huge pot of boiling water, plus pungent garlic in the air, signified Wednesday—and that we'd shortly enjoy spaghetti for supper.

My mother called Thursday "pick-up

By Marie Grant
Monroe Township, New Jersey

night". By this she meant we'd be having whatever she could pick up from the corner grocery store on her way home from the PTA meeting.

Anyone who came into our house on Friday and didn't smell fish had

absolutely *no* sense of smell. This was by far the easiest day of the week to determine via the "dinner test".

Saturday night was when we kids got our hair washed, shoes shined and clothes inspected to make sure everything was in order for Sunday school. So much activity necessitated a quick and easy dinner, which always meant beans and franks.

And how could anyone not know it was Sunday when we passed our plates to Father, who loaded them with thick slices of roast beef and steaming mashed potatoes smothered in rich brown gravy?

As you can see, it was easy for me to keep track of the days when I was young.

I admit that Mother's cooking wasn't always a chef's delight, but it was a lot better than today's soggy hamburgers served in Styrofoam boxes—with nary a clue as to what day of the week it is!

I Survived the 'War of the Worlds'!

By Robert Tefertillar
Springfield, Illinois

HALLOWEEN EVE fell on a Sunday in 1938, so the usual festivities in my hometown of Centralia, Illinois were rescheduled for the following night.

I was one disappointed 11-year-old, more or less resigned to a boring evening at home, listening to radio programs with my family.

None of my favorite adventures or serials were on...and even Edgar Bergen and Charlie McCarthy didn't seem very funny that night.

No one objected when Gramps began twisting the dial in search of more interesting fare. He paused at a music program and was about to move on when we heard a news flash.

The announcer quickly had our complete attention. He said that a Chicago scientist has just observed several big explosions on the planet Mars!

"Mars, huh?" Gramps grunted and grumbled. "That's a million miles away —what's that got to do with us?"

The music started once again, but it was almost immediately interrupted by a frantic announcement about a "fiery, unknown object from space" that had crashed in a farm field near Grovers Mill, New Jersey.

Now my ears were really riveted to our old Philco! When the announcer promised to keep us posted on any new developments, an awful premonition began to turn my stomach inside out.

Music Stopped for Good

My fears were not quieted when the music stopped for good a moment later.

"There are fragmented, unsubstantiated reports of many people dead or injured in New Jersey," the announcer said in a trembling voice.

"What in billy blue blazes is going on?" my uncle stammered.

Grandma gasped. "Mercy, that man said people were dead and injured."

"There's got to be some mistake," Grandpa snapped. "I don't care how scared that announcer sounds. There'll be a commercial soon, and we'll find out this is all made up."

This isn't made up! my mind screamed. *It's real!* After all, I'd read all about Superman coming from another planet, and I kept up with all the adventures of Buck Rogers.

Spaceship from Mars?

I knew exactly what that thing in New Jersey was—a spaceship from Mars, filled with terrible monsters that were killing people. They'd probably get all of us—including me!

On the radio, another voice cut in...it was a reporter actually on the scene at Grovers Mill!

"This is unbelievable!" he gasped. "I am standing on a small hill observing what is just not possible. What has landed here is a silver spacecraft of some sort...

"These creatures," he continued, "are huge slug-like beings. Their weapons are some sort of ray guns, shooting a deadly green flame. Another cylinder has just crash-landed...the police are moving in...Arrrgghhh!"

Just then, a tremendous pounding at the front door sent me cowering behind Grandpa's chair. Our neighbor, Jessie Collins, barged into the room, ashen-faced and shaking.

"What's...what's going on?" he stammered. "Is this for real?"

"It can't be real!" Grandpa insisted.

Outside our house, there was commotion in the street. Grandma threw open the front door, and I peered cautiously around her skirts.

Neighbors were streaming from their houses. Some had guns, others carried pitchforks and baseball bats. All eyes were scanning the clear, star-filled sky, searching for signs of those dreaded silver cylinders from Mars.

Some folks, who'd tuned in the program from the beginning, said it was only make-believe. They tried to convince their hysterical neighbors it was all a put-on. But nobody believed them.

We stayed awake for hours watching for Martians. When finally we decided to go to bed, Gramps was grumbling about how easily people had been taken in.

I, on the other hand, was not completely convinced. Just to be safe, I slept on the floor of my grandparents' room. Meanwhile, a few neighborhood diehards kept a lonely all-night watch from their porch swings, with loaded shotguns in their laps!

Truth Was Embarrassing

Next morning, the newspaper revealed the embarrassing truth—*The War of the Worlds* broadcast by Orson Welles had frightened not only our neighborhood, but a good portion of North America.

Welles himself professed amazement that his make-believe performance had been taken literally. I think he was secretly pleased!

I know I will never forget the genuine terror I felt that night. Nowadays, modern "space-creature" movies just don't seem as scary. After all...I survived the Martian attack of 1938! ☎

Orson Welles

By Richard Mathewson
Norman, Oklahoma

Knitting For Victory

DURING WORLD WAR II, everyone in Owosso, Michigan was involved on the home front, even grade-school kids like me who were asked to knit afghans for wounded veterans.

All of us had relatives in the service and realized we were part of the war effort. I was 10 years old in 1943 and really enjoyed the knitting. I think I did it for a while before I drifted onto other things.

This photograph (above) appeared in the *Owosso Argus Press* along with an article about our efforts at Emerson Elementary School in my hometown, west of Flint.

Because of the labor shortage, my mother was working at the newspaper. Another man at the paper who had a student at the school thought our project was worth reporting—people were always interested in what the children were doing to help.

The story noted that 30 of the 45 boys in the fourth through sixth grades had made at least one afghan square as a Junior Red Cross project.

"The boys are really very patient and are willing to do the squares over and over again to get them right," one teacher said in the story. "My son has had to rip one of his out four times."

"It is a lot to expect that youngsters in the fourth grade turn in perfect knitting, but we do get some fine pieces of work," another fourth-grade teacher said.

We did the knitting after our lessons were done in school or took the work home to do.

"My pupils can knit better than I can," one teacher remarked. "There's not a single thing these youngsters of mine can't do."

The afghan that we worked on actually went to a wounded veteran who was a relative of one of the kids in the school. That made our work even more rewarding. ☎

Our Blue Magic Christmas

By Glenna McClish, Issaquah, Washington

I WAS 16 in the spring of 1938 when I met Arthur at a dance at our Dunkirk, Indiana high school. He was a marvelous dancer, and we were amazed to discover we had the same birthday.

We had similar interests, too. We both sang in the church choir and were avid bicyclists. We began dating, and by late fall, it was generally known at school that we had become "an item".

We had such fun together! Fantasizing that we were Nelson Eddy and Jeanette MacDonald, we'd sing duets from operettas while I provided piano accompaniment.

On Christmas Eve, our church choir was scheduled to sing the *Messiah*. Arthur came early to pick me up and brought along my Christmas gift, a beautiful rose-petal necklace he had made. As he placed it around my neck, he said, "I have something else for you." Then he fastened his Hi-Y pin on my blouse.

Taking me in his arms, he kissed me tentatively and gently, and I felt my world coming to life. How wonderful it felt to be young and in love!

After church, he walked me home

THEIR BLUE HEAVEN became a reality when Arthur and Glenna (above right) reunited after being teen sweethearts.

through the snow. Along the way, we were enchanted by a cottage beautifully decorated with blue lights. Standing behind me, Arthur put his arms around me and said, "I hope we have blue lights on *our* house at Christmas."

Tremulously I whispered, "Yes." With those words, the magic of the night closed about us and time stood still.

That magical Christmas became a memory as we continued to date and have fun together. In the fall of 1939, Arthur went away to college in another state. I, too, went away to school.

As time passed, our letters became less frequent. In fulfilling our goals, we'd lost each other. Arthur eventually became a landscape architect and I a medical records technician.

Still, I never forgot our wonderful "blue magic" Christmas. During World War II, Arthur went into the Army while I eventually married a fine man with whom I spent 25 happy years.

When my husband died suddenly of

a heart attack, I felt bereft without him and had difficulty adjusting to being alone. I returned to the medical field, and slowly my heartache eased.

Then, in the spring of 1983, I flew to the West Coast to attend a medical conference and meet an old school friend. Sometime before, she'd run into Arthur, who'd also moved to the West Coast. When she learned I was coming to see her, she invited him to have dinner with us.

I was nervous and apprehensive, but when the front door opened and I saw him standing there, the years fell away and the young man I knew so long ago greeted me with open arms.

After dinner, we took a long walk and talked of the twists and turns our lives had taken. Later, after I'd returned home, he called and asked if he might come visit sometime.

Proudly, I showed him my home and the town where I lived. During his visit, we became reacquainted anew. Then, while we walked in a beautiful botanical garden, the old magic surrounded us and he asked me to marry him.

"Oh, yes!" I gasped.

So, at the age of 62, we recaptured the romance of our youth. We retired to the northern woods of Washington after our wedding, which was held in a beautiful apple orchard. The two of us went camping, took long hikes and rode a tandem bike for miles.

We even toured Europe and bicycled through Holland at tulip time. Each day was an adventure to look forward to.

Then, on our first Christmas together, Arthur invited me to take a walk in the snow. When we stepped outside and I saw our house aglow with blue lights, I was overcome with emotion.

Unknown to me, he'd hung them while I was busy with the Christmas baking. Taking me in his arms, he said, "I told you I hoped our house would have blue lights, didn't I?" ☎

A Hanukkah Gift from The Heart

By Florence Paul, Santa Ana, California

IT WAS DECEMBER—a month in which two different festivals of lights would be commemorated. First began the Jewish Hanukkah, then Christmas.

I was 7 that year, 1927, and living in a New York City neighborhood partially surrounded by cemeteries. Visitors would shudder and wonder aloud how we could live so close to a graveyard. We'd laugh and answer, "The dead are certainly more harmless than the living."

The holiday of Hanukkah passed quietly for us that year. There wasn't enough money for necessities—let alone a menorah, candles and gifts. Instinctively, we knew that if our wonderful mom had been able to, we'd have had a festive holiday.

After Hanukkah came Christmas. My Christian friends all had trees in their homes, hung with delicate colored balls. Some even had silver stars on top with beautifully wrapped presents underneath.

I felt in awe, but what I didn't realize was most of the gifts were practical items. Although better off financially than we were, few of our neighbors could splurge on gifts.

One day when my ball went over the fence and into the cemetery, I climbed through an opening to retrieve it. Many of the tombstones were decorated for Christmas with wreaths and pine branches with poinsettia leaves.

Lying near my ball was a pine branch about 12 inches long. I took a needle off, rubbed it between my fingers and sniffed—the scent of fresh pine was heavenly.

Branch and Box Gave Her an Idea

Then I picked up my ball and left, holding the pine branch. On the way home, I spotted a small cardboard box, slightly soiled but in fine shape. An idea came to me and I decided to take it home, too.

In my bedroom, I made a pencil hole in the center of the box, stuck about 2 inches of the branch into the hole and was delighted when it stood up straight.

To decorate my "tree", I took little balls of cotton and dipped some in blue ink, some in red ink and left the rest white.

Next I rummaged through my junk drawer for a vial of tiny, colored glass beads. With needle and thread, I made several strands of beads and tied each to a branch.

When the cotton balls were dry, I strung thread through them and hung them on branches. Standing back to admire my handiwork, I thought it was beautiful.

Thrilled to find more beads in my drawer, I sat down to make a double strand, then wrapped it in a paper napkin and tied it with some ribbon I'd saved.

When Mom came home, I took her hand and led her into my bedroom to show her my "tree". As she stared quietly at it, I pointed to the gift. "Mom, it's really a Hanukkah present, but it looks pretty under the tree."

GIFT OF GIVING. Author (above in 1927) and her mother (top) shared a memorable holiday years ago.

What Would Mom Say?

She hadn't said a word yet, but I noticed tears in her eyes. She opened the package, held up the necklace and said, "How lovely," as she put it on over her head.

Then she sat down on the bed and held me close. How I loved the clean scent of her.

"My darling," she said, her voice a little husky, "thank you so much—I will always keep and enjoy this lovely necklace. And from today on, we'll save our pennies so that next year, we'll have a real Hanukkah celebration."

Years later, I found out that Mom started doing domestic work 1 day a week to supplement my dad's meager salary. Every week, she put $2 into a Christmas Club account, so the next year each of us would have a little gift for the holidays and a special dinner.

At the time, though, nothing could have dimmed my satisfaction at her pleased reaction—not even my brother saying, "What a dumb thing that is."

It was a holiday gift to *me* that I will treasure forever. ☎

Harold M. Lambert

When Smokey Bear Wore Pink Pajamas

By Dereck Williamson, Annandale, New Jersey

IN THE GOOD OLD DAYS, talking dolls had no batteries to wear out—all you had to do was turn the key and wind them up.

Now most of those dolls are packed away in dusty attics. And somewhere, there's one special windup doll that, if her key is turned, is going to give someone quite a start!

The story began when "Patti" dolls made their debut in Clinton, New Jersey in December 1955.

Patti was a talking doll, and one Patti in particular became the most famous doll in the state. People came from all over to hear her! I remember the details well because, back then, I was working as a cub reporter and covered Patti's story for the local newspaper.

The special Patti arrived without much fanfare at Attaway's Department Store on Main Street, packed in a shipping carton with six identical-looking blond sisters, each wearing pink pajamas and a silver ribbon that said "Patti Prays".

Each doll had a key on its back. When wound, Patti would say, "Now I lay me down to sleep, I pray the Lord my soul to keep. God bless Mommy. God bless Daddy. Amen."

Patti Growls a Warning

Mr. Attaway took the dolls from the carton and tested them one by one. Each recited her little prayer nicely—until he got to the last one.

When he turned her key, she looked up with her bright blue eyes and growled: "I'm Smokey the Bear! I'm Smokey the Bear! Running and looking for smoke in the air! I warn careless people, and tell them 'Take care'. Prevent forest fires, says Smokey the Bear!"

Mr. Attaway dropped baby Patti like a hot potato! When he regained his composure, he picked up "Patti Bear" and set her aside. "That's going to scare some kid half to death," he muttered.

Word of the growling Patti soon spread, and Mr. Attaway was kept busy

> ## "*M*r. Attaway dropped baby Patti like a hot potato!"

taking her down from her shelf in the back room, winding her up and letting visitors hear her deep-voiced warning about fires.

Some investigation revealed that the Patti dolls had been shipped from a Georgia factory that also had an order from the South Carolina Forestry Commission for Smokey Bear dolls. Sure enough, someone had mixed up the voice boxes!

Patti Bear Finds a Home

Eventually all of bear-voiced Patti's sisters found homes, but she remained on the shelf, unsold.

Her story had a happy ending, though. One little girl kept coming back to the store, winding up the doll and rocking it, as if to soothe the snarling beast within. The little girl had fallen in love with the fire-obsessed Patti. On the day before Christmas, Mr. Attaway quietly gave her the doll.

Mr. Attaway declined to reveal the girl's name, saying he wanted her and the doll to have a happy, publicity-free holiday.

A decade later, Mr. Attaway retired and moved away, taking with him the secret of Patti's placement. I have the feeling that she is still out there somewhere, waiting to deliver her special message. But exactly where she is, only her owner—now grown up—knows.

There's another unanswered question. Whatever happened to the Smokey doll who inherited Patti's voice? I can still imagine a barrel-chested bear in a ranger hat who, on command, lisps a falsetto "Now I lay me down to sleep...". ☎

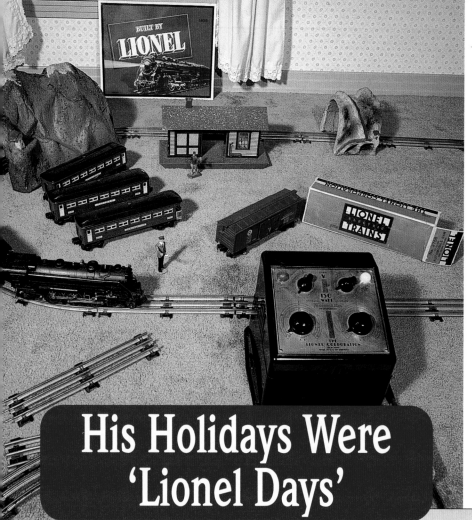

His Holidays Were 'Lionel Days'

By Frank Finale, Bayville, New Jersey

MY CHRISTMAS MORNINGS will be forever linked to my uncle and the Lionel train set he started for me in 1950, when I was 8 years old.

The first box I found under the bubbling lights of the Christmas tree at my aunt's Bronx, New York home that year was heavier than a metal bank full of pennies. I reached in, and out came a black beauty of a locomotive with six silver wheels reflecting the lights of the tree.

Other boxes contained a tender, small transformer and enough 027-gauge track to encircle the Christmas tree.

I remember my aunt whispering, "Do you really think he's old enough for such an expensive gift?"

My uncle, always calm and logical, replied, "Of course." He then instructed me how to set up the transformer and warned against touching the live wires. My worried aunt's countenance changed to one of admiration for her brother as she offered him a glass of eggnog. She still wasn't so sure about me, but she trusted her brother. So did I.

One Car Each Christmas

The Christmas tree didn't burn down that year, or in the many years that followed. My aunt's fears diminished, and my uncle continued giving me a car a year—gondola, boxcar, tank car, coal car.

I'd run that train for hours, until I *became* the great steam locomotive, pulling freight under tunnels of chairs and bridges of blocks, steaming past the tall forest of the Christ-

mas tree wrapped in cotton snow, wailing like a coonhound in the night.

The sharp, warm scent of electricity filled my nostrils, and faraway names rattled in my imagination—Erie, Wabash, Rio Grande, Santa Fe.

One Christmas, a figure dressed in a red suit and white beard came in, stomped the snow from his shiny black boots, shook his belly and "Ho, Ho, Ho'ed" us kids awake. From his bulky sack he began withdrawing presents. I remember the wrapping paper on mine was still cold with melting snow.

Santa stayed only a short while. After his departure, my uncle appeared, claiming to be disappointed that he'd missed him.

Dream Came True

I wasn't disappointed at all, though. That was the Christmas I received the car I'd dreamed about night after night—the refrigerated milk car. It was white as the milk it delivered, with seven silver miniature milk cans I could load into the hinged roof hatch.

I'd pull the car onto the remote-control track and endlessly buzz the little man to deliver the milk. Watching him was like watching the cuckoo pop out of the clock without having to wait an hour between performances. I reloaded that car so often, my thumb showed the dark indentations of the milk cans.

The last car I received from my uncle, before he and his family moved away to Ohio, was a red caboose. Although he wrote and visited, Christmases were never quite the same afterward.

Sometimes I'd daydream about catching a boxcar on a long freight train, riding it to Ohio and showing up at my uncle's doorstep. He'd hug me tight, and then we'd sit and reminisce about past Christmases and trains.

But I never hopped that freight train. So now, when Christmas carols drift through the air and the department stores set out their displays, I make my way to the model train setup.

There I catch a whiff of that old electricity and feel the warm glow of the past...the Lionel days of my youth. ☎

ELECTRIC MEMORIES. Young Frank Finale (top) got his first train from his uncle (above). That started a lifetime of memories of those great Lionels, as each Christmas brought another piece for the railroad.

Would Christmas Even Come?

By Janet Heller, Raymore, Missouri

IT WAS December 1918. The United States was at war, and a terrible flu epidemic was taking as many lives as were lost on the battlefield. But I was a 7-year-old girl in a small Missouri town, and my only thoughts were of the Christmas soon to come.

My father had died the year before of "pernicious anemia", so my aunt and uncle had taken charge of his small grocery store. I still liked to walk there every day to visit and help myself to a little penny candy.

On the way, I'd pass our town hardware store. Its front window was filled with a wonderful display of toys, and in the middle of that display sat the most beautiful baby doll I'd ever seen. With sky-blue eyes and a sweet smile, she reached out with chubby arms as if waiting for someone to claim her.

Each time I went by the window, I stood for a long time and stared at her, longing to hold her.

No Doll in the Window

One day as I hurried to my usual spot by the window, my heart just fell—there was an empty space where my baby doll had been. I turned and walked home so sadly in the cold, with tears running down my cheeks.

The only bright spot I had left was my oldest brother, Tom, who was home on Christmas leave from his job at a munitions factory in Virginia.

I was "his little girl" ever since Daddy had died. When Tom returned from his job and we met him at the train station, I broke into a run and jumped into his arms because I'd been so lonesome for him. Whenever Tom was around, I was on his lap—and if I wanted something, he'd take me to town to get it.

As Christmas drew nearer, Tom came down with the flu. Soon after, my other two brothers and I also had it and were bedridden. Mother spent every moment taking care of the four of us. We suffered with night sweats, but Mother saw to it we had clean blankets and sheets.

It was an enormous job, and to this day, I still don't know how she did it using only an old-fashioned wringer washer and trying to dry wet cotton blankets that froze up stiff as a board out on the line.

We were all so ill that when the doctor came to our house, he warned Mother that it was likely none of us would live through the night. Fortunately, three of us survived. But my beloved Tom died before morning.

He was buried on December 24, and with the snow so deep and everyone sick, my brother's only funeral service was a few words of comfort spoken to us by the minister.

In a solemn procession, Tom's casket was borne in a farm wagon pulled by four horses, while a crew of men trudged ahead to shovel out the drifts.

A Somber Christmas Eve

What a sad Christmas Eve. With all that had happened and my mother still busy caring for the rest of us, I went to bed thinking there wouldn't be any Christmas this year.

The next morning, I opened my eyes as Mother walked into the room. "Don't you want to see what you have by your bed?" she asked.

Beside me was a small cedar chest. I opened it slowly, and there lay my beautiful dream doll from the hardware store window.

"Tom bought it for 'his little girl'," Mother said softly.

This final precious gift from my brother was loved as no other. Even today this doll remains one of my most precious possessions.

Now she wears a long white dress I made. Someday she will live with my granddaughter, who every year at Christmastime asks me to tell her this story. ☎

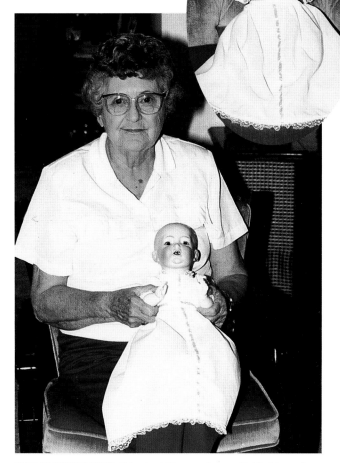

GIFT REMEMBERED. It looked like a sad seventh Christmas for Janet Heller (seen then, at top left, and now, above)...until a special gift arrived. She still has the doll today.

❧ NICEST THING ANYONE HAS DONE FOR ME ❧

There Are Still Heroes

MY UNCLE, Harry K. Morrison, was fighting in Europe during World War II. In November 1943, when I was 6, I received a box from Uncle Harry. It was full of chewing gum and chocolate bars—items almost impossible to get at home because of rationing.

In the box was a letter, which read:

Dear Pudgy (I was actually a skinny kid):

When I was a little boy, I would have liked it if I had a package waiting for me containing the things money won't buy —the thought that someone remembers.

These are for you. But be generous. Give more than your possessions, but of yourself, and when you grow up, you'll be a big man, inside and out, and the world will like you, for such men are hard to find.   Your uncle, Harry K

When I'm asked today if I have any heroes, I have to say, yes…my father, my father-in-law and my Uncle Harry K.   *—Karl Kolk III*
Columbus, Ohio

ADVICE BY AIRMAIL. Karl Kolk (below, on the right) received many letters from his Uncle Harry (left) during WWII, but one would contain a priceless message.

Speller Was Doubly Happy

ALL YEAR LONG, the citizens of Wayne County, North Carolina look forward to fall and the Wayne County Agricultural Fair. The year I was in fifth grade, I was eligible for the annual spelling bee held at the fair.

I had always been a good speller, and when I won the preliminary contest in our school class, I qualified to appear at the fair.

That year, my parents had to work on the day of the spelling bee. My brother, Dennis, who was 11 years older, agreed to take me.

Dennis was already married, with one child. Not only was he trying to support his family by farming, he was also going to college part time.

Dennis was a serious person who appeared gruff and distant to me. We didn't talk much on our way to the fair, so I took the opportunity to study a list of words given to me by my teacher.

As we entered the fairgrounds, Dennis sensed my uneasiness. He squeezed my hand and said, "It'll be okay. Just take your time and you'll do fine."

It wasn't much of a speech, but it helped calm me down. As Dennis sat in that smelly livestock barn, my competitors went down one by one until I was handed the blue ribbon.

I looked at my big brother, who was on his feet, clapping as hard as he could.

As we toured the fairgrounds, every time we stopped to talk to people he knew, Dennis introduced me, told them about my victory and prodded me to show off my blue ribbon.

Winning the spelling bee was great, but even greater was the warm recognition shown by my brother.
—Renee Futrelle
Mt. Olive, North Carolina

A Shovel Full of Love

MY GREAT-AUNT FAYE was the treasured love of my life, and her house in Port Townsend, Washington was my favorite place to visit. We spent many happy hours sitting on the front porch swing, which overlooked a country lane at the end of a huge yard dotted with flower gardens and giant evergreen trees.

When those trees filled with snow in winter, Aunt Faye spread the branches with bread crumbs, oatmeal and a

DIGGING UP MEMORIES of Great-Aunt Faye is easy for Patrice Sanders, thanks to her keepsake shovel. That's Patrice above at age 3, back in 1945, with her favorite Faye.

dried fruit concoction she made up daily to feed the birds.

Aunt Faye had chickens, and I'd help collect the eggs. Her cat, "Calico", lived for 18 years, and she had a mixed Lab named "Rowdy", who also enjoyed a long life. They were great playmates.

Aunt Faye loved to garden, and at age 3, I loved to "help". One day in 1945, Aunt Faye bought me my very own little shovel, which I used in the garden and to shovel snow in winter.

After I grew up, our visits dwindled. When Aunt Faye passed away in 1976, I discovered she'd kept my little shovel over 30 years as a keepsake.

Years later, in 1981, my husband, Robert, surprised me. He had taken the shovel and had it framed with a gold plaque that carries my nickname, "Li'l Bug".

Having that precious shovel to display on my wall is the nicest thing anyone has done for me. It's a constant reminder of Aunt Faye, who also demonstrated in so many nice ways how much she loved me.   *—Patrice Sanders*
La Grange, California

May the Circle Be Unbroken

OUR NEIGHBORS, Laurence and Bertha Wiest, were such close friends to my parents that they were almost like brother and sister. We kids called them Uncle Laurence and Aunt Bertha.

The Wiests helped take care of my crippled sister and me when we were small. I still remember the rabbit pull-toy and overalls they gave me during the Depression, as we didn't have any money.

Later, when I was in college and struggling with finances, Aunt Bertha periodically sent checks to keep the wolf from my door. Uncle Laurence had since passed away.

After graduation, when I found a job, I went to pay back Aunt Bertha. She said it was a gift and there was no need to repay her.

She did suggest that I use the money to invest in another young person's

HE WAS COVERED. John Mayer received the coveralls and pull-toy from close family friends in '29.

education, as she had done with me. I did just that, and that young man in turn helped another struggling student.

Because of my friend Aunt Bertha, a circle of unselfish love and concern had begun, and where it will end, no one knows. —*John Mayer*
Bakersfield, California

TV Boxing Was Fun For Family

By J.D. Brookhart
St. Marys, Ohio

THE CLANG of the bell, the *thud* of punches, the crowd noise and the announcer yelling out the split decision—those were the sounds of boxing in the 1950s.

Boxing was big in our family. We listened to radio broadcasts and later watched on television. Dad had been in the Marine Corps in World War II and learned jujitsu and boxing. He was so enthusiastic that he bought my brothers and me boxing gloves for our own Sunday night fights in the dining room.

We'd push the table and chairs out of the way and move the rug, and my older brother, Gary, who outweighed me by 15 pounds, would pummel me into submission.

I was every bit of 60 pounds and built like the skeleton that hung in our family doctor's office. I did have one terrific defense, though. I bled profusely when Gary hit me square in the face, ending the bout with Mother pleading for Dad to stop the Sunday night fights.

PINT-SIZE PUGILIST. Author with his dukes up back in the '50s, when he and his brother sparred under the tutelage of their father.

Brother Threw in the Towel

Eventually, I grew enough so I could land a few lucky punches, and Gary lost interest in fighting.

Our family didn't lose interest, however. We listened to the Wednesday night fights sponsored by Mennen Skin Bracer and the Friday night fights sponsored by Gillette Safety Razors with their slogan offered up between every round.

Grandfather Brookhart loved listening to the radio accounts of the championship boxing matches. He never missed a Joe Louis bout, although he claimed Louis always worked over the opponent's eyes before going for the knockout.

We listened to bouts with all the famous fighters of the time. And who could forget the third man in the ring, Ruby Goldstein?

For the Friday night fights, Mom popped a large pan of white popcorn and we'd drink Dad's Old Fashioned Root Beer. What memories!

In 1951, the Topps Bubble Gum Company came out with small cardboard boxing cards—excellent renditions of the famous boxers, usually the champions. We collected and traded these and learned a lot about the combatants from the backs of those cards.

Boxing continued to be a spectator sport for Dad, my brothers and me as we watched the newer fighters on TV. But the '50s remain my best memories of boxing—the taste of freshly popped popcorn, the flickering black-and-white screen, and Grandpa, Dad and my brothers all rooting, booing and yelling for their favorite boxers. ☎

The Pork Chop Incident

By Ruth Dipper, Willow Grove, Pennsylvania

MY PARENTS had two simple rules about dating: I had to wait until I was 16…and before I could get in a car with a boy, he had to come to dinner so my family could look him over.

The first test came in 1952, when a tall good-looking senior at Pitman High School in Wenonah, New Jersey began showing interest in me. One day in the hall, Al made his move.

"Would you like to go out?" he asked. "How about Saturday night? I'll pick you up about…"

Noticing the look on my face, he asked, "What's the matter? Don't you want to go out with me?"

"Of course I do," I responded. "It's just that… well…I'm not allowed to date until I'm 16."

"When will that be?" he asked.

When I told him it'd be another 3 weeks, his face lit up. "That's no problem," he said. "I can wait."

Continuing awkwardly, I explained that he'd have to come for dinner first.

Al shrugged. "Fine," he replied. "Tell me when, and I'll be there."

Planned a Dinner Party

I couldn't believe how easy it all was. When I told my folks the news, Pop looked at Mom and said, "She doesn't have to be *exactly* 16, does she?"

With a smile, Mom replied, "Of course not," and suggested I invite Al that very Sunday. After he accepted the invitation, I began planning the nicest little dinner party I could imagine.

Mom wisely insisted on making most of the meal, leaving me to concentrate on my special recipe for stuffed pork chops. I put out our nicest tablecloth and even arranged some daffodils into a centerpiece.

Desperately wanting everything to go well, I warned my three brothers to behave themselves.

"Al comes from a nice, refined, well-to-do family," I explained. "Please don't act like idiots."

Just Warming Up

After Al arrived and we began eating, the conversation was polite but tense, punctuated by several long pauses. Finally, with an air of sophistication, my brother Carl exclaimed, "*My*, these stuffed pork chops *are* delicious, Ruth."

"You *really* outdid yourself this time," George added politely.

Brother Marty chimed in, "Is there *no end* to your talents, Ruth?"

I knew that this meant trouble—the idiots were just warming up! The tension increased, and I was afraid to say a word. Al just sat there eating.

After a particularly long, embarrassing silence, Carl picked up his pork chop bones, reached across the table and placed them neatly on my plate. "You can chew on these now," he said. "I'm finished."

I sat there totally dumbfounded

George

Carl

Marty

THREE WISE GUYS. Ruth Dipper's brothers (above) increased the tension of an already nervous occasion when she invited a beau to dinner for the first time (that's her and Al at left).

RP Photo

as George and then Marty also placed their bones on my plate. Looking up, I pleaded, "Mom! Please make them stop!"

She reprimanded the boys, asking them to behave themselves and stop acting like children. But then, after another awkward silence, Mom discreetly picked up *her* bone and placed it atop the others on my plate!

Everyone at the table burst out laughing. Totally embarrassed and almost in tears, I looked over at Al, only to see him trying in vain to hide his laughter behind a napkin. He looked so ridiculous that *I* started laughing, too.

For the rest of the dinner, we all relaxed and enjoyed ourselves. After dessert, Pop turned to Al and said, "The boys and I will help Mom with the dishes. Why don't you take Ruth out for a ride in your car?"

Al and I dated for the next 2-1/2 years, and it was that first night when I realized how lucky I was to have such a fun family. ☎

Buddy Lee Is Her Longtime Pardner

By Yvonne Fine, Prescott, Arizona

WHEN my family moved from the affluent city of Evanston, Illinois to the humble "cowboy" town of Prescott, Arizona, my two sisters and I soon found out that the bows and ribbons on our dolls were out of style. We wanted boy dolls!

Those were hard to find, but Mother persevered. In the window of a Goldwaters Department Store, she found three little boy dolls advertising Lee jeans and bought them.

I named mine "Dickie". We went horseback riding and climbed trees. I even made a raft for him to float on in a nearby creek or in the basement when it flooded.

After high school and college came the war. In 1942, I worked at Lockheed building airplanes, then joined the Navy. All the while, Dickie followed me in a box. Marriage brought five little girls and four boys, so my doll was never without attention.

Yes, he is worn, but he can still stand by himself. He was loved by my children, grandchildren and great-grandkids. I so often hear, "Granny, can I hold Dickie?"

"Of course," I say, "just be gentle. He's like Granny—old. But, like Granny, he loves your attention." ☎

HER BUDDY. Yvonne Fine called her doll "Dickie" (in cameo), but he's actually Buddy Lee, the trademark figure for Lee jeans (at right and top).

Brown Brothers

He Went from Heel To Hero in a Pair Of Button Shoes

By Peter Rienstra, Modesto, California

I STOOD all alone at the side of the Sanborn, Iowa grade-school playground, just watching the other kids run and jump and play. How I wished I could join them....

The year was 1924, and there I was, a skinny, sickly kid with allergies. But the main reason I felt so left out was because I was ashamed of my hand-me-down clothes.

I wore a pair of oversized knickers, gathered about my waist and held up with a belt cinched down to the last notch, to school every day. How I envied those boys who came from the big farms—they wore bib overalls and miniature work shoes with hooks for the laces instead of eyes. I called them "men's shoes".

If I only had a pair of men's shoes, I thought, then maybe the others would like me.

Then one day I noticed that I'd worn a hole in the sole of one of my old shoes. I was elated because now I could finally get a pair of men's shoes.

Skipped with Joy

It worked. After I showed Mom the hole, we set out for the shoe store. As we crossed the vacant lot on the way, I skipped and danced for joy.

I could not have known that Mom didn't share my excitement. With worry in her eyes, she was sweating over just how she'd ever be able to buy me a pair of shoes and still have enough money left to feed a family with seven children.

When we walked into the store, I tugged on Mom's arm and guided her to the display exclaiming, "There they are!"

Mom priced the new shoes with a scowl, then turned her attention to a barrel of leftover shoes near the counter—at a giveaway price of 25¢. Some of those shoes were relics from the days when button shoes were in style. Mom hesitated, then asked me to try on a pair.

I walked out of the store wearing a brand-new pair of button shoes. Mother's dilemma was solved but mine had just begun. Things would be worse than ever!

Too Awful to Wear

With knicker pants, those button shoes stood out like beacons—and they were the ugliest shoes imaginable. Long rows of buttons up their sides required a buttonhook to pull them through the holes in the stiff, tough leather.

When I returned to school on Monday, there was just no way to hide the shoes under my knickers. The teasing was immediate and almost unbearable.

"Hey, 'Button Shoes'!" yelled the class bully. Soon, he was leading everyone in a sing-song chant: "Button shoes, button shoes, Peter's wearing button shoes!"

As noon, I ran home crying. I burst through the door and breathlessly informed Mom that I'd never go back to school in those shoes.

Mom tried to calm me down, and promised I'd feel better after I ate some lunch. I told her I didn't want any and stomped outside. I even thought of running away…but where would I go wearing button shoes?

My older brother Dick, home for lunch from his job, stepped outside and put an arm around my shoulders. "What's wrong, Peter?" he asked. I told him.

"Don't pay any attention to those kids," he said. "They're just jealous because you have better shoes than they do. Why button shoes are the best in the world for running!"

This I didn't believe at all. But Dick nodded and kept up his pep talk. "If you don't believe me, just try running down the street and see."

Right on the Buttons

I started down the street, and my feet did feel lighter. When I turned to run back, I was sure Dick was right!

By then, it was time to head to school. I took a hurried bite of my lunch, then ran all the way back.

The bully and his buddies were waiting for me. They'd no sooner started a reprise of the chant when I told them, "My shoes are better than yours…these shoes are made for running." He snorted at that and challenged me to a race.

I really was no match for the bully—he was bigger, stronger and longer-legged than me. But I had three things in my favor: First, the confrontation had my adrenaline surging. Second, I was warmed up and loose from my earlier run. And third, I'd hardly eaten my lunch, while he'd probably eaten heavily.

A crowd gathered around us as we toed the starting line. Someone called out, "One for the money…two for the show…three to get ready—and four to go!"

I exploded from the line. I never even saw the bully, because he lagged behind me and he stayed there all the way to the finish. Everyone erupted into cheers and waving. I could hardly believe it—I felt like a hero!

Never again would I be the poor, skinny kid with hand-me-down clothes. I had outrun the biggest, toughest kid in the class. As the rest of the kids kept cheering, I realized that I finally was part of them.

And I owed it all to my good old button shoes. ☎

By Oneta Aldrich Dernelle
St. Petersburg, Florida

Papa Lived In the Attic

WHEN I WAS a girl in Lansing, Michigan, I came down with some illness every spring. Mostly it was colds or flu …but when I was 8, in 1927, I came down with something *serious*—scarlet fever.

I learned just how serious it was when I overheard the county doctor conferring with Mama after he had examined me.

"You must send her to the contagious hospital right away!" the doctor said.

"No," Mother replied firmly. "I won't send her to that pest house."

"If you don't, you'll lose her…and maybe one or two of your other girls," the doctor warned. "I can't put it any stronger than that!"

"There's a bigger chance of losing her if I send her to that terrible place," Mother insisted. "I'll take care of her myself."

Unable to change Mother's mind, the doctor left. Soon afterward, a man came by and tacked up a quarantine sign on our front door. Our whole family would be confined to home for weeks.

Papa needed every cent he earned to support us, so he couldn't live under quarantine and stay out of work. But he couldn't afford to pay room and board elsewhere, either.

It was decided that he'd live in our attic. The door from our regular living quarters to the attic was sealed off. The only way for Papa to reach his new home was to climb a long ladder leaned against the side of the house. He carried up a portable kerosene stove, some canned goods and utensils.

Downstairs, things changed, too. I was put in my parents' bedroom, and Mama slept on a cot in the living room. My sisters shared the back bedroom. Rosie, 18, Violet, 17, Iva, 16, and Ella, 14, all slept sideways across one bed!

Liked Happy Sounds

They didn't seem to mind—I often heard laughter and singing coming from that room. Sometimes Mama quieted them down because she thought the noise bothered me, but it didn't. I liked hearing those happy sounds.

Mama gave me excellent care. She changed the bed sheets every morning, bathed me, fed me special food on her best dishes and kept a close watch on my temperature.

Meantime, Papa left for work every morning before I was awake. Every night, as he climbed back up the ladder to the attic, he'd stop by my window to wave at me. Smiling broadly, he'd "speak" to me through the glass with exaggerated sign language. Seeing him was the highlight of my day!

Of course, Papa was not allowed to come into the house. But late one night after I'd begun to get better, I heard his voice. Peeking through the bedroom door, I was surprised to see him and Mama sitting at the kitchen table holding hands. "Papa!" I exclaimed.

A Late-Night Surprise

"Back to bed, honey," he said quietly. "I'm glad you're almost well."

The next day, Mama showed me the new wedding band Papa had given her in celebration of their 20th anniversary.

Not long afterward, the doctor declared me well. The quarantine sign was removed from our door, Papa moved back downstairs, and my sisters and I returned to school.

Looking back now, I don't remember feeling really sick. Instead, I recall the love and attention my family lavished on me, and the fun and laughter I heard in our house.

But the thing that stands out most clearly in my mind is Papa smiling at me through the window before climbing the ladder back up to the attic! ☎

Neena Mitchell/Stock Art Images

MEMORIES KEPT FRESH. Longing for an old-fashioned icebox like the one above, this reader recalls the iceman's reliable delivery.

Bring Back the Icebox, Please!

By Anne-Marie Nilsen, Ann Arbor, Michigan

THE SALESMAN at the appliance store promised that a brand-new refrigerator would not only keep my food cold, but it would fill me with joy every day I used it.

How wrong he was. For that empty promise, I paid a ransom price for a large appliance that doesn't always work. Twelve house calls in 12 weeks have failed to make this unwelcome newcomer perform as advertised.

As the repairman opens it up in yet another attempt to repair this infernal machine, I can't help but remember the good old icebox. I long for one of those oak iceboxes with a zinc lining from 1920. It dependably chilled my foods and provided chipped ice whenever I wanted a glass of ginger ale.

To relive those almost-forgotten luxuries, I would gladly empty the drip pan underneath. It's a task I used to regularly execute with nimble efficiency.

But the best part of having an icebox was knowing the man who filled it. Our iceman in Ann Arbor, Michigan was Mr. Bent, a friendly giant with old-world courtesy. On hot summer days, he was the Pied Piper to all the children in our town.

We'd follow him around his route from stop to stop, and he was more than happy to share the little daggers of ice

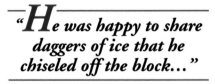

> *"He was happy to share daggers of ice that he chiseled off the block…"*

that he chipped from the great frozen blocks he carted throughout our neighborhood.

Mr. Bent knew to a millimeter the size and capacity of each icebox on his route. He chiseled and trimmed until the blocks of ice fit as perfectly as the keystones the Romans dropped into their arches. With his sharp tongs, he'd lug those sculptured blocks up long stairways to recharge the cold in each waiting icebox.

Dapper Mr. Bent sat up in his yellow ice wagon like a king, his round derby hat pressed firmly on a crop of red hair.

He tipped his old derby to everyone, from the town busybody to us kids on the street, each of whom he called "Little Sweet Pea". That hat, we learned, was the same one he'd worn as he marched off to fight Kaiser Willy.

Our iceman's team of Belgian horses was the steadiest in town. Though they passed the noisy switchyard every day, not once were those horses spooked by the chuffing engines or banging railroad cars. They clip-clopped along the streets, looking every bit as proud and well-groomed as their master did.

In a sense, Mr. Bent was our town crier, for he always knew what was going on. And he was more than glad to pass along the news of the day. Mr. Bent was also a true connoisseur of pastries. A housewife wouldn't dream of putting away any baked goods before Mr. Bent passed judgment on them.

Whether she'd made a lemon pie with mile-high meringue, a black walnut cake or mince tart laced with rum, the iceman's approval was critical. If her baking passed muster, word of her excellence spread like wildfire!

Today, I'd love to have the chance to offer some lemon pie or burnt sugar cake to a friendly iceman—even though my brain tells me it would be foolhardy.

After all, every delivery person works out of a truck these days. An iceman without a team of steady Belgians just wouldn't be an iceman at all.

H. Armstrong Roberts

neck by a leather strap. On the bottom was a wooden pole, which enabled him to rest the organ on the sidewalk.

He could stand the organ on the ground and play his music with one hand, using the other to hold the leash attached to the monkey's harness.

That bright-eyed little creature was dressed in a red coachman-style coat trimmed in shiny black braid with brass

"*We could hear the music from blocks away...*"

buttons and big pockets. A matching pillbox hat completed the outfit.

When his master was walking, the monkey was swung up by the leash to sit on top of the organ. After enough people had gathered, he was lifted off his perch and put down onto the sidewalk.

There he'd stand, with that little coat hanging to his knees and his curly tail poking through the slit in back. His lively eyes darted from child to child as the festive music filled the air.

Pennies, Please!

Some lucky child with a penny would stick a hand out. The monkey would take the coin, nod his head, doff his hat and put the penny in one of his capacious pockets—then start looking around for more.

When the crowd's supply of pennies was exhausted, my sister and I showed our grapes to his master, who would nod. One by one, my sister and I gave the grapes to the monkey, who repeated his same movements—except instead of putting the grapes in his pocket, he'd eat them.

My sister says he peeled the grapes first, but I don't recall that...perhaps another reader will.

When no one had anything else to offer, the organ-grinder would swing the little fellow onto the box and move on to the next block. My sister and I were not allowed to follow. For a long time, we'd stand on the corner and listen to the disappearing strains of music.

Then came a summer day when somebody in the neighborhood said, "Say...we didn't see the organ-grinder and his monkey this year."

We were sad to think that our friends didn't come back around to see us, but our memories of those special visits will always bring music to our lives. ☎

The Organ-Grinder's Coming!

By Elaine Wojenski, Burlington, New Jersey

DOES ANYONE remember the friendly organ-grinder and his little monkey?

When I lived in North Philadelphia, Pennsylvania during the '20s, we kids looked forward to his visit every summer with great anticipation.

We could hear the music that announced this delightful duo's arrival coming from blocks away as it was carried to us on the warm summer air.

I still remember rushing into the house to tell my mother, "The organ-grinder's coming!"...and being told I had to wait until he got to our block.

Pennies were scarce in those days, so we seldom had any to offer the organ-grinder. But we often did have green seedless grapes in the kitchen. Mother would dole some out to us, then we'd wait at the corner as the music drew nearer and nearer.

When they finally reached our street, we tried to get as close to the performers as we could. We did, and were absolutely enchanted!

The monkey's owner always had a wide grin on his face as he cranked away at the magical box hung from his

When FDR Came to Warm Springs

Brown Brothers

By Doris Starrett, Victorville, California

I RECENTLY FOUND a letter my late husband wrote to his parents over 50 years ago from Warm Springs, Georgia.

Ed was stricken with polio in 1940 and went to Warm Springs in '43 to exercise in the mineral springs. Imagine the excitement this 23-year-old felt seeing the President!

Franklin Delano Roosevelt first tried Warm Springs in 1924 and found the waters helped his own symptoms. He bought the property and established the Georgia Warm Springs Foundation to offer low-cost treatment to others with polio.

I'm glad to share Ed's excited note to his parents about meeting FDR:

Dear Mom and Dad,

Here's a big scoop! It won't be in the papers for another week. The President of the U.S. was here tonight and had dinner with us.... I have just gotten into bed and wanted to write down these notes while they are fresh in my mind.

I'm the guy who shook the President's hand. I had a swell place in the dining room—just opposite the first table in front of the speaker's table.

A Secret Service man sat at our table—a very interesting fellow and he answered all of our questions. He was in charge of a detail of Secret Service

men that went to Africa (the Casablanca Conference) with the President and was one of the few persons who knew where they were going.

I was impressed with the fine condition the President seemed to be in. He looked to be in very good health. Sometimes you'll notice that his pictures produce a tired look and dark spots under his eyes. These were not apparent.

We had a delicious turkey dinner. President Roosevelt made a short talk after dinner.

I was very interested in the fact that the President's legs seem to be in as bad shape as mine. He does wear two locked braces.

When he rose to give his address, an attendant held his chair, and he got up with the difficulty that all us polios know about. He stood behind his chair, using the chair for support. He came in through the private dining room in a wheelchair and shifted to the other chair. All the guests rose and applauded. He finished his address by saying he would go over to the dining room door and greet everyone as they went out.

It is now Friday morning and I just saw the President drive by in Mr. Botts' car. FDR was driving. This is a very exciting occasion. The President's dog, "Fala", was also here. Fala is a Scottie—a very friendly dog.

We asked the Secret Service man about Eleanor Roosevelt. She won't have any Secret Service men following her. He said that they couldn't keep up with her anyway.

The last time President Roosevelt was here at Warm Springs was November 30, 1941. One week later, Pearl Harbor was attacked. He said he had an uneasy feeling while he was here, and that is why he returned to Washington before he intended to.

The President does have a wonderful personality. I have a great deal of respect for a man who is a polio and has done the things he has accomplished.

We have never seen pictures of him walking or getting in or out of a chair. I have seen him do it the same way the rest of us polios have to do it. Just think of standing before Congress for a couple of hours! He must be quite tired.

These are about all the notes I have for the present. Please send them back to me as I want to keep them. I hope you'll let everyone read about my experience.

In 1939, I, too, contracted polio as a senior at the College of the Pacific in Stockton, California. My dean of women wrote to Eleanor Roosevelt, who helped me get into Warm Springs in 1944.

It was fun. There were movies, and soldiers from Fort Benning came by on weekends. I met people there from all over the world—and one of them was Ed. ☎

PRESIDENTIAL PLATE. Author's husband posed with FDR's car at Warm Springs, Georgia in 1943 (left), as the First Swimmer participated in a game of water polo (top).

To MaryLou — with good good wishes to you — Lena Horne

Young Reporters Scored Scoop with Famous Singer

By Mary Lu Leon, Grass Valley, California

EVERYTHING HAPPENS in San Francisco, my friend George and I silently sighed after reading the headline in the *San Francisco Chronicle*.

"Lena Horne to appear at the Fairmont Hotel" the headline read. San Francisco was only 12 miles away from Oakland, where we lived. Yet the two cities shared nothing but a bridge.

"Wouldn't it be fun to see her?" I asked George. By 1951, Lena Horne was a big star in the music and movie world. Her renditions of *Stormy Weather* and *The Lady is a Tramp* were already classics. At 16, she worked as a chorus girl at Harlem's famous Cotton Club, where she was influenced by Duke Ellington, Cab Calloway and Billie Holiday. She debuted on Broadway, then the silver screen before returning to singing as a top-paid nightclub performer.

"Hey, I know," George said.

LUCKY WITH LENA. Author (left, at age 15) lucked out and got an interview with Lena Horne (above).

"Why don't we interview her? It would be more interesting than that boring school stuff you always print."

I liked the idea. At 16, I was a senior and editor of our high school paper, and George and I had formed a teenage show troupe that entertained troops regularly in the Bay area. We considered ourselves up-and-coming stars.

With the brashness of youth, I called Miss Horne's press agent, announced myself as editor of *Green and Gold* and requested an interview. To my delight, and surprise, he agreed!

We were told to be there an hour before show time. We nervously knocked on the door of Miss Horne's suite and were invited in.

Miss Horne rose to greet us. She was an absolute vision in her flowing white chiffon gown, glossy hair, liquid eyes and adorable spatter of freckles on her nose.

She gave us her famous grin, then sat back at the dressing table to finish her makeup, while George peppered her with questions.

Miss Horne spoke frankly about the racial prejudice she'd encountered in her early days, and about her love for jazz and popular music. But she also asked us about our troupe and our aspirations. After the interview, she handed us each an autographed photo.

"I wish we could see you perform," George said. "But we can't get in," I added. "We're underage."

Miss Horne thought for a moment, then snapped her fingers. "I have an idea," she said. "I'll ask the light man if you can watch the show from his booth. No law against that."

"Great!" we answered.

We waited in the lobby, dwarfed by the opulence of the hotel. Soon Miss Horne swept in, winked at us and pointed to the stairs near the Tonga Room.

We raced up the steps as Miss Horne glided in for her entrance, then dashed into the lighting booth and sat entranced through her performance. Here we were, two unimportant 16-year-olds from a high school newspaper, being treated as honored guests by a top star.

Lena Horne probably forgot about us that night. But I have never forgotten her charm, her humility at her fortune and her spontaneous gesture that allowed us to watch her show.

At the height of her fame, Lena Horne gave two strangers an example of graciousness and greatness. Truly, this lady is a lady. ☎

I Once Invented a Problem Potion

By Janet Lee Friesorger, Pinconning, Michigan

"IF ONLY I had a chemistry set!" I muttered, kicking at stones in the schoolyard. "I'm sick of those dumb boys bragging all the time…how come *girls* never get good stuff to play with?"

This obvious discrimination didn't seem to bother other girls in my sixth-grade class in Bay City, Michigan in 1952. But it made me—an inveterate tomboy—all the more determined.

Mom, knowing her mischievous daughter well, didn't think a chemistry set was such a good idea, so there was no use begging. And with money tight in our neighborhood, it'd be tough for me to find enough odd jobs to raise the necessary cash.

Never one to stand around and wait for wishes to come true, I began to scrounge through all the junk barrels on Elm Street for curiously shaped bottles. Mom became increasingly nervous as I also raided her laundry, cleaning and baking supplies.

The resulting assembly of chemicals was colorful and probably dangerous, as several nose-burning experiments and other minor mishaps hinted. But what I lacked in sense, I more than made up for in confidence.

Certain a breakthrough was just around the corner, I could already see the headlines: "Janet Lee McComb, Scientist Extraordinaire, Makes Amazing Discovery!"

Scientific Announcement

On the way home from school one day, I announced to my friend Jimmy, "I'm inventing a miracle beauty cream." Jimmy was unimpressed, but his little sister, Judy, listened intently as I expounded on the virtues of my cream.

By the time we got home, I was beginning to believe my own sales pitch. Emptying bottles with abandon, I mixed and stirred until my beauty potion felt "right". Its "fragrance" was strange, but nothing a generous dose of Evening in Paris toilet water couldn't fix.

The result was a colorful green cream that more closely resembled pond scum than Oil of Olay. But Judy didn't mind—she couldn't wait to be the first to experience its benefits.

I applied the goo liberally to Judy's trusting face. It spread easily like cake frosting. We waited breathlessly for a miracle, and it soon occurred—the cream hardened into a ghastly green shell that resembled a moldy plastic bowl.

I noticed that my palms were sweating. "Don't worry; that's how it's supposed to work," I assured Judy with more confidence than I felt.

"Take it off!" she whined.

Mad as a Wet Hen

I tried wiping the stuff off with a dripping washcloth, but it wouldn't budge. Judy's whining escalated to loud yelps and angry tears, which was quite an accomplishment since she could hardly blink her eyes.

I rubbed harder with the cloth. Nothing changed. I felt like crying, too, but I didn't dare. Then Mom appeared on the scene, squawking like a brood hen who'd just been dunked in water.

This didn't bode well for my future as a chemist. There followed much soaking and scraping and more whining. The process was a bit like removing varnish from an old table, only noisier.

Then came the uncomfortable phone call to Judy's mom, preparing her for her daughter's new look. My miracle cream had indeed changed Judy's appearance—her swollen face looked like a patchwork quilt of pinks and reds, dotted green with remaining traces of the relentless "beauty cream".

Fortunately, Judy's face recovered. Later, after my "chemistry set" had been disposed of, I was left to sadly ponder an age-old question: Are great scientists never appreciated by their mothers? ☎

RP Photo

Back in the early '50s, our 6-year-old son, Albert, would sit much too close to our 10-inch TV watching his hero, Captain Video, every weekday evening before supper.

Much like Buck Rogers or Flash Gordon in the '30s, Captain Video captivated '50s kids with his outer space crime-fighting.

Attired in his silvery "Nehru-style" space hat, a safari bush jacket, white whipcord breeches and star-studded boots, Captain Video was Earth's crusader against alien wrongdoers. No star was too far and no unearthly perpetrator went unpunished.

One memorable autumn day in 1953, Captain Video stepped out of his spaceship and invited young fans to come see him in person!

"Space Rangers," Captain Video announced, "it's easier than zapping a Martian worm-rat! Simply have your parents remove the label from a jar of my Mallowmarsh Syrup and carefully print your name, age and address on the back.

"Send it to me in a self-addressed envelope, and tickets to my Empire State Building headquarters will be mailed to you posthaste. First come, first served!"

Blast-Off Set

We did as the space master bid, but it wasn't until the following July that a familiar self-addressed envelope reappeared in the mail at our Levittown, New York home. The promised tickets had arrived, and Albert's joy knew no bounds!

The day of our visit to the show was sweltering hot. Arriving at Studio C on the 66th floor of the Empire State Building, we and the other bewildered parents were herded into a large room where a harried-looking guide waited.

"At precisely 4:45," she explained, "the children will be escorted to the set for a quick warm-up. At 5:02, Captain Video will appear and interview his young Space Rangers. You parents will sit in the adjacent viewing room equipped with a TV monitor.

"Last, but far from least, the rest rooms are at the far end of the corridor. Please make sure that all, uh, precautions are taken *before* we go on the air," the guide concluded.

At that point the door opened, and in walked Captain Video himself. He was greeted with shouts of joyous recognition from the children and polite applause from the adults.

Doffing his silver cap, he bowed

Everett Collection

Captain Video's One-Man Cleanup Crew

By Albert Sohl, Port St. Lucie, Florida

modestly, saying, "Thank you. Thank you one and all."

The Captain had even more instructions. At the end of the show, his little Space Rangers were to line up and accept a jar of Mallowmarsh Syrup from him.

"It is most important that you take the gift with both hands," the Captain emphasized. "Both hands," he repeated, looking at his young charges. "How many hands, Space Rangers?"

"BOTH HANDS!" the kids yelled.

"Excellent. Now, let's blast off!"

In the parents' viewing room, out-of-focus images of our children faded in and out. We struggled with the controls, but it was 20 maddening minutes before

we got a tiny but clear picture of Albert accepting his jar of Mallowmarsh... with both hands.

A Sticky Situation

The show over, we hurried down the hall to join our junior celebrities. Happy and excited, Albert ran toward us. Then the unthinkable happened—he dropped his jar on the marble floor, where it shattered into a thousand pieces!

Like a giant amoebae, the syrupy puddle extended sticky tentacles in every direction. For a moment there was a stunned silence, which was then broken by Albert's loud, anguished shriek.

We were attempting to console Albert when, from the corner of my eye, I saw someone rushing toward us with a cloth and a pail. It was Captain Video himself!

"Just an accident...couldn't be helped," he muttered to no one in particular, dropping to his knees and swinging the cloth in sweeping arcs. When Albert saw his space hero kneeling on the floor in full uniform, his crying stopped.

Later, as we took the elevator back down to Earth, my son, holding his new jar of Mallowmarsh, looked up at me with a wisdom beyond his years.

Yes, I'm afraid the humbling sight of the Champion of the Universe mopping up that sticky mess had probably shattered his youthful dreams forever.

STUNNED SPACE RANGER. Young Albert Sohl (below in 1954) was surprised when his hero, Captain Video (above left), landed back on Earth.

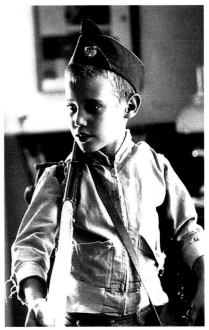

OVER THE BACK FENCE

AMUSING MORSELS AND BITS OF WISDOM
...OVERHEARD AND READ HERE AND THERE.

Car-Eating Cow

MANY YEARS AGO, when I was a girl, we went to the farm of a distant relative we had never met.

When we arrived at the farm, a cow came up to our car, pulled the cover off the spare tire and ate it. Next she pulled a hunk of the border off the cloth roof and ate that, then she took a bite of the roof!

"Your cow is eating my car," Dad complained to the farmer relative.

"That's okay," the farmer replied. "It won't hurt her." —Lorrayne Clafin
Jackson, Michigan

In Name Only

GROWING UP, I was addressed by my initials, M.B. When I applied for my first driver's license and the clerk asked my name, I said "M.B."

She wrote down "M (only) B (only)", filled out the rest of the information and sent it off to the state capital. About 4 weeks later, I got my license. Imagine my surprise when I read my name—"Monly Bonly Lavender"!

I quickly sent the license back to the capital for a correction.
—Moses Lavender, Ozark, Alabama

In the Army Now

A YOUNG MAN, not thrilled by being drafted into the Army, was called to take his physical. He figured he could fail the physical with a few well-placed answers to the doctor's questions.

"What do you see on that wall over there?" asked the doctor.

"What wall?" the man replied.

"Good," the doctor said. "You just passed the hearing test."
—Carolyn Joyner Freebairn
Salt Lake City, Utah

English Major

EMPLOYER: Sure, I can give you a job. Sweep out the store.

Employee-to-be: But, sir, I'm a college graduate.

Employer: Don't worry. I'll show you how.
—Sister Marie Scaletty
St. Louis, Missouri

Walk This Way

A YOUNG college student was trying to convince his father to buy him a car.

The father said he'd consider the request if his son would read the Bible more often and get a haircut.

"But, Dad," the son protested. "In Biblical

times, all the men wore their hair long."

"Quite true," the father replied. "And all of them walked everywhere they went." —Laura Nitkowski
Baltimore, Maryland

What...No Smiths?

WE GREW UP in Swartz, Louisiana during the 1930s and '40s. It was a boomtown then because of the abundance of natural gas.

There were a lot of families with unusual names. We remember Couch, Roach, Spear, Hare, Music, Fiddler, Crow, Glass, Sweet, Pool, Farmer, Berry, Sapp, Fields, Rasberry, Ford, Carpenter, Case, Gray, Cobb, Keyes, Woods, Gaar, Crane, Crumb and others. We might have left out a few.
—Newty and Birdie Jeansonne
Baton Rouge, Louisiana

Heated Discussion

I WAS TELLING my granddaughters about the old-time tradition of St. Nicholas Night, when we hung our stockings for treats. "In the morning," I explained, "naughty boys found coal in their stockings."

The girls looked puzzled for a moment and asked, "Grandpa, what's coal?" —Les Tobiason
Eugene, Oregon

Do the Buck and Wing

A COUPLE went into a pet store to buy a canary. They told the salesman the bird had to be a good singer.

They heard a canary singing loudly and remarked, "It's beautiful, and it sings great."

But when the salesman took the bird from the cage, the couple said, "Hey, it's got only one leg."

"What do you want," the salesman asked, "a singer or a dancer?"
—Louise Caterson
Stratford, Connecticut

Friends and Relatives

WHEN MY MOTHER, Nettie Kellow, died, I sent the obituary information to the local newspaper. I made sure to include the names of both her husbands, Floyd Phillips Anthony, my father, and her second husband, Harry Albert Kellow.

When the obituary appeared, I saw that someone had put commas after each name, so it read that Mother was predeceased "by her husbands Floyd, Phillips, Anthony, and Harry, Albert,

If you are calling from a Touch-Tone phone, hold for modern music. If you are calling from a rotary phone, hold for music from the Big Band era.

This is good, but it doesn't compare to slivers snitched from the iceman's wagon.

Kellow," making it look as though she had six husbands.

The funeral director's wife came to our house, apologized and said there would be a correction in the next day's paper.

I assured her my mother would have thought the mistake was as funny as I did. I know some folks would have been horrified, but we're not that kind of people.   —*Josephine Dunn*
Newark Valley, New York

¿Por Qué?
PUPIL: Teacher, you flunked me in Spanish. I can't understand it.

Teacher: That's why I flunked you.   —*Sheldon Glassman*
Brooklyn, New York

Hopping Mad
I WAS a spunky youngster, but Mom always managed to get in the last word.

One time I was so mad at her that I swallowed a great big grasshopper.

Mom just looked at me and said, "Son, when you swallow your food whole like that, you lose a lot of the flavor."   —*Ernest Webber*
Lake Placid, Florida

Doggoned Smart
WHEN I was growing up in the Missouri Ozarks in the '30s, my most treasured possessions were a gun, a pocketknife and a dog.

I had a bluetick hound I called "Blue" that I got as a puppy from a neighbor. Blueticks are good hunting dogs, and smart too. After I had the dog for a couple of years, I had the chance to tell my neighbor just how smart.

I said that when I came out of the house in the morning to go hunting, all I had to do was show Blue the barrel of the gun and he'd know what to hunt.

If I showed him the shotgun, Blue would hunt only quail. If I showed him the .22, he'd only hunt squirrels.

One day, I played a trick on old Blue and came out of the house with my fishing pole. Blue looked at the pole, looked and me, then turned away and ran around the house.

I worried that I had embarrassed Blue and that he'd never hunt again. But a few minutes later, Blue returned. In his mouth he had a can of worms.   —*Bill Hinkle, Cheyenne, Wyoming*

What Goes Down...
HALLOWEEN was eagerly awaited by us "juvenile delinquents" in Le-shara, Nebraska back in the late '20s and early '30s.

Only about four or five families in the town of 101 had indoor plumbing. We didn't go trick-or-treating. We just tricked and went around tipping over outhouses.

Our favorite target was the school, where there were two outhouses, one for the girls and one for the boys. We saved those for last, then tore home to beat the 8 p.m. curfew our parents set.

But I'd be awakened early the next morning by my dad to help him set up those last two outhouses—he was the school custodian!   —*Norman Stevens*
Verdugo City, California

Let There Be Light
THE CONGREGATION of a small country church was having a meeting to discuss the possible purchase of a chandelier. Most of the deacons were enthusiastic, but one man held out.

"I have three reasons for objecting," he said. "First, nobody here knows how to spell the word, so we couldn't order one.

"Second, even if we got one, there's nobody in our church who knows how to play it.

"Third, if we could come up with the money, I say what we need more is a new light fixture."   —*Helen Needham*
Chicago, Illinois

Just Ask Newton
MEDICAL STUDENT: Professor, why do we have to take physics? It has nothing to do with our profession.

Professor: Because it saves our lives.

Student: How on earth can a physics course save lives?

Professor: It prevents idiots from graduating.   —*Giles Millspaugh*
Aurora, Colorado

Slow Down, Son
MY daughter-in-law was driving through town with her children in the backseat when she was pulled over for speeding.

While the officer was writing the ticket, with the lights from his cruiser flashing, my 5-year-old grandson piped up, "Can't you turn off those flashing lights? Everybody's looking at us."   —*Lyle Getschman, Baraboo, Wisconsin*

'Vacation' Meant 2 Weeks in a Tent

By Theo Smeenk Sr.
London, Ontario

IT WAS 1960, and a family vacation was long overdue.

My wife, Pauline, and I had emigrated from the Netherlands to Canada 8 years before with three children and one crate of keepsakes.

As the years passed, we worked diligently, acquiring a home and filling it with furniture, household items and more children. By the summer of 1960, we had seven children ages 12 to 1.

It seemed like time for a holiday… but with seven kids and a limited budget, camping was our only option. Of course, the kids didn't mind a bit—it would be their first camping trip!

Our 12-year-old, Frankie, was especially enthused since we'd be camping at beautiful Beausoleil Island Provincial Park in Georgian Bay. It was accessible only by "water taxi", and Frankie was crazy about boats.

In fact, once our plans were made, Frankie decided to build his own boat. He began scrounging scrap wood, and his brothers and sisters watched excit-edly as he hammered together a 6-foot flat-bottomed craft. He painted it green and ivory and christened it *Alley Oop*.

Meanwhile, I hunted for a tent and other gear. Camping with seven kids and two adults would be quite different from the backpack trips I'd taken as a teenager in Holland. Just packing 2 weeks' worth of clothes, toys, balls, baby supplies, groceries and camping

> ## "*We* didn't have enough sleeping bags, so three kids slept in two bags…"

equipment would challenge my logistical ability.

Some friends had an old army tent we could borrow. It weighed a ton, had no floor and was missing its center pole. No problem there—we'd lay a tarp on the ground and substitute a 6-foot four-by-four for the post.

To transport all our gear, I bought a homemade open-topped trailer for $35, cleaned it up and painted it silver. When the big day arrived, we packed the trail-er and lashed everything down securely.

Into the car went loads of groceries plus suitcases, seven kids and Mom and Dad. *Alley Oop* was tied on top.

The kids were good as gold as we drove along. The older ones held the younger ones on their laps, and things went well for 100 miles, until we drove into such a downpour that it was impossible to see.

We pulled over to wait out the storm and watched through fogged-up windows as our cargo in the open trailer got a good soaking.

The delay put us at the dock for the water taxi shortly before sunset. The kids eagerly grabbed soaked stuff from the trailer and carried it to the boat. As a sodden cardboard box was lifted over the gangplank, its bottom fell out, and a number of our groceries went to the bottom of Georgian Bay.

The trip across the bay was uneventful. Night fell as we unloaded our gear onto the dock at the island. We'd have to find a camping spot in the dark.

All the sites near the dock were taken, so we stumbled and fumbled along. Finally, I found a nice grassy spot

campground supervisor had paid us a visit around midnight to say we were set up in a private area. In the dark, we'd missed the *No Camping* sign posted near our tent.

We'd had other visitors during the night—raccoons that raided our food. Boxes had been torn open, and bacon, bread and cookies had disappeared. There were some chicken bones left.

After we got resettled, the kids hit the beach. Frankie very proudly took *Alley Oop* out for her maiden voyage, and she proved seaworthy.

However, he lost some enthusiasm when he saw the gleaming speedboats of the other campers. He soon abandoned his crude craft to his little brothers, who happily splashed around in it.

Some Vacation for Mom!

Mom, meanwhile, was airing out sleeping bags, doing laundry and cleaning up dirty dishes. As the days went by, she would sit down very seldom.

Cooking was done on an open campfire, and as our remaining provisions were used up, other campers kindly shared freshly caught fish with us.

At night, the kids had fun around the fire, toasting marshmallows on straightened coat hangers. What a treat those blackened marshmallows were!

As the flames flickered and wood crackled, the smoke added to the unique camping fragrance we'd all acquired. We didn't mind...we sang around the fire, feeling in harmony with nature.

The days passed quickly, and we enjoyed every one. In spite of all the mishaps, nothing before or since has brought our family as close together as that first camping trip.

To this day, we treasure our memories of it...rain, mosquitoes, thieving raccoons and all! ☎

with no other tents.

We dropped everything and began to set up our camp. The kids pitched in, since I had never put up an army tent before.

Later, exhausted and riddled with mosquito bites, we crawled inside. By lantern light, we zipped together wet sleeping bags. We didn't have enough for everyone, so three kids would sleep in two bags.

The baby slept cozily in a blown-up dinghy. Pauline and I worked ourselves into a single bag and took turns breathing. It was a long night.

In the morning, we were all up bright and early...to move to another site. The

"WE'RE CAMPING!" The kids thought this family outing was great, but their tired mother (above) likely had another opinion. Oldest son Frankie (right) was so excited that he built his own boat for the trip.

Dad's Love Was Unspoken

By Venus Bardanouve, Harlem, Montana

I GUESS my father never actually *said* he loved me, but I know without a doubt that he did. How do I know? From the memories I have—such small ones, but memories made of the stuff that bonded me to my father.

My father, Edgar Potts, who was known as "Bea", had what they used to call a dray line. He used small trucks to deliver packages, groceries, freight and coal to the houses in St. Paul, Nebraska.

He also delivered cans of cream to trains and mail pouches to and from the post office. On Sundays, I got to ride with him, along with any other friends or cousins who wanted to come.

Dad worked hard and long hours during those Depression days. But he saw to it that there were some pleasant times, too.

Among my memories are small things from winter evenings when my parents and I were sitting in our combination dining/living room.

I was an only child, and when I was little, I'd comb my father's hair as he read his paper. I would fashion tiny braids with small ribbons, make spit curls and anything else I could think of. Looking back, I marvel at his patience.

Special Nights

Then there were those special evenings when Dad would bring home a bag of peanuts. I remember the warm feeling I got as we sat around the round oak table, shelling and eating this treat.

Sometimes he brought home cookies. Mostly they were plain, but there would be a few chocolate-covered delights or pink marshmallow ones covered in coconut. Dad was always so pleased when he opened the bag and showed me the fancy cookies. I felt showered with love.

Summer days were hot in Nebraska, and an-

other of my pleasant memories is of the picnic suppers we had along the Loup River just outside of town. We kept a piece of tin hidden in some bushes that Dad used to cover a hole where he built a fire. Our supper was cooked on the tin.

One time when Mother forgot the utensils, Dad just took out his pocketknife and sharpened some small sticks. We ate baked beans by stabbing each one separately—such fun!

Water Tester

After supper, I liked to go wading with the friends I was allowed to bring along. None of us could swim, so Dad would roll up his overalls and check the depth with a long stick before he allowed us to go into the water.

I can remember only one time when I brought on my father's displeasure, and even then I think it was motivated by his love.

I was walking home from school for lunch, and for some unknown reason, I picked up a tin can and threw it at a girl walking behind our group.

I know now that the girl was one whose life was far from easy. My father saw me do this and gave me a small spanking. I learned then that we do not hurt anyone, especially those less fortunate.

Some years after I grew up, I was emptying the pockets of my father's suit when I came across a ticket to a high school play I had been in years before. He had kept it all those years.

As I held the little yellow ticket, my heart was warmed. It was just another way of knowing—as with the braided hair, peanuts, cookies and suppers at the river—that I was my father's precious child, and he loved me. ☎

LOVING FAMILY. Author, at about age 5 in 1922, posed with her parents, Edgar and Emma Potts.

Sit a Spell with Uncle Dave

WATCHED THE WORLD GO BY. Author's Uncle Dave (right) decided his sturdy old chair out on the porch was the perfect spot to spend the rest of his days.

By Madolyn Jamieson, Clearwater, Florida

"GONNA BE pretty cold this winter," said Uncle Dave, settled snugly in an armchair on the front porch as an easy September breeze crept up from the apple orchard. "Wooly cattypillars say so."

I recalled this scene recently on a trip back to the farm my great-grandparents homesteaded in Pennsylvania. Uncle Dave died there in 1943 at the age of 92.

Uncle Dave had worked hard for many years. Then one day he decided he'd had enough of the seeding, slopping hogs and harvesting. He vowed that the rest of his days would be spent on more leisurely pursuits.

Uncle Dave went to the parlor, selected the strongest chair and moved it to his front porch. Made of sturdy oak, that chair had reinforced legs and broad arms. Uncle Dave settled his 200-pound frame into it and began watching the world go by.

Not having advanced beyond the fourth grade, he had no interest in books or newspapers. But his dog-eared Bible was always within reach, as were his mellow pipe and a pouch of sweet-smelling tobacco.

Uncle Dave announced he planned to spend the rest of his life seated contentedly there from sunup to sundown. And as the seasons changed, he never deviated from this plan.

A Sedentary Naturalist

Because he spent most of his hours outdoors, Uncle Dave became a keen observer of nature. In spring, it was he who heard the first tentative peeps from the tiny frogs in the pond across the lane.

"Time to plow," he'd say. "Days are gittin' longer now."

He learned the habits of returning birds and delighted in the pear trees' blossoms. He reveled in the scent of Aunt Carrie's rambler roses as summer dusks brought fireflies that winked and danced in the yard.

In the evenings, other family members joined him on the porch to listen to his tales of bygone times. One time, Aunt Carrie came running up from the springhouse shrieking about a skirmish with a skunk.

"Hope you didn't give him too much of a scare, Ma," Uncle Dave teased, his ample belly quivering in a soft chuckle.

Braved the Cold

As he continued to sit, Uncle Dave metamorphosed into a great bear of a man.

When fall came, he counted flocks of southbound geese. On October nights, when the harvest moon hung low on the horizon, he hated to relinquish his chair for bed.

Even winter didn't deter Uncle Dave—he's just don long underwear and bring out his worn buffalo robe.

With the bowl of his pipe warming his fingers (and mugs of steaming hot coffee from Aunt Carrie), he was so comfortable, he often had to be coaxed to come inside.

When he did join us inside in the warmth of the lamp-lit kitchen, we kids pressed him for stories, then listened round-eyed to tales of Indians, rattlesnakes and wolves.

Over the years, Uncle Dave's beard grew long and white. With his soft chuckle and the pipe smoke encircling his head, he began to resemble Santa Claus. Folks came from all over to visit and carry home bits of wisdom.

Meanwhile, that chair seemed to age along with Uncle Dave, groaning each time he lowered his bulk into it. Finally, one day when he was in his 90s, his beloved chair collapsed, leaving him sprawled on the porch. Neighbors helped him to his bed, which he never left.

Uncle Dave died not long afterward. His passing left a huge void because he wasn't only *my* uncle—he was an uncle to everyone who'd had the pleasure of knowing him. His stories and his old oak chair remain happy memories for us all. ☎

My Family Found Freedom In This Country's Welcoming Arms

By Edith Jacobs, Sarasota, Florida

BY MORNING of February 27, 1940, the luxury liner *S.S. Hamburg* had been at sea for 24 hours. My parents, brother and I were heading farther and farther into the Atlantic, away from Germany.

My grandparents had accompanied us on the long trip from Schweinfurt, Bavaria to Hamburg. I'd cried bitterly at the time of our final parting because I feared we'd never see each other again.

My grandfather tried to reassure me, "Things will return to normal. You'll be visiting us soon, you'll see."

At the pier in Bremerhaven, we'd said our last hurried good-byes, then departed on a calm sea. By the next morning, the weather had changed, and the Atlantic was displaying its awesome might with powerful winds and fierce waves that swept over the bulkheads.

I prayed the captain wouldn't be deterred by the storm and return to Germany. Even at age 9, I knew each day brought us closer to freedom.

A Better Life Ahead

My mother had told us there were no signs on store windows reading "Jews Forbidden" in America. And public places like schools, libraries and swimming pools were open to *everyone*.

In Germany, I'd learned that I could only watch while other children enjoyed those kinds of things. Even my class-mate Inge, who'd vowed we'd be best friends always, eventually joined the Hitler Youth.

"I had to do it," she told me. "I didn't want to be an outcast."

From that day on, she would cross the street to avoid me. Yet on the night

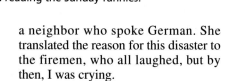

SAFE IN AMERICA. Author (above right, with her brother) and her parents (below left) found safety, family and friends in America after they fled Nazi Germany in 1940. It wasn't long before she was speaking English and reading the Sunday funnies.

before our ship's departure, an envelope was pushed under our door. In it was a picture of Inge, who had written "Remember Me" on the back. I still have that picture.

In time, black-uniformed S.S. officers picked up my father for questioning. He was detained and jailed, and after he was released, our final immigration papers had arrived.

Our American cousins had sent us visas and accepted the responsibility for our welfare until my father could find a job. We finally met them when we disembarked at the pier in Manhattan. Since they spoke no German, I couldn't even *talk* to these strangers who'd saved our lives. Luckily, my parents knew some English.

They'd rented two rooms for us with another refugee family. We lived there until my parents found their own apartment, and a day after we arrived, I was already enrolled in a public school.

The neighborhood quickly became aware of my existence one Sunday when my mother asked me to mail a letter at the corner mailbox. In Germany, mailboxes were red, and I accidentally pulled the fire alarm by mistake!

The fire trucks came within minutes. Some kids who'd seen me, and knew I couldn't speak English, ran and found

a neighbor who spoke German. She translated the reason for this disaster to the firemen, who all laughed, but by then, I was crying.

An Alarming Gift

One of the men put his arm around me and wiped away my tears with his handkerchief. The translator explained that the fireman had to make a report, but that there would be no fine. They even joked that this would be their welcoming gift to me.

Everything was so different in America. A new friend acquainted me with the five-and-dime store and we shared a "black-and-white sundae" at the ice cream counter. I couldn't understand *why* it was called a "Sunday" if it could be bought any day of the week.

Other friends treated me to egg creams—chocolate syrup and milk swished together with seltzer—at the corner candy store.

Movies cost a dime, but the lady who took the tickets always waved me in when my friends explained I was a refugee with no money.

By summer, I was speaking and reading English fluently—I'd even discovered the Sunday funnies. No longer on the outside, I now "ran with the gang".

My childhood had truly begun…and I was learning to love America. ☎

Sonja's Sparkle Was No Accident

By Grace Case, San Diego, California

DRESSED THE ICE QUEEN. Grace Case (above) had some interesting times when she was in charge of costumes for Olympic champion Sonja Henie (right) when the skater began her Ice Revue career.

SONJA HENIE reminded me of spun sugar, a sparkling confection twirling across the ice. Barely 5 feet tall, she was pure glamour on skates. And *where* she got the energy for all those spins and turns was a mystery.

Commissioned to costume her Hollywood Ice Revue in the late '40s, I first met Sonja at a rehearsal in the Pan-Pacific Auditorium in Santa Monica, California. That day, she was hardly the fairy-like creature of the show.

Sonja wore old black rehearsal tights and had her hair in pin curls under a scarf. A star all the way, she was also a no-nonsense performer who expected the best of her crew.

With an unlimited budget for costumes, plus the fine workmanship of fitters, embroiderers and lighting experts, I knew I could please her.

Costumes Were Fancy

Still, I recall trembling as I unrolled my costume sketches for a Hawaiian number she loved. To embellish one of her costumes, she wanted a 20-foot turquoise velvet cape bordered with a 3-foot band of ranch mink, to be carried onto the ice by six male skaters.

I thought the cost would be prohibitive, but the producer said, "Give her anything she wants. She's terrific!"

Sonja could let you know in six languages when things weren't going the way she expected.

I came close to feeling her wrath when we opened the show at the Indianapolis Coliseum. There'd been a blizzard the day before, and all flights had been canceled. To make matters worse, the costumer in New York was late delivering Sonja's outfit. I had the hat, but the costume was still in New York.

Before each show, there was a dress parade to check all costumes for possible alterations, then the dress rehearsal—a complete run-through of the show with full orchestra. Sonja's costume still hadn't arrived, and it was my responsibility.

Sonja was very upset, and the producer was irate. After a rehearsal that ended at 3 a.m., he called my hotel at 7 a.m. "The show starts at 8:30 tonight," he snarled. "Sonja's due on the ice in that costume at 8:40. The flight from New York lands at 8:20. How're you gonna get the costume here on time?"

High-Speed Delivery

My career on the line, I could think of only one solution: "You're going to get me a police escort to and from the airport," I managed to croak.

And he did. At 8 p.m., a car, driver and four motorcycle policemen escorted me to the airport. As soon as the plane landed, we practically kidnapped the frightened fitter who was carrying the boxed costume.

With sirens screaming, we roared back across the city at over 100 mph. At the Coliseum, I rushed to Sonja's dressing room with the beaded chiffon costume in my hands. She smiled, stepped into the costume and skated onto the ice amidst wild applause.

The show was a sellout everywhere we went. The producer felt he could sell any show with "Hollywood" in the title, but I knew it was Sonja who sold the show.

Of course, stars have their own lives, too. A few months later, I attended Sonja's wedding reception at the New York Plaza Hotel. The event was mobbed with theater people and half of Hollywood as well.

Sonja wore her favorite color—turquoise—and the five-tiered wedding cake, which the bridegroom cut with his Navy sword, was also frosted in turquoise with tiny silver candles.

Much like the mink-edged cape I'd designed for her ice show, that cake was guided into the ballroom by six busboys. It was a fitting reception for one of the brightest stars of her generation.

What Are You Waiting for?

HAVING SERVED aboard an aircraft carrier for nearly 2 years in WWII, I had enough points to be sent home shortly after the Japanese surrender.

We sailed on the battleship *Iowa*, and as we were not part of the crew, we were assigned different duties each day. One day we had no duties, and that was bad —you didn't want to be caught doing nothing.

A higher-ranked shipmate went to the chief's office for instructions. I was waiting for my buddy when an officer approached and angrily said, "Sailor,

AS YOU WERE
★ ★ ★ Where fond military memories fall in ★ ★ ★

what are you doing just standing there?"

He called me to attention and chewed me out for not turning to (getting back to work). But as I continued to stand there, he asked, "What are you waiting for?"

"I'm waiting for Christmas," I meekly replied.

That made the officer *really* mad, and he tore into me again. About this time, my shipmate returned, and he was questioned by the officer as to who he was and what he was doing there.

"I'm with him," my shipmate said, pointing to me. "I'm Christmas. Dale Christmas."

The officer was speechless. He gave both of us one more look, then walked away and hollered, "Turn to!"
—*Gilbert Lopez, Denver, Colorado*

Thanks Fir the Memories

ON CHRISTMAS 1944, I was at a naval base in the Philippines when my inventive father sent me a Christmas "tree" in a small wooden cheese box.

The box actually contained a number of small Douglas fir boughs, with instructions on how to make a tree from a short piece of broom handle.

I drilled holes in the broom handle, fastened it to a block of wood, then stuck the boughs in the holes.

It made a small, but pretty good, tree. And the best thing was, the boughs had been so tightly sealed in the box that they still gave off that wonderful aroma. Guys came from all over the island just to see and smell that tree to bring back memories of home.

Dad brought a good Christmas to a lot more guys than he ever imagined.
—*George Bostwick*
Hood River, Oregon

G-E-R-O-N-I...Ouch!

I WAS STATIONED at Rosecrans Field, St. Joseph, Missouri, during the

early part of World War II. I worked in the flight dispatch office and was able to go on flights when I was off duty.

I went along on one training flight with a student who had the habit of taking a nap in the rear of the airplane when he wasn't scheduled to be in the pilot's seat. This perturbed the instructor, who decided to cure the student of his habit.

The student flew the first half on the training flight, then went to the rear for his nap. He was still sleeping when we landed, and the instructor put his plan into action.

With the rest of us in on the plan, we taxied to the ramp, cut the engines, then, with our parachutes still on, went to the rear shouting, "Bail out! We're going down!"

The student scrambled into his 'chute, released the safety pins on the cargo door and bailed out to the concrete ramp 4 feet below.

He never again napped on a training flight...and he became a good pilot.
—*Howard Jones*
St. Joseph, Missouri

GREAT KIDDER. "This photo of my son Jackie and me was made in the spring of 1942 outside Oran, Algeria, following the invasion of North Africa the previous November," explains Bill Wilson of Princeton, Indiana. "I sent a copy of the photo home to Hampton, Iowa, where it appeared in the rotogravure section of the *Des Moines Sunday Register*, captioned, 'Little Iowan Goes to North Africa'. The paper was flooded with calls and mail from angry readers protesting Jackie's being allowed to visit me in North Africa during wartime. They failed to read the explanation below the photo. Jackie's grandfather, L.H. Davis, a skilled amateur photographer, made a life-size photo of Jackie, mounted it on cardboard and mailed it to me. It's that photo I'm holding, not the real Jackie."

UNAUTHORIZED GEAR. When then Corporal Joseph Hopkins was ready to ship out to Iceland in 1943, his daughter Pat wanted to go along. Joseph, from Annapolis, Maryland, says Pat didn't want him to go, but like all GIs, "I had no choice." She did not accompany her dad.

Through the Cracks

MY BUDDY and I were both recalled to active duty in 1961. We were corporals in the National Guard in Virginia and were sent to Fort Campbell, Kentucky.

We were put up in World War II-era barracks, where the sergeant tried to impress us by having a "GI party" upon our arrival.

He put us in charge of the upper floor, which he wanted scrubbed, then rinsed down with buckets of water. I told him it wouldn't work, but he insisted. So we did as we were ordered and soaked those old floors with water—which ran through the cracks and all over the bunks and possessions of the guys on the first floor.

That was the last time for that type of GI party. —Tom Bertsch
Sandusky, Ohio

Read All About It...If You Can

IN 1951, I was in basic training at Lacking Air Force Base, San Antonio, Texas.

One morning, some buddies and I were coming out the door of the chow hall. There was a little boy at the door selling newspapers. He was yelling, "Buy a paper! Buy a paper!"

My buddy Cox joked to the kid, "I can't read."

The boy shot back, "Then buy a paper and put it in your back pocket so you won't look so dumb."
—Gene Brooks, Fairfield, California

Stars Watched Movies, Too

AS ANYONE who served in the South Pacific during World War II knows, the first thing the Navy Seabees built were outdoor theaters. I think they built some of them before the islands were secured.

One night on Orete Point, Guam, I

was watching a movie, sitting on one of the coconut tree log "theater seats". The guy on my right looked familiar, and I was trying to place his face.

"Don't I know you from somewhere?" I finally asked.

"I'm Tyrone Power," he said. "You probably saw me in a few of my movies. At least, I hope you have."

So there I was, sitting next to a movie star, instead of watching him on the screen. —Eugene McClintock
Suffern, New York

Never Mind, He'll Swim to Safety

IN THE EARLY '50s, our destroyer was at Guantanamo Bay, Cuba for refresher training. This particular day, we were to have a "man overboard" drill.

A kapok life jacket, nicknamed "Oscar", represented the "man" overboard. The ship started a 360-degree turn, the rescue crew assembled their equipment and Oscar was thrown over the side. It promptly sank to the bottom.

A second Oscar was thrown over the side as the ship made another turn. This Oscar floated, but the ship ran over it.

I doubt I have to say it, but we failed our man overboard drill.
—Richard Gillette
Anderson, South Carolina

One Less Girl in Port

I WAS A Navy Armed Guard gunner on a merchant tanker in the Pacific in 1945. All of the pinup girl photos next to my bunk were of my dream girl, Susan Hayward.

One day, I was called to Lieutenant Hughes' quarters. He admired my pictures each morning during inspection, and he told me to sit down because he had some shocking news.

The blood drained from my face. I just knew something awful had happened to my family back in Chicago.

PHOTOGRAPHIC MIND. When Casey Prunchunas was wounded in Italy in 1944, he eventually ended up back in the States for recuperation and rehabilitation. Required to attend school, Casey, of Chatsworth, California, settled on photography. He was good enough that his lieutenant told him to keep up the work after his discharge. Casey kept his day job in civilian life, but he kept up his photography and even made a little money at it. He also had a number of his photos accepted by the Chicago Historical Society for its permanent collection.

HOT SUBJECT. Before Doris Griffin (left), Lee Styles and Anna Dybings were posted to New Caledonia in 1942, they had some memorable training.

Nurse Heats Up Training Site

BEFORE HEADING to the South Pacific in October 1942, we Army nurses were required to learn to use the flamethrower. It was very heavy and hard to control.

My first attempt to steady it and aim for some brush was almost a disaster. The instructor jumped in to help me steady it before I nearly wiped out some onlooking medical staff.

I can still see the looks of alarm on the doctors as they quickly backed away. Thank goodness we never had to use flamethrowers when we got to our post in New Caledonia.
—Lee Gelott Styles
West Peabody, Massachusetts

Seeing my distress, the lieutenant got up, put his hand on my shoulder and said in a somber voice, "Susan Hayward just had twins." —James Horan
Chicago, Illinois

Camo Passed the Test

I WAS assigned to Camp Roberts, California for infantry training in 1944. After learning to shoot, throw grenades, give first aid, march and peel potatoes, we went on a 2-week bivouac.

We hid in slit trenches by day and slept in them at night. Each trench was covered with a canvas "shelter half".

We were ordered to camouflage our trenches by breaking up their outlines. I used dirt, twigs and leaves.

The sergeant, coming down the hill one day, stepped on my shelter half and fell into my slit trench. "It doesn't have to be *that* good," he growled.
—Edwin Utvick, Tracy, California

Brown Brothers

Sailor Never Forgot Act of Kindness

By Darrell Cavolt, Hemet, California

BACK IN SPRING of 1943, I was a young sailor in a tight spot.

I was on leave from the Norfolk Naval Training Station in Virginia and about to head home to Terre Haute, Indiana. I'd just bought a diamond engagement ring for my girlfriend and planned to pop the big question.

But when I stepped up to the ticket window at the Norfolk train station and asked the agent the cost of a ticket to Terre Haute, I was plumb out of luck! That ring had cost more than I'd planned to spend, and I didn't have enough money for a ticket to Indiana.

I left the window, perplexed over what to do. Should I take the ring back and exchange it for a cheaper one?

Suddenly, a pretty young woman walked up and handed me a round-trip ticket to Terre Haute. She'd seen me turned away at the window and wanted to help. I was flabbergasted!

When I told her I couldn't accept such a gift, she explained that she was married and her serviceman husband was in Europe. She wanted to do this in the hope that if he were in a similar predicament, someone would help him.

We boarded the train and rode together as far as Charlotteville, Virginia, where she got off. I asked the young woman for her name and address, but she refused to tell me because she knew I'd try to repay her.

48 Years Later...

Through the years, I often wondered about that young lady who helped me. I'll bet I told the story of her kindness a thousand times. But I never dreamed I'd get to see her again...until January 20, 1991. I'll never forget that day.

The telephone rang as my wife, Mary, and I were eating our supper. Mary answered, and the caller asked to speak to me.

That caller asked if I'd been in the Navy in Norfolk, Virginia during the spring of '43. When I told her I had, she asked if I remembered someone giving me a ticket to Terre Haute.

"Yes!" I yelled. "Are you that lady?"

"No," she replied with a laugh. "My name's Mary Dawkins. The lady who bought you that ticket is my neighbor, Blanche Dunsmore."

It seems Blanche had shared her memory of that day with Mary, and Mary decided to try and find me. It took her 3 hours and several phone calls, but there she was, asking me to call Blanche—collect.

Of course, there was no way I'd reverse the charges...I'd waited 48 years to make that call!

But I was so excited that I couldn't even dial the phone, so my wife did. When Blanche answered, my wife started joking with her, saying how I didn't look remotely like that handsome young sailor anymore. That was when I figured I'd better grab the phone.

Blanche and I reminisced for quite a while about the train trip and the roads our lives had taken. She'd worked in a bank after the war and now lived in Chapel Hill, North Carolina. She and her husband were soon to celebrate their 50th wedding anniversary.

I told her I'd married after the war and continued serving in the Navy. I moved to California in '52 and eventually retired as vice president and senior loan officer of a bank.

In July 1991, Mary and I paid a 4-day visit to Blanche and her husband (and Mary Dawkins, too). It was the best trip we've ever taken.

While there, I "fessed up" and told Blanche the rest of my story. My wonderful wife, Mary, is not the girl I'd proposed to after our train ride. That romance ended before I rejoined my ship in Norfolk, and I didn't court Mary until I went back to Terre Haute! ☎

REMARKABLE REUNION. Darrell Cavolt never forgot Blanche Dunsmore's good turn. Nearly 50 years later, they reunited to recall.

I Was in the 'First WAVE'

By Jean Talcott Wicks
Omak, Washington

CARRIED on the tide of patriotic fervor sweeping the country at the outset of World War II, I enlisted in the U.S. Navy late in 1941.

As part of the first class assigned to the newly formed WAVES (Women Accepted for Volunteer Emergency Service), I took my physical exam and aptitude test in Des Moines, Iowa.

It wasn't until my classmates and I were lined up to take the oath of service in the United States Armed Forces that I realized what my enlistment really meant—the Navy had just taken charge of my life.

In January 1942, I was sent to boot camp at Iowa State Teachers College in Cedar Falls. Basic training consisted of drills, calisthenics, classes, lectures and lots of inoculations. Every spare minute in between was filled with more drills and calisthenics.

Eventually I received a uniform allowance—two $100 bills. I'd never seen that much money in my life! The excitement was short-lived, however...I was handed the bills at one table, and at the next table, the Navy took them back. My uniform was paid for.

Alterations Included

Our class was bused to a Waterloo department store, where we were given uniforms to try on. A size 12 fit me perfectly...so, of course, I was issued a size 14, which had to be altered!

When the uniforms arrived several days later, we put them on and stood outdoors for an hour in 5° temperatures, waiting for dress inspection.

Unfortunately, our overcoats had *not* been delivered. I learned quickly how hard it is to stand at attention while shivering from head to toe!

There were other lessons to be learned in boot camp that weren't included in the training manuals. I learned how to live with all kinds of people, from debutantes to factory workers, schoolteachers to career girls.

I also learned never to volunteer unnecessary information. One day I casually mentioned that I had been in a high school marching band...and I was promptly made platoon leader!

Another important lesson involved

U.S. Navy

PLANE JANE she wasn't! Jean Wicks flashed a winning smile in 1943, when she served in the U.S. Navy as an Aviation Machinist Mate, Third Class.

food. The first time the mess crew plopped beans and ketchup on my tray for breakfast, I dumped them.

The next time, I ate the beans, ketchup and all—you can get mighty hungry doing drills all morning on an empty stomach!

After basic, I was assigned to aircraft engine assembly work at another base. That's when my training—the part about not divulging information—proved especially useful.

I fell in love with a sailor from Tacoma, Washington. Since married couples on base were forbidden, we married without permission and kept it secret!

We served together on that base, secretly married, for quite some time... and I never told a soul! ☎

Three Years Late For Graduation

By Raymond Goin, Boonton, New Jersey

MY HIGH SCHOOL EDUCATION was interrupted for 3 years during World War II while I served in the Navy in both the Atlantic and Pacific.

When I came home from the service, I was determined to finish my studies even though, at 21, I'd be the oldest student by far at Morristown (New Jersey) High School.

The local paper, the *Morristown Sunday Sentinel*, had photographer Joe Zeltsman tag along with me to chronicle my return to civilian life. Some of his photos appear here.

I finished high school in 1947, went on to Rider College and ended up with a degree in journalism. I later earned a master's degree, and after 17 years working for the *Morris County Daily Record*, I switched professions and became a teacher. ☎

1. NO REVEILLE. His first morning home, Ray could get up when he felt like it, not when someone told him to. But 10:30? What a slugabe

4. NO NAVY BLUE. After 3 years of wearing nothing but blue or whit uniforms, the array of colors in shirts and ties had Ray a little surprise

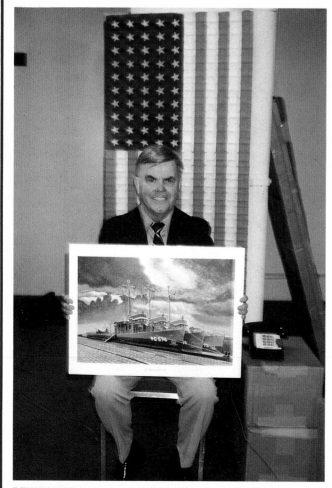

REUNION TIME. Determination took Raymond Goin, seen above at a reunion of his shipmates in 1984, through World War II, back to high school, on to college and into a professional life that included journalism and teaching. His first days back home from the war are chronicled here.

7. PRINCIPAL'S OFFICE. Being sent there was not punishment for Ray this time. He had to see Principal Wiley to get back in school.

2. HOME COOKIN'. At last, breakfast with no lines, no trays, no "mess". Being waited on by Mom—that's the life!

3. BUYING CIVVIES. Trying on civilian clothing at the local menswear store must have seemed a bit odd for Ray. Imagine…hats with brims!

5. MAKING IT OFFICIAL. Just to keep it legal, the draft board wanted to make sure Ray had his battleship discharge papers.

6. FRESH WATER. After Ray's 3 years at sea, a little fresh water in the Morristown YMCA pool felt good. No waves either.

8. SCHOOL PALS. Ray's return included a stop at the sweet shop.

9. I WAS THERE. History class (right) was something of a snap for Ray. He had a small part in making it while serving in the Navy.

PARENTS · SERVICE · CLUB INC. FREE · CANTEEN · STREATOR · ILL
SUPPORTED & SERVED BY ORGANIZATIONS OF THIS & OTHER CITIES

Photos: Helen Knoedler

CANTEEN DEPOT. One of the founders of the Streator, Illinois canteen, Mary Plimmer (in white uniform with tray) waits with her helpers to serve soldiers during World War II.

FREE CANTEEN SERVICE

Our Canteen Was an Oasis of Kindness

By Mary Plimmer

Editor's Note: This story, recounting Mary's experiences organizing and working at the Streator, Illinois Free Canteen during World War II, was shared by her niece, Sister Ann Rena Shinkey, a Reminisce reader from Streator.

IN 1943, the residents of Streator, Illinois often went to the busy Santa Fe Railroad depot to watch the many troop trains that traveled through our city. We saw the hungry young men and women run across the street to a small homey restaurant to get something to eat…but the trains never waited long enough for all to be served.

To deal with the problem, the Parents Service Club, of which I was a member, founded the Streator Free Canteen. We eventually served some 1.5 million servicemen and women—absolutely free!

We set up a work table in one corner of the train depot and began contacting local merchants to ask for donations of food and kitchen utensils. On a very cold November 28, 1943, we opened our canteen. It was 5 a.m., and 10 ladies were on hand.

We'd made coffee at home and brought it to the station in thermos jugs. Since we had no cups to serve it in, we'd gone door-to-door asking for empty cottage cheese containers.

When the first train rolled in, we handed out paper sacks containing sandwiches and homemade cookies to everyone. On that first exciting day, we served lunch to over 300 soldiers, most of them traveling from Chicago to San Francisco. Although it was hectic, we all agreed that it was worth the warm feeling that filled our hearts.

Workers Went Without

We realized just how many service people were passing through our town the first time we ran out of food! Undeterred, we ladies took up a collection among ourselves to buy more for the next day. Some of the club members even went home and ground up their family's roast to make sandwiches.

Coffee was perked in every home we could contact, and when the next train arrived, we were ready to serve. The project grew like wildfire— it seemed like everyone in town was eager to do their part for the war effort.

Someone donated an icebox, and ice was furnished free every day. Merchants gave us large coffeepots, carpenters built long tables and farmers dropped off sides of beef and pork. Other generous farm families gave us bushels of apples and pears. There never seemed to be enough tomatoes to satisfy hungry soldiers, who said the tomatoes reminded them of their gardens back home.

Sometimes, though, these young soldiers needed more than just food. Quite often, boys would ask us to call their parents and tell them they were okay. We made a special effort to handle all such requests.

The Word Spread

As word of our project spread, we were visited by some famous celebrities. The day Amos and Andy of radio fame stopped by was memorable. And when Claudette Colbert and Shirley Temple visited the canteen, they told us how amazed they were at the generosity of our town.

But I think the troops were the most amazed. They didn't hesitate to tell us that, in all their travels, they never found anything like our canteen—and all for *free*!

In the beginning, some doubted we could feed so many hungry servicemen, but those of us who believed in the canteen never once thought it would fail. We served the soldiers every day without fail between November 1943 and May 29, 1946, when the canteen finally closed.

We shed some tears and had a few laughs on that closing day, but we were proud. The Streator Free Canteen was our contribution to our country—a contribution we were happy to make. ☎

'Brownie' the Churchgoing Dog

Hugh P. Smith Jr.

By Evelyn Olson, Ogilvie, Minnesota

Sunday mornings are a leisurely time in many households—but they certainly weren't in our Ogilvie, Minnesota home in the late '20s.

Church services began at 9:30 a.m. Mother was the organist, so she had to be there early. That meant all of us kids had to be washed and dressed with our hair neatly combed by the time Mother left the house.

As you'd expect, there was a lot of hurrying around to make sure everyone was ready on time. That was trouble enough, but there was a bigger problem—our little dog, "Brownie".

Every morning during the week, Brownie was let out by the first person who got up. When we called him back in, he'd usually come running right away…but not on Sundays!

On that day, we could call and coax as much as we liked, but Brownie was simply nowhere to be found. Unable to locate our disappearing dog, Mother would finally give up in despair, and we'd all head off to church leaving Brownie outdoors somewhere.

After we arrived at church and got settled in with Mother at the organ, there would suddenly come a loud scratching at the church door. That was followed by the plaintive sound of a lonesome dog howling.

Took Sunday Stroll

This wailing would continue until the usher had no choice but to open the door. In would come Brownie with a smug look on his face! He'd stroll up the aisle to where Mother sat at the organ, plop down and sit quietly until the service ended.

On the rare Sundays when we didn't go to that service, Brownie attended anyway. As usual, he'd make a commotion at the church door until let in.

After he was allowed inside, he'd proceed down the aisle to where the organist was playing. Once he'd determined that Mother wasn't playing that Sunday, he'd go back to the door and make it known he wanted to leave and go home.

As you can imagine, this was quite embarrassing for Mother. There were some people who weren't all that happy to see a dog in church—plus, each time we got a new preacher, Mother had to explain our unusual situation to him.

A Heaven for Hounds?

Since Brownie lived to be 19 years old, quite a few preachers got used to having that little brown dog interrupt their Sunday services. Finally, though, Brownie grew too old and sick to go to church anymore.

Not long after Brownie passed away, our minister came to call. After inquiring about our signs of grief, he made a comment that gave us some comfort and helped put our little friend's life in perspective.

This is what he said:

"If there is a heaven for dogs, you can be assured Brownie will be scratching at the door—and when it is opened, he will be given a place right up front with the best of them." ☎

HEAVENLY DOG. Brownie (above with neighbor Joey Niemann) was a regular churchgoer during the '20s.

The Little Brown Church in the Vale

"HOW MANY *Reminisce* readers have taken a look inside The Little Brown Church in the Vale?" asks Cheryl Casjens of Santa Rosa, California. "This photo (above) gives them a chance to do so."

The Little Brown Church is the subject of a famous hymn sung by generations of worshipers. Built between 1860 and 1864 near Nashua, Iowa, The Little Brown Church still stands in the vale today.

Cheryl's husband's parents were married in a simple ceremony there, and the photos seen here were taken on their wedding day, June 8, 1940. Cheryl says she's happy to share her in-laws' cherished photos and their memories of a true storybook wedding.

Dorothy Mae Whitsell wore a peach dress with a sweetheart neckline, lace bodice and a full double net skirt that she made herself. Cheryl still has that dress and intends to pass it on to her daughters.

The bride's only jewelry was a gold locket, a gift from her groom, Clarence Casjens. She carried a bouquet of red and yellow roses and sweet peas.

After the ceremony, a luncheon was served in Dorothy and Clarence's honor at the St. Charles Hotel in Charles City, Iowa. Their guests enjoyed a four-tiered wedding cake decorated with a miniature bride and groom.

After a honeymoon trip to Yellowstone National Park, the couple settled in George, Iowa. They raised two sons, Jerry and Judson—the latter became Cheryl's husband.

That old-time hymn, known and loved so well, holds special meaning for many—but especially for Cheryl, Judson and family. It recalls for them the memorable summer day when Mr. and Mrs. Clarence Casjens spoke their wedding vows at The Little Brown Church.

WEDDING IN THE VALE. The famous Little Brown Church in the Vale really is a church, as Dorothy and Clarence Casjens (right) showed when they were married there on June 8, 1940. The church still stands today in Nashua, Iowa. Most people have heard the song, which was actually written before the church was built.

First the Song...Then the Church

WHEN he first visited Bradford, Iowa on a bright June afternoon in 1857, Dr. William S. Pitts saw a setting of rare beauty. "There was no church there," he later recalled, "but the spot was waiting for it."

Back home in Wisconsin, he wrote a song he called *Little Brown Church in the Vale* or *The Church in the Wildwood*. Then he put the manuscript away in a drawer.

In the spring of 1862, Dr. Pitts moved to Iowa and settled in the town of Fredericksburg, just east of the spot he'd visited 5 years previously.

Meanwhile, the citizens of Bradford had decided to build themselves a modest little church. By early winter of 1864, that church was ready.

One evening that spring, Dr. Pitts went to the new church with a choir and brought along the manuscript for his song. There, for the first time ever, he sang the song in public.

The response was so positive that he took the manuscript to Chicago and had his composition published. It rapidly gained popularity and eventually became one of the most beloved songs of the era.

It wasn't too long

before the church became known as "The Little Brown Church in the Vale" ...just as William Pitts had envisioned it back in 1857. ☎

Little Brown Church In the Vale

There's a church in the valley by the wildwood,
No lovelier spot in the dale;
No place is so dear to my childhood,
As the little brown church in the vale.

Refrain:
Come to the church in the wildwood,
Oh, come to the church in the dale.
No spot is so dear to my childhood,
As the little brown church in the vale.

How sweet on a clear, Sabbath morning,
To list to the clear ringing bell;
Its tones so sweetly are calling,
Oh, come to the church in the vale.
Refrain

There, close by the side of that loved one,
To the trees where the wildflowers bloom,
When the farewell hymn shall be chanted
I shall rest by her side in the tomb.
Refrain

From the church in the valley by the wildwood,
When day fades away into night,
I would fain from this spot of my childhood
Wing my way to the mansions of light.
Refrain

Short Food Memories

Saved from Stale Sandwiches

I TOOK a bus trip from Newark, New Jersey to Los Angeles, California in 1949. I was on a tight budget for the trip, so before I left, I made 25 peanut butter and jelly sandwiches to eat along the way.

The first day, a group of GIs on the bus got so hungry watching me eat that they bought out my supply at 25¢ each. Instead of stale sandwiches, I was able to enjoy food at rest stop diners all along the way. —David Knoderer
Nevada City, California

Homesick for Homemade

BACK in 1945, I was a homesick 17-year-old freshman from Dallas, boarding at Texas Tech. I only went home twice that year.

After riding on the bus for hours, I would finally see the "Red Horse" that marked the Dallas skyline. What a thrill that was!

Right then I could almost smell banana pudding and goulash, which would be waiting for me at home.
—Jody Lloyd Cousins, Hockley, Texas

Dad Could Feed an Army

DAD was an Army cook during World War I, so everything he made thereafter was in large quantities. This came in handy during World War II, as we had 30 some boarders living in the loft of our barn while they worked nearby at a war plant.

Sourdough buckwheat pancakes were made in 5-gallon crocks, dozens of eggs were scrambled in gigantic skillets, cakes were baked in fours, pies numbered 10 at a time, and soup was pre-pared outside in a 10-gallon canner over an open fire. Everything always tasted wonderful. The only "flop" happened when Dad tried to bake *one* angel food cake. He couldn't remember how to scale down the ingredients! —Sandra Litchet
Wichita, Kansas

Dried Apple Pie

I REMEMBER fall in the '30s, when my grandma cored and sliced freshly picked apples, tied them in a cheesecloth bag and hung them in the attic to dry.

When Christmas dinner came, we saved some room to enjoy a piece of her delicious dried apple pie. That was a once-a-year treat. I even liked to eat the dried apples right out of the bag.

—Ina Armstrong, Lansing, Michigan

Make Room for Limburger!

AS A CHILD, my uncle was very small, so whenever the kids in his one-room schoolhouse crowded around the pot-bellied stove to warm up, he could never get near.

Then one day he put a piece of Limburger cheese in his overalls pocket. Pretty soon, he had *lots* of room, once the cheese began to warm and share its "aroma". What a stinky trick!
—Margaret McQuary
Salem, Oregon

Even Neck Bones Were Good

DURING the Depression, Grandma often made a meal of neck bones and rice, both of which were inexpensive.

Years later, Mom made the same meal—she could make *anything* taste good. Now I sometimes make neck bones and rice simply to feel close to my family. —Gail Stevens
Largo, Florida

Don't Hold the Onions

MY FAVORITE TREAT as a child was a mustard onion sandwich. When my twin sister and I came home from school, we'd go straight into the garden and dig out a large onion.

While one of us cleaned the onion, the other got out the cutting knife and a loaf of Mom's homemade bread. I can still taste those slabs of bread, spread with a generous layer of butter and mustard and hugging a thick slice of onion in between. —Lorretta Pfeffer
Breckenridge, Minnesota

Dessert Was Deserted

I DECIDED to surprise my mother by baking our favorite spice cake for our evening meal. While she was away, I mixed up the ingredients, all from handy canisters in the pantry.

The finished product looked flat, but I carried it to the table with great pride. When my dad took a bite and noticed a gritty texture, I soon learned a cup of coffee meant *brewed*, not ground. —Doris Romstad
Plentywood, Montana

Pooled Their Efforts

FOOD WAS SCARCE in our house during the Depression, but there was plenty of spot fish in Chesapeake Bay. I recall my father and our next-door

TEEN KEPT HER HUMOR. "Even as a teenager in 1939, I waited for the Good Humor man to come down the street," admits Marion Brantley, Winter Garden, Florida. "Here I am with the good-natured driver, who graciously let me pose alongside his truck."

neighbor would leave at sunup and later come home with a big catch.

Then we all pitched in to scale and clean the fish, salt them down and store them in barrels for the winter. The heads, tails and innards were used for fertilizer.

In this photo (at right), I'm in the front row, the first girl on the left. I was 10 at the time. —*Zora James*
Chesapeake, Virginia

Maytag Featured a "Butter Cycle"

UNHAPPY with low milk prices in 1957, some desperate dairy farmers dumped their milk on the ground.

Mother couldn't bear to be so wasteful. So she sanitized our Maytag washing machine, filled it to the brim with cream and turned on the agitator. Soon we had mountains of butter, plus plenty of good buttermilk. Everything we ate was topped with a big dollop of butter! —*Marilyn Smith*
Fair Grove, Missouri

Gathering of the Greens

I CAN'T let a spring go by without at least one good "mess of wild greens".

Back in the '30s, my mother used to gather greens. She even sowed wild mustard seed near the house to have handy to add to her combination of poke, lamb's-quarter, dandelion, bluestem, curly dock and chickweed.

Those cooked greens—along with ham, potatoes and homemade bread—made a feast fit for a king.
—*Scharlotte Klein*
Boonville, Missouri

Nuts for Ice Cream

BACK in the '30s, my Uncle Bob had a hand-cranked ice cream freezer that made slightly less than 2 quarts of ice cream at a time. My Aunt Louise's scrumptious mixture of sugar, eggs, cream, vanilla and Grape-Nuts cereal was a rare Sunday treat.

We cousins all gathered around to watch the makings as our appetites reached an almost painful level. No one dared leave my uncle's little house, lest he miss out on his serving. It was always worth the wait.

My aunt served the dessert in cobalt blue cereal dishes that had a photograph of Shirley Temple imprinted in the bottom of the dish. Those pretty dishes made the occasion all the more special.

The only downside of this gathering was the fact that there were eight anxious mouths to share in such a moderate amount, and there was never an offer of a second helping.
—*Patricia Munroe, Solon, Maine*

Creamed Dish Was Snow Job

DURING the '40s, we lived on a farm outside Muscatine, Iowa. We had a big garden and canned almost everything.

Carrots were not one of my favorites when I was 4, so my mother cooked them up with a white sauce to get me to eat them. She told me they were creamed *peaches*, one of my favorite fruits! —*Peggy Schmidt*
Springfield, Missouri

Mother's Invention Of Necessity

MOTHER knew how cold New England was in the winter months, especially for a young child who walked to school and got breakfast on her own.

During the '50s, she worked and usually didn't get home until after midnight, but she managed to set up a double boiler of cornmeal mush on the stove. When I woke up, the mush would be warm and ready for me to eat while she was still sleeping.
—*Christine Akiona, Kaaawa, Hawaii*

Granddad Jammed

WHEN my grandparents hosted their six grandchildren for vacation or holidays in Thorndale, Texas in the mid-'40s, my granddad always prepared our breakfast.

He put a large chunk of freshly churned butter into a hot iron skillet, placed a slice of bread on top and fried it to a golden brown. He kept turning out fried toast with homemade plum ↻

A PINCH OF THIS... "This was my mom at 95 years old," says Anne Kulick of Phillipsburg, New Jersey. "She baked until age 97 and always just measured with her hands. It took me 2 years, at Easter and Christmas, to translate her measurements into cups and spoons. Now my breads look like these and continue to be a part of our family's Easter tradition."

FAMILY TRADITION. "My father-in-law started holding clambakes in 1952," says Fay Yoder of Hamburg, Pennsylvania. "A big iron kettle was put over an open fire. In the bottom were rocks and a little water, then the kettle was lined with burlap feed sacks. Potatoes and corn circled the outside, with onions in the middle and sweet potatoes on top of the onions. The clams went over the top, so the juice dribbled down over the rest of the bake as it cooked for about 2 hours. We'd also have pepper cabbage and lots of desserts. Pop made the best clam bakes and passed his knowledge on to my husband and son."

jam as long as there were "customers" to eat it.
—*Carroll Wilson*
Olney, Texas

Tasty Hand Warmers
MY MOTHER grew up in Plattsburgh, New York during the '20s. She and her sisters had a long walk to school and many winter mornings had to walk atop 6-foot snowdrifts.

My grandmother would cook two hard-boiled eggs for each of them to put in their pockets. Mama said it kept their hands warm and cozy, and at noon, their lunch was ready. —*Mabel Stevenson*
Wildwood, Florida

Greeted Grits at Every Meal
I WAS born and raised in New York, but Mother spent her childhood in Florida, where grits had been a staple at just about every meal.

We ate grits mixed with eggs, sausage or bacon for breakfast, and in winter, we ate them as cereal with lots of butter and brown sugar. Lunchtime found us eating grits with butter, salt and pepper or grits fried with butter.

Grits greeted us at suppertime, too...on the plate covered with rich

gravy and complementing steak, roast beef, pork chops or ham.

All those grits with trimmings, however, didn't fatten me up one bit!
—*Jerry Nostrand*
Colorado Springs, Colorado

Hurrah for Bread and Milk
TIRED OUT from caring for her brood of nine children, Mother would sometimes say with a pang of guilt, "You kids can have bread and milk for supper."

We'd all jump up and down and yell, "Yea! Yea!"

Bread and milk was homemade bread torn into pieces, soaked with whole milk and sprinkled with sugar. What a departure from the pork chops, fried chicken, pot roast, fish, venison, vegetables, homemade cottage cheese, jam and pickles that Mother normally served.

It never failed to amaze her how much we loved bread and milk!
—*Michelle Negaard*
Vernon Center, Minnesota

Anyone Else Eat Fried Catsup?
SOME DAYS were very lean during the Depression, so we ate *fried* catsup.

This delicious filler was prepared by browning a tablespoon of butter in a cast-iron frying pan until it was close to burning, then mixing in a half cup of catsup until bubbly.

After removing it from the heat, we dipped fresh white bread into this tasty sauce!
—*Tom Vatsula*
Pocahontas, Arkansas

Hog-Wild for Meat Treats
EVERY FALL my parents and relatives butchered a pig in a building called the summer house. While they were busy, my cousins and I played in the main house, watching from the window and anticipating the taste of freshly cooked liver, which our parents

LAST LICK. "Mother had just finished filling up the jars with homemade jelly when this photograph was snapped in 1928," relates Ruth Fanger of Monroe, Oregon. "My brother, Lee, and I are enjoying every little taste left in the pan on the steps of our farmhouse near Coquille, Oregon. Two years later, my parents lost the farm early in the Depression."

would bring to the house for lunch, and scrapple later on. It was the best part of butchering day. —*Kathleen Unger*
Nazareth, Pennsylvania

Rhubarb Took Revenge
DURING the 1930s, our family lived in Chicago. Despite living in the big city, we had a garden patch and a grape arbor. My favorite yield from the garden was rhubarb. Mother made wonderful pies and a pudding she called rhubarb stew.

One day she made a bowl of stew and left it on the table. I was little but couldn't resist sneaking a taste. One thing led to another, and before I realized it, I'd eaten the whole bowl!

Mother didn't even have to punish me...Mother Nature did that with a tummy ache I never forgot.
—*Joy Dunn, Corpus Christi, Texas*

Sundays at Grandma's
SUNDAYS were special days for me whenever I could go to Grandma's for dinner. Homemade applesauce, sweet corn from the Victory Garden, yummy mashed potatoes and an occasional fresh cherry pie from a tree in the yard was a menu to look forward to.

Grandfather would not stand for any nonsense at the table, and we had to be absolutely quiet while he listened to Gabriel Heatter say, "Ah yes, there's good news tonight." —*Marge Dwan*
Rockford, Illinois

Goose Grease Was Best
I WAS A KID during WWII, when just about everything was rationed. I remember my mom baked a goose as a special treat, and the gravy was great.

But the best part came later, after the gravy had been refrigerated. The grease rose to the top and Mom made goose grease sandwiches.
—*Richard Kirchner*
Blaine, Minnesota

By Madeline Huss
Bowie, Maryland

'Aluminum Party' Was An Affair to Remember

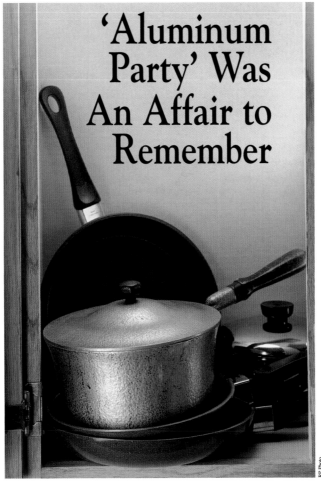

WHILE CLEANING up after dinner one recent evening, I stopped to examine an old pot. Suddenly, childhood memories flooded back of the Depression era in my home in Lyndhurst, New Jersey.

It seemed nothing exciting ever happened in Lyndhurst until the day in 1936 when Mama announced, "I'm having a Club Aluminum party tomorrow. I want you to behave and watch your little brother in the backyard."

My ears perked up immediately. "What's an aluminum party?" I asked. "I never heard of it."

Tightening her apron, Mama said, "Soon you will see."

The next day, our house buzzed with excitement. Mama placed a freshly ironed linen tablecloth on the seldom-used dining room table. With help from her friend Mrs. Alex, she set out her good china and silverware.

At the sound of the doorbell, I raced through the house to see who was there. At the door stood a short, balding man surrounded by boxes filled with pots of every description.

A *Man* Was Cooking

"Good morning, little lady," he said. "Is your mother at home?" Before I could answer, Mama appeared beside me. "Come in, Mr. Harris, come in," she gushed, holding the door open wide.

After lugging the heavy boxes into the house, he returned to his Model A to get the supplies for the brunch he was about to make.

While he went about his preparation, the other ladies who'd been invited poured excitedly into the house. Conversation hummed—a *man* doing the cooking! What a wonderful treat!

From the back porch, nose pressed against the screen, I watched the proceedings with great interest. Soon delicious aromas began wafting out the

door and it was time to serve the meal.

Plates were filled with lacy browned pancakes topped with yellow cling peaches, mounds of scrambled eggs and browned link sausages.

The women ate eagerly, happy to partake of a meal they hadn't prepared themselves. Later, after the table was cleared, Mr. Harris lined up his pots and

pans for all to see. He explained that only *his* cookware could produce a meal like the one the ladies had just consumed. They listened to every word, then a few dared ask, "How much?"

There were gasps when the answer was received. But soon a couple of the women were rummaging in their purses.

A Small Deposit...

"Ladies—ladies," said Mr. Harris reassuringly. "With a small deposit, you can select your cookware now. Then I'll come around every week to collect on the balance."

At that news, a collective sigh of relief filled the room, and the ladies began fingering the pots in earnest. Mama and Mrs. Alex certainly bought their share that day.

With her shiny new pots, Mama could often be heard humming a cheerful tune while she prepared meals. When Mrs. Alex died years later, she left her entire collection of Club Aluminum to Mama. When I married, Mama passed them on to me.

Now, over 60 years later, my cupboard bulges with modern cookware. But when I reach for something to cook with, I invariably grab one of those sturdy old aluminum pans.

I can't help but feel a link to the past—sometimes I even find myself humming as I turn on the stove to cook yet another meal. ☎

LOTS O' POTS. Madeline Huss shows that her Club Aluminum pots and pans aren't just for show. She often cooks in them, and when she does, they bring back fond memories of her mother.

By Jayne Walton Rosen
San Antonio, Texas

Toast to The King of Champagne Music

I WAS the second "Champagne Lady" to sing with Lawrence Welk's orchestra. Our adventures between 1939 and '47 could fill a book!

I grew up singing for local radio stations and dance bands in San Antonio. After graduation, I worked as a singer at WOW radio in Omaha.

Touring Nebraska, Lawrence heard one of my shows. His singer had left, so he called the station manager to see if he could talk to me about joining his band. In summer of 1939, at age 22, I went on the road with Lawrence Welk's Champagne Orchestra. It was an interesting life.

Many of our appearances were one-nighters in small ballrooms with no dressing rooms. Have you ever tried putting on a formal in the backseat of a car in zero-degree weather?

Played Top Ballrooms

Imagine putting a coat over that formal and donning snow boots to venture out behind the ballroom and wait in line to use the outdoor privy.

Playing the wonderful Trianon and Aragon Ballrooms in Chicago got us off of one-nighters for a while and offered the chance to get our formals cleaned. (After 3 months of one-nighters, they could practically stand up alone!)

While on the road with the band, I did most of the driving. Lawrence would get out the map and tell me which highways to take, then go to sleep.

One time in Wisconsin at 4:30 a.m., I slammed on the brakes when I came to a large body of water with a chain across it and a sign reading "Next ferry 6 a.m."

Lawrence woke up and wanted to know what the trouble was. Well, the trouble was I couldn't drive on water! We lost 80 miles that night.

Small towns often had hotels along Main Street, typically on a second floor above a restaurant. Rooms usually had a thick rope tied to a radiator to use as a fire escape.

We were in a little Iowa town one night when I woke to sirens and people screaming in the street below. The hotel was on fire! Lawrence and all the boys had run downstairs before the flames blocked the stairway. They were yelling up at me to grab the rope and jump!

I did, and endured rope burns for weeks. After that, I asked Lawrence to buy me a folding rope ladder that attached to the windowsill. I carried it on the road for years.

I'll never forget when Lawrence rented a sleeper bus to take us on a tour of one-nighters. One rainy night when the main highway had flooded, the driver told Lawrence he knew a shortcut. At about 4 a.m., the bus overturned in a muddy ditch!

Our instruments were broken, the sheet music was everywhere and the

"*O*ur adventures could fill a book!"

Hammond organ flew to the front of the bus. Luckily, no one was hurt.

All 21 of us climbed out the windows and stood there on the highway in the pouring rain.

Lawrence hiked to some farmhouses, and in a few hours, three huge tractors came up the road to help right the bus.

Meanwhile, the boys and I had started walking to get something to eat. We found a truck stop 6 miles away and ate everything in the place. Lawrence rented cars and instruments, and we continued on.

Visited Veterans

Once during World War II, Lawrence took his accordion and I took my voice to Walter Reed Veterans Hospital. We spent hours going from bed to bed trying to bring a smile to those boys' faces.

Some of them had danced to our music during better times. I'll never forget one boy who'd stepped on a land mine. He was terribly injured, yet he smiled at us. Lawrence and I both left his bedside in tears.

I've stayed in touch with the Welk family and was with Lawrence and his wife, Fern, in 1992, a short time before he passed away.

Today, this old Champagne Lady has nothing but sweet memories of Lawrence Welk—a great bandleader and a wonderful man. ☎

AN' A ONE AN' A TWO. Great musical experiences in the Lawrence Welk band were shared by Jayne Rosen (lower right).

No One Was Sweet on
Candy Bars Until the '20s

By Ray Broekel, Ipswich, Massachusetts

THE 1920s was a decade of new beginnings for much of the United States. Railroads were the way to travel to distant destinations and the automobile was fast catching on.

Radio was bursting onto the scene, while Hollywood's fledgling movie industry was just beginning to capture the imagination of the American public—and the candy bar industry was experiencing an unprecedented boom.

Way back in 1894, Hershey had come out with the first American machine-made "candy bar". It wasn't much of a hit, nor were the other bars that followed before World War I. Soldiers returning from Europe had gotten used to the candy bars supplied to them during the war, and they retained their fondness for them.

Most of the numerous brands of candy bars made between 1894 and the end of the '20s are now gone. But a few of those early ones survived—besides the Hershey bar, they included Cherry Mash (early 1900s), the Goo Goo Cluster (1912), Mountain Bar (1914) and Clark Bar (1917).

Among the non-survivors were many bars that were popular for a time, then disappeared forever. The IT bar is a good example. Clara Bow, popular film star of the '20s and early '30s, was known as the "IT girl". She was the actress for whom it was said, "Either you have it or you don't." The Imperial Candy Company of Seattle tried to cash in on that fame with the IT bar.

Perhaps the most widely made kind of early American candy bar was the "nut roll" (peanuts, caramel, fudge and chocolate). Many companies made their own version—two still around today are Baby Ruth (1919) and Oh Henry! (1920). Not quite as successful, the Love Nest bar first came out in the '20s and lasted into the '50s.

Another very popular nut roll that started in the '20s was the Chicken Dinner candy bar. Curious how the unusual name for this bar originated?

Well, during World War I, it was thought that a family was indeed fortunate if it had one good meal a day. Since the words "chicken dinner" brought to mind a good hearty meal for most people, the Sperry Candy Company of Milwaukee decided to use the popular name for its new candy bar.

To add to the effect, the trucks that delivered the Chicken Dinner candy bars had large chickens formed out of sheet metal on their hoods and tops. So, for a time, people in the Midwest chuckled at these "Chicken Trucks". Chicken Dinner bars were actually quite successful. For a while, in the '30s, there was a small 1-cent version of it offered, and the bar did not disappear from candy counters until the '60s.

Since the '20s, the candy bar business has stood up well, weathering the Great Depression and the social changes in the ensuing decades. It's been estimated close to 100,000 different brands of candy bars have appeared on the scene over the years—with new ones popping up all the time.

Why are candy bars still so popular? Part of the reason may be that they provide a delicious, convenient easy-to-eat snack…and another reason, may be that, for some of us at least, they bring back fond memories of childhood days and kinder, gentler times. ☎

Tub o' My Heart

By Mary Secanky, Sturtevant, Wisconsin

PA HAD SCANNED the Sears Roebuck catalog for several evenings, creating an atmosphere of excitement and anticipation in our Racine, Wisconsin household. Usually, Pa was too tired for anything after he came home from working 10 to 12 hours at a local foundry. He started the furnace at 3 a.m. and faithfully performed his duties for 44 years.

Many men in our neighborhood during the 1920s worked with Pa, and none of them spoke fluent English. Our neighborhood of Poles, Slavs, Russians, Hungarians, Italians, Germans, Irish and French produced a smorgasbord of sounds as phrases of the various languages blended together.

Each group had its traditions, but all had the same goals of elevating their standards of living and educating their children. There were no problems, only challenges that took hard work.

Mom Bartered Sewing Skills

Ma was the neighborhood seamstress (she had the only sewing machine) and had borrowed the catalog from the Statz Sisters Dry Goods Store, where she got most of her sewing supplies. Customers often browsed through the catalog.

We had a steady flow of ladies through our house giving Ma sewing orders. Ma rarely received money for these jobs. Sometimes the pay would be in help at canning time, housecleaning, whitewashing the basement or other exchanges of services.

Eventually, Pa ordered a collapsible, rubberized bathtub from the catalog. It sounded modern and magical—5 feet long and mounted on a crisscross wooden stand that folded up for storage. He dreamed of leisure moments soaking the dirt out of his pores. When the tub arrived, Ma and Pa filled it with water, admiring its size and thinking about the luxury of being able to stretch out, almost full-length, and soak. But my sister and I were the first ones to actually bathe in it.

Sweet Dream Turned Sour

Our pride and joy soon became a source of frustration because many of our neighbors, shyly at first, then more insistently, asked to borrow our new tub.

Ma just couldn't refuse. Soon one neighbor neglected the courtesy of asking to pass the tub to someone else. In a short time, to our distress, no one really knew where the tub was or who was the last to have it.

The worst part of all came when Pa was ready for his hot bath and soak one night. Ma could not explain the whereabouts of the tub.

Pa consoled himself with the knowledge that someone in the neighborhood was now experiencing the luxury of an indoor bathtub, even though he was not.

One day, the tub appeared in the utility room off of our kitchen…in sad shape. Someone had ripped the fabric between the wooden mounting from top to bottom.

Pa became silent, and poor Ma was so apologetic that she kept trying to please him in every way. People who visited felt uncomfortable because most of them had experienced the ecstasy of a warm soak in our wonderful modern contraption.

We never solved the mystery of the ripped tub.

Couldn't Move *This* Tub

But Pa was not to be denied. One Saturday afternoon he walked over to Pete's Plumbing Shop, where there was a white bathtub displayed majestically in the front window. Made of cast iron, it couldn't be passed from house to house and Pa bought it, even though it took months to pay off.

Our family was the first in the neighborhood to have a stationary white tub. When Saturday morning came, our neighbors filed in to view it. With a towel draped over their arm, they anxiously hoped to be invited to take a bath.

Pa explained that we only had hot water when the furnace was running. Otherwise, we had to heat water in Ma's boiler where she boiled her bed sheets and cottons to keep them white.

Pa soon bought a hot water tank. Until it arrived, Pa boiled water in Ma's boiler and let the neighbors enjoy a bath in our tub…but for special occasions only.

We were richly repaid by being the guests of honor at all neighborhood festivities, and my sister and I had a taste of what it must be like to be famous. ☎

SQUEAKY CLEAN. Author and her parents were regular neighborhood heroes in the '20s.

My Kaleidoscope Of Memories

By Sarah Wealti, Belleville, Wisconsin

I GREW UP on a farm near Belleville, Wisconsin and married a local boy, so we stayed in the same area. I'm 75 years old now, and my children wanted me to write down some of the things I'd told them as they grew up. Perhaps these snippets of memories will remind others of their yesteryears.

I REMEMBER...

...my mother spending all day Saturday making pies and cakes, and cleaning chickens for Sunday dinner.

...picking violets in early May, and how there were so many in the field that it looked like a blue-purple blanket spread over the hillside.

...how I'd sit with a large bowl in my lap and stem strawberries that were to be canned, made into jam or mashed up for sauce to be eaten with whipped cream.

...before falling asleep, we'd make shadow pictures with our hands on the bedroom wall.

...when black raspberries were so thick in the woods that I could get a pailful just going after the cows in the upper pasture.

...I was supposed to weed a row of vegetables one time, but I pulled up the beets and left the weeds!

...lying in the sweet-smelling grass on a warm June day, imagining all sorts of shapes in those big puffy white clouds above.

...spending the morning picking and snapping green beans, then canning them in boiling water for 4 hours to make sure they didn't spoil.

...how good fresh rhubarb sauce tasted after a long winter of canned and dried food.

...sitting in a dark corner of the hay barn and listening to my sister scare us with ghost stories.

...how we could hardly wait for the first ripe tomato.

...sitting on the porch on a July evening and listening to the frogs in the creek and smelling the new-mown hay—and if that hay was sweet clover, the hayloft would smell like summer all winter long.

...the afternoon our mail carrier and his wife came to visit, and how embarrassed I was when my mother had to tell me who he was—even though I'd seen him every weekday for years! I guess I thought he was attached to his car and mailbag.

...how the windfall apples from the Duchess tree in the front yard were large enough to use for apple dumplings. They were so-o-o-o good.

...the time I was an angel in the first-grade Christmas program, with gauze wings and all. The next day, we learned I had chicken pox and had infected all the other kids.

...the morning my dad came in the house with icicles in his beard, then bundled me up and carried me to the barn to see a litter of baby pigs.

...how in the evenings, I felt like God was in His Heaven and all was right with the world as we sat around a cozy fire, eating popcorn and apples—the whole family safe from the outside world. ☏

Dad Kept Wrigley's Rolling

PACKED IN MEMORIES. Jerry Witt (above) saved plenty of mementos (right) from his job at Wrigley's. He gave the collection to son John, who notes "Army Ration" gum was made for the military during the war. So were Commando "Milk Snacks", but they were called "chewy sticks of delicious food", not gum.

By John Witt, Hayward, Wisconsin

W hen I was a boy in the late 1930s, my dad brought me a treat from work every day. This was a benefit of his job with the Wrigley Chewing Gum Company, which was located at 35th and Ashland in Chicago.

Every afternoon, I'd walk a mile to meet Dad at the "El" train and we'd stroll home, talking about school and such. Dad always brought something different. Sometimes it was licorice or peppermint gum (my favorite was Juicy Fruit). Candy-coated "Tips" gum was a rare treat.

Gum was never in short supply at our house, because Wrigley's workers got to take home four packs every day. These were usually the "reject" packs that weren't properly wrapped.

Dad also received a discount on regular boxes, which held 25 packs, so friends and relatives who visited our house never left without taking along plenty of gum.

Though he worked as a maintenance man, Dad wore a suit and tie to the plant *every* day. He'd change into his tan uniform at work, then back into his suit

100

before taking the train to go home.

He was proud of his work and had lots of good friends there. Dad often told stories about the huge conveyor system he worked on. It ran from the first floor of the plant up to the eighth floor.

As he explained, empty boxes started out on the conveyor at the first level, and by the time they reached the eighth floor, they were filled with packaged gum ready for shipping.

Not Always Easy

Dad's job was to oil and grease the system each morning before production started. As long as the system was running, his job was easy, but when the system broke down, production halted on all eight floors and the bosses would come flying out of their offices!

There were quite a few times Dad had to work long hours into the night so things would be ready to roll the next morning.

Major planned maintenance was scheduled for weekends, starting on Friday nights, and sometimes didn't finish up until Sunday night. Of course, Dad still had to be back at his normal

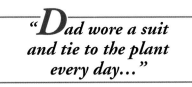

"Dad wore a suit and tie to the plant every day..."

job on Monday morning before the plant started operation.

The Wrigley plant was never open to the public for tours, so I didn't get the chance to see where my father worked.

I remember him telling me there was one floor where they cooked tree bark to extract the chicle. Another floor had the ovens and cutters, where each stick was cut after it was cooled, then coated with powdered sugar. Another floor housed the wrapping machines.

Good Work Rewarded

Dad stayed with Wrigley's for nearly 40 years. He was hired during the Depression in 1937 to wash walls, and his good work was rewarded with a promotion to the maintenance staff. There he stayed until retiring in 1974.

Dad saved an assortment of gum and other items from the late '30s through the early '50s. I now have his collection as a memento of this wonderful man and his dedication.

I still chuckle remembering how shocked my family and I were when Dad finally decided to retire. For the first time in decades, we had to *buy* gum at the store. How spoiled we had become! ☏

He Hunted Potato Bugs in Grandmother's Garden

By Wallace Johnson, Crescent City, California

WHEN I WAS A tyke, I had the privilege of spending my summers with my grandmother and uncle, Herb Ericson, on their 80-acre farm near Conover, Wisconsin.

This was in the late '20s and early '30s, and times were tough. But they raised most of their food, so they never went hungry. Cows, chickens and pigs provided them with meat. They also grew vegetables in a large garden, which they harvested and stored in bins in the basement.

I remember helping Grandma in the garden (right), picking potato bugs from the potato plants. Uncle Herb handed me a can with oil in the bottom and showed me what to look for.

As I recall, the garden consisted of three or four rows, 15 to 20 feet long. I diligently went about my duty.

When I finished the task, I handed the can to Grandma, hoping that now we could head for the house for biscuits and a glass of milk. Instead, Grandma gave the can back and told me to go over the potato patch again. I ended up with as many bugs as the first time around!

I don't remember getting homesick at Grandma's, probably because I got so much attention there.

I'd guess that's the reason my visits ended. My two brothers and cousin became jealous and demanded equal time, so I had to stay home.

It worked out fine. I didn't miss the farm as I grew older. I enjoyed the summer with the boys who lived in my neighborhood, playing baseball and other games and also building shacks. ☏

My Double Date With Jimmy Stewart

By Elsie West Duval, Newport News, Virginia

NOT OFTEN does a girl from Newport News get to spend a day with the likes of Jimmy Stewart and Olivia de Haviland…but that was just one day of a star-filled week I spent around Hollywood in 1940.

I'd had some prior experience with stars—my best friend was Kay Aldridge, who in the 1930s was one of the 10 most photographed girls in the world. After 8 years as a model, she was in the movies for 8 more years, appearing in 21 features and three serials.

Kay had moved from rural Virginia to live with relatives in Newport News, where she and I were classmates. Later, after she moved to Hollywood, we corresponded occasionally.

In 1940, Kay was pictured on the cover of *Life* magazine. Feeling mischievous, I dug out an unflattering girlhood photo of her and sent it with a letter to the editor.

Well, *Life* ran the letter and photo, and Kay saw it. She immediately wired me an invitation to visit her in Hollywood. I saved up enough money to take the 3-day train ride across the country and spend a week with my friend.

Besides seeing movies and meeting movie stars, I also got to "double-date" with Jimmy Stewart and Olivia de Haviland.

Picnic with the Stars

At the time, Kay was dating John Swope, a photographer who shared a house with Jimmy Stewart and Henry Fonda. John and Jimmy both had remote-control model airplanes and were eager to fly them in the desert, so a picnic was scheduled at Mirage Lake. Kay was to be John's date, and Jimmy would bring his steady, Olivia.

As luck would have it, Kay had a wardrobe fitting that day for her next film, so John invited me to "pinch-hit". I was ecstatic but determined not to act like a starstruck fan. I didn't ask for autographs and took only a few snapshots.

I felt perfectly comfortable, as I'd been with all three of them 2 days before at Jimmy's house for dinner. Jimmy had played the piano and sung silly ditties before we went to the MGM studio for a private movie showing.

It was a great picnic. Olivia brought a delicious catered lunch with matching paper plates and napkins. What I recall most of all is that Jimmy—whether playing piano or flying model airplanes on the desert—seemed just like he was in the movies.

Now that Jimmy is gone, I often think back to that day in the desert and my double date with that tall, dark and handsome "Gee, whiz" guy. ☎

LIFETIME OF MEMORIES. Author (on the left) and her actress friend, Kay Aldridge, posed for *Life* magazine in Los Angeles in '40, but the photo was never published. Jimmy Stewart and his model airplane are shown above.

Olivia de Haviland

Jimmy, the model airplane pilot

Olivia's picnic

On a visit to Wichita, Kansas some years ago, my husband and I went shopping for antiques. One of our "finds" that day was an old wooden doll cradle …and little did we realize what a *find* it really was!

Back at home, I began to strip the paint from the cradle. But after while I had to stop when the stripping solution became irritating to my skin.

A few days later while talking to my father on the phone, I mentioned my problem. He offered to finish the job if my husband and I would bring him the cradle.

Carved into Memory

Dad was in the kitchen when we arrived at his place. When we put the cradle on the table in front of him, the *strangest* look crept over his face.

Mom walked into the kitchen just then, and when she saw the cradle, she stopped

The Cradle That Came Back Home

By Loretta Wilson, Raytown, Missouri

LUCKY FIND! A coincidence helped the author (holding toy cradle) recover a priceless heirloom 40 years after it was stolen from her parents (above). As a child (far right in picture at right), she and her siblings got handmade gifts from their dad.

in her tracks. She and Dad looked at each other for a moment, then Dad blurted, "I *made* that cradle 40 years ago!"

"I know!" Mom exclaimed.

Dad showed us a scar on his finger. He explained that his knife had slipped while he was carving one of the cradle's rockers, leaving a cut on his finger and a nick in the wood. He also remembered gluing together one of the cradle's spindles that had cracked.

Telltale Nick

We quickly turned the cradle over, and sure enough— there was the nick in the rocker. And the cracked spindle was still in place!

For a moment we all just stared in disbelief. Then Dad broke into a huge grin and told us the rest of the story.

He'd made that cradle for my very first Christmas in 1929. He'd also made a wooden wagon for my older brother and a china cabinet for Mom.

That spring, Dad lost his job as a carpenter. He and Mom decided to move to Kansas City, Missouri, to look for work. They left behind Mom's china cabinet, the wagon and my cradle, stored on my grandmother's porch. Unfortunately, those items were stolen.

Incredible Coincidence

All of this was news to me —I'd never even heard about the cradle. That made it all the more remarkable that I'd decided to buy this antique. For some strange reason, it had really appealed to me!

When Dad finished the stripping job and asked how I wanted the cradle finished, my answer was easy: "Restore it just the way it used to be!" And he did.

A few years after the cradle "came home", Dad passed away.

Today, I'm *so* grateful for that lovely little antique. Somehow, I believe it was meant for me to find his cradle, because for me, it remains a permanent and priceless reminder of his love. ☎

How I Met My Spouse

Love at the Laundry

AS SINGLE AIRMEN stationed at Lincoln Air Force Base, Nebraska in 1965, my friend Phil and I drove to Lincoln to use the self-service laundries in hope of expanding our social life.

One afternoon while waiting for our clothes to dry, I noticed a cute gal very neatly folding her clothes on the next table. I told Phil, "I believe I'll have that gal fold my clothes, too."

With her permission, I joined her and proceeded to make a real mess of folding my whites. She couldn't help but notice and soon offered to show me the correct way to fold clothes.

That was 36 years ago (below), and I'm still making a mess out of folding my clothes, and Bea is still showing me the correct way. —*Larry Luksik Adkins, Texas*

Shared Kindergarten Blanket

IN SPRING 1935, our family moved to the south shore of Long Island, and I went to my first day of kindergarten as a "new kid" who didn't know anyone.

When the usual nap time came, all the children got out the blankets or mats they had brought from home. As the only one without a blanket, I stood there confused and dismayed.

Suddenly, a pretty little girl with long wavy curls came over and said her blanket was big enough to share.

From that day on, we were boyfriend and girlfriend. We dated through high school, were engaged afterward and got married in 1952 after my discharge from the Marine Corps.

Now, after all these years, Jane and I are still boyfriend and girlfriend! —*John Belzak, Patchogue, New York*

Mistake Changed His Life

IT WAS the first Monday in 1948.

An ad in the previous day's newspaper had offered part-time employment at a downtown Omaha, Nebraska office. I was in high school, and right after my last class that Monday, I dashed downtown.

I found the corner building, walked inside and told the receptionist I was there about a job. She called the foreman. While waiting for him, I noticed an attractive young lady working her way through a tall stack of filing.

She paused occasionally to answer the phone and chat with passing co-workers, smiling warmly. The entire office seemed to be brightened by her presence!

I was staring at her when the foreman walked in, so I was momentarily flustered when he stepped up to introduce himself. But that was nothing compared to how flustered I felt when he mentioned his company's name.

I was in the wrong office building! The company that had run the ad was across the street!

I may have been flustered, but I decided then and there that I'd much rather work for *this* company, with *that* girl! Amazingly, there happened to be an opening.

I took the job. Anne, the friendly young lady, and I worked together, then we began courting. We were married within a year.

There hasn't been a day since that

KINDERGARTEN SWEETHEARTS Jane and John Belzak remain sweet on one another to this day (see story above left).

I haven't thanked my lucky stars for guiding me to the wrong office building way back in '48! —*Robert Kreymborg Louisville, Kentucky*

Bananas Were No Slip

I WAS WORKING at a small restaurant in Cuba, Illinois in 1945 when a handsome Marine sergeant came in and ordered a banana split.

The war was still on, and I hadn't seen a fresh banana in months, so I told him, "You get the bananas, and we'll *both* have one."

He marched right out to his car and came back with two ripe bananas! My boss, who was one great lady, let me fix two banana splits and sit down and eat one with him.

It turns out that the owner of the local grocery store was a good friend of the sergeant's and had saved him some of that rare fruit so he could come to the restaurant and meet me. We were married a few months later.

Three children and five grandchildren later, the memories remain as sweet as our first ice cream treat.

—*Audrey Jacobus, Cuba, Illinois*

Romance Off to a Cold Start

MY FUTURE HUSBAND, Bob, was a Navy student stationed at the University of Pennsylvania in Philadelphia in spring of 1944.

One Sunday night, he missed the streetcar back to school and decided to visit the canteen for a sandwich. I was a hostess at the canteen that night, and Bob asked me to dance.

Later, we enjoyed a cold root beer, and while we were talking, a sliver of ice popped out of Bob's mouth and down the front of my dress!

Embarrassed to no end, we both started to laugh. Bob then asked for my phone number, which I gave him, even though this was against the rules.

That night, when I told my mother about it, I couldn't remember Bob's last name. She said, "Watch out—the name you can't remember is the one you take." She was right.

—Barbara Hockett, Vista, California

Toasting a Memorable Toaster

I WAS WAITING for a bus to downtown Evanston, Illinois to pick up a toaster I'd bought for a Mother's Day gift. That's when a friend drove by and asked if I wanted a ride.

He had a buddy with him, and I later learned the buddy thought I looked pretty good and convinced him to offer me the ride.

That ride changed my life, because I eventually married Neville, and my mother never got the toaster—we did. We used that toaster for 45 years, and our four children laughed every time I told them how we got it.

The toaster finally gave out just

before we retired. I went shopping for another, and quite by accident found one just like the old model.

When the clerk asked if I wanted an extended warranty, I told her that I didn't think I needed it, as the other one lasted 45 years.

Two years later, Neville passed away. It may seem silly, but whenever I look at that shiny toaster, I think of him. *—Joan Bicknase, Cary, Illinois*

He Really Fell for Her

AFTER I CAME HOME to the Boston area from overseas in World War II, my sister asked me to attend a gathering of her youth drama group. She'd met her husband there.

While there, I noticed one girl I could not take my eyes off. I knew right away that she was the only girl for me, so I walked across the room to introduce myself.

I was about 10 feet from the girl, when I tripped over my own feet and fell. She and everyone there, except me, laughed. But the girl, Gloria, came over and said, "My parents always told me to take care of any old man who falls down."

Well, at least we met. And we met again about a month later when I volunteered to be in one of the plays.

There was a scene where Gloria was to be kissed. I asked the director to let me do the scene and requested that he not tell Gloria.

When the scene came, I said, "This is for me," and kissed her. She was stunned and wouldn't talk to me for the rest of the night.

In fact, it took several calls and some flowers before Gloria relented and accepted the offer for our first date—a double-header Braves baseball game in

WIRED WEDDING. "After months of hard work in 1936, I finally mastered the backward somersault on the tight wire and applied to the Avalon troupe because they were looking for a wire walker," writes Jerry Tricomi of Murphysboro, Illinois. "I joined the troupe at the Shrine Circus in Sudbury, Pennsylvania. Walking from the train station to the hotel, I encountered this vision—a lovely young lady walking a Russian wolfhound. I later found out she was a member of the troupe, so I made sure I excelled in my tryouts. I was hired, and 6 months later, I married the vision, Eva Lorine (pictured with 'Mickelhoff' at left in 1934)."

Boston. I knew after that date, I could not let her get away. We were married in 1950. *—Tony Galinis
Tewksbury, Massachusetts*

She Was a Knockout

IN JUNE 1951, I was an 18-year-old WAC private who had just finished basic training. I was terrified of anyone with any kind of rank, for fear I'd forget to salute or show proper respect.

I had been assigned to Fort Hamilton, New York, which was a beautiful ivy-covered campus, much like a country club, complete with swimming pool and other amenities.

One day I was in the pool and had just come out of a dive. I had my hands extended and punched the jaw of a good-looking soldier, who yelled, "You knocked out my teeth!"

I immediately envisioned ending up in the stockade, especially when I found out he was a corporal. But the teeth I knocked out were attached to a new partial, which was easily replaced.

Two weeks later, Joe Price and I were dating. We were married Feb. 13, 1952 (below). *—Janice Wasden Price
Seattle, Washington*

We Were Married on Network Radio!

By Shirley Pope Waite
Walla Walla, Washington

MANY YOUNG WOMEN dream of a big wedding, but few can imagine having thousands of guests from all across America. That's just what happened to me, though, when husband Kyle and I were wed in 1949. We exchanged our vows "on the air"!

It all began a year earlier in Twin Falls, Idaho, where I was teaching high school. On winter weekends, we single teachers often rode the bus to Magic Mountain ski area along with our students. A few of us in our early 20s were sometimes mistaken for students ourselves.

One Saturday at the ski lodge, I ordered a hamburger. The cook looked like a rough-cut cowboy, and the hamburger he served up was *awful.*

"Who taught you to make hamburgers?" I asked him. To my surprise, he leaped over the counter, picked me up, carried me outside and threw me in a snowbank! He thought I was a little high school "brat". I gave that rude cook a swift kick in the shin and stomped off.

Days later, I bumped into him on the street. Sheepishly, he asked, "How about buying me a moldy doughnut and a cup of coffee?" He looked contrite, so I reluctantly agreed.

Kyle apologized for mistaking me for a student and then invited me to a chicken and noodle dinner at the lodge. He'd made the noodles himself—and they were delicious!

Love Blossomed

We began seeing each other every day. Before a week had passed, Kyle told me he loved me. Two weeks later, I confessed my love for him.

Then the school year ended, and I had to return home to Michigan. I thought I'd never see Kyle again.

We wrote regularly, and a few months later, he came to Michigan. The first evening he said, "I know a guy who's come 2,000 miles to ask a girl a question."

"Then why doesn't he ask her?" I responded.

He did...and I answered "Yes".

I returned to Idaho to be closer to

BRIDE AND GROOM. Kyle and Shirley Waite were married in '49 (above). She kicked his shin when they met—and he has the scar to prove it (right)!

Kyle while he finished his college degree. In my little apartment, I often listened to the popular radio show *Bride and Groom.* Couples were actually married on the air during this program and afterward showered with gifts.

Bride and Groom producers were looking for unusual love stories to share with their listeners. So—despite the fact that they received over 100 letters a day—I wrote to them about ours.

What a thrill it was to receive a telegram that read: "Your application to be on *Bride and Groom* has been accepted. You have been given the date of Friday, August 26, 1949."

A flurry of activity started. My parents came out from Michigan with my younger brother, who would be Kyle's best man. I asked a friend to be my matron of honor, and the six of us drove to Los Angeles in time for Kyle and me to get our wedding license.

On the program, we shared our love story with master of ceremonies John Nelson. Then we exchanged vows, and Jack McElroy sang our lovely wedding song, *'Tis You.*

Showered with Gifts

Next we were presented with $2,000 worth of gifts, including a vacuum cleaner, radio-phonograph, gas range, luggage, a recording of the show and our wedding rings.

An all-expenses-paid honeymoon was included, too. Since our destination was Virginia City, Montana, one of my gifts

was a four-piece dress for square dancing. I've kept that dress to this day, and I can still wear it...if I hold my breath!

Kyle still has a "memento" of our first year, too—a small scar on his shin from the day I kicked him with my ski boot!

He occasionally makes noodles for me, but never hamburgers! And, on every anniversary, we listen to our recording of that memorable day when we were married on the air. ☎

My First Job Was in a Tree

By Ronald Ford, Redwood Valley, California

IN THE DAYS when service stations actually gave you service (wiping the windows, checking the oil, topping off the radiator), they often gave you interesting architecture to admire as well.

There were stations built to look like Swiss chalets, oil derricks and Chinese pagodas. One even featured a dinosaur. But the most memorable service station I ever saw was built inside a tree!

Billed as "The World's Largest Redwood Tree Service Station", this unique attraction stood on the outskirts of Ukiah, California, a small town about 120 miles north of San Francisco. The station was built in 1936 from the butt cut of a huge redwood tree that was said to have been 1,500 years old! The log used to build the station was 18 feet long and 17-1/2 feet in diameter.

It had been cut into six segments and hollowed out to a thickness of 10 to 24 inches. The wood removed from the inside of the log would have equaled at least 25,000 board feet, enough to build 15 houses! The station's rest rooms were made from hollowed-out sections of smaller redwoods.

My first job was at this station in the 1940s—keeping the soda case filled and passing out postcards to the thousands of tourists who found their way to this roadside attraction each summer.

The soda case was nothing more than a large metal box filled with water, ice and as many bottles of Coca-Cola, Orange Crush and Delaware Punch as I could cram into it. During those sweltering 100° days, I worked pretty hard

> ## "*Local loggers gathered at 'The Stump' to trade yarns...*"

keeping that box full for all the thirsty customers!

Some of the tourists turned out to be even more famous than the station. Heavyweight boxing champ Max Baer and his brother, Buddy, came through several times. Bing Crosby stopped once and so did Clark Gable and Carole Lombard, on their honeymoon trip!

I always enjoyed listening to the comments of the tourists—plenty of them suspected that the service station was not built from one tree, but cleverly crafted from several trees. Obviously, these nonbelievers had yet to visit California's magnificent redwood forests!

The region was a bustling logging and lumbering community back then, and every night a bunch of the local loggers would come to town and gather at "The Stump" to trade yarns. Often, they had a little good-natured fun at my expense.

"Sonny, go get that can of compression behind the seat in my truck," one would order.

Or: "Hey, kid, ask the boss for a skyhook so we can unload that trailer over there."

Those dead-end assignments, along with being sent to fetch left-handed monkey wrenches and pre-sized postholes, became valuable lessons in human nature as I grew up.

Most unique service stations like The Stump are gone now. But my memories of the hot summer days stocking the soda case and the cold winter nights huddled around the coal oil stove inside that big redwood tree listening to the loggers' stories will live on forever. ☎

'How Do They Fit?'

By Dorothy Smith, Hanover, Indiana

WHEN my brother and I were growing up in Chicago in the 1930s, it was only a hop, skip and a jump to the neighborhood shoe store. In fact, the two of us did a lot of hopping, skipping and jumping back then—much to Mother's dismay.

Roller skating, jumping rope and playing baseball in the alley made our shoes wear out fast. Trips to the shoe store might have made Mom and Dad wince, but we kids relished them.

As we swept into the store, the clerk greeted us like old friends. During the depths of the Depression, it must have warmed his heart to see Mother arrive with the two of us hand in hand. He knew we wouldn't leave without shoes for each child—maybe even a pair for Mother.

We sank deeply into the upholstered chairs, and I became the center of attention. The clerk expertly slipped off my right shoe and slid a measuring board under my foot. It felt cool beneath my stocking foot as the clerk moved the metal guide up to my toe.

"Look at how her foot has grown!" he would marvel. "She'll need a size larger than the last time."

I, of course, would beam, for growing was one of my easiest and favorite accomplishments.

A Treat for the Feet

After Mother described the shoes she had in mind, I'd wriggle my toes in anticipation while the clerk disappeared into the back room. Soon he emerged with three or four boxes.

He drew a silver shoehorn from his pocket and skillfully slipped my foot into a gleaming leather oxford or a shiny black "Mary Jane". Then I'd stand and walk a few steps while both the clerk and Mother would watch carefully and ask, "How do they feel?"

After we agreed on the style, we'd move to the rear of the

COUPLE OF SHOE-INS. Dorothy and her brother, Phil, have white shoes on here...but their shoes didn't stay white for long.

store to make use of the miraculous X-ray machine.

"Step right up here and put your feet in," the clerk would say. Peering into the eyepiece, I could look right through my new shoes and see my bones! Wonder of wonders—that X-ray machine showed my feet from the inside out!

Mother and the clerk would look into their viewers and comment on the great fit while I watched my bones do their dance inside a vague outline I knew to be my shoes.

My brother had to look, too, of course, and our giggling soon filled the air. He'd have his turn at the machine as soon as I was finished.

Treasures Behind Glass

But the best was yet to come. The store kept an account of our purchases, and when they reached a certain level, we got to pick out a gift from behind a glass counter.

As I pressed my nose against the glass, I weighed the possibility of new roller skates against a doll. But I loved baseball as much as my brother did. He'd chosen a new mitt last time, so this time I picked a bat—I hit a few good ones with it that summer, too!

We traded at that shoe store for years. They were so friendly, and, let's face it, my brother and I *loved* choosing gifts. The tennis racquet I took to college was picked from that glass case.

And the store provided service you can't find today. One time the clerk took the streetcar to our house on his lunch break and brought several pairs of dressy shoes when Mother decided I needed a new pair of flats for a dance class after school.

Those days are long gone. But to this day, I have fond memories of seeing my bony toes wiggling beneath that X-ray machine...and standing before a glass counter filled with childhood dreams. ☎

That Was Swing!

By Tom Swafford
Asheville, North Carolina

I'LL NEVER FORGIVE rock music for replacing swing. After all, my generation grew up in the Swing Era—the glory days of the Big Bands of Tommy Dorsey, Glenn Miller, Artie Shaw, Benny Goodman, Jimmie Lunceford, Gene Krupa and so many others.

In its day, swing was every bit as big as rock—maybe bigger. Youngsters could reel off the names of every musician in a band, their songs and all the lyrics.

In the 1930s when swing was just beginning to captivate the nation, my family lived in Harlingen, Texas. It was too far off the beaten path for traveling bands, so my brother, Hal, and I saved our allowances to buy the latest RCA, Columbia, Decca and Bluebird records.

On radio, we'd get a lot of dance band "remotes" on KRGV, just up the road in Weslaco. If they weren't carrying one, we'd start dial-hopping and pull in WOAI and KTSA in San Antonio...KPRC in Houston...KWKH in Shreveport...WWL in New Orleans or, on clear nights, WLW in Cincinnati.

As the program began, the announcer would say, "From the College Inn of the Hotel Sherman in Chicago, it's the music of the Sentimental Gentleman, Tommy Dorsey, and his orchestra!"...or perhaps "From Lavaggi's in the Back Bay section of the city of Boston, it's the King of the Clarinet, Artie Shaw, and his orchestra!"

We'd sit there with our heads practically on the radio's speaker, tapping out the tempo with one foot. We'd sing along with Frank Sinatra on *I'll Never Smile Again* or wait impatiently for "Liltin'" Martha Tilton to finish *And the Angels Sing* so we could hear Ziggy Elman's wild trumpet solo.

For me, the highlight of the Swing Era came in 1938 when our family drove to Los Angeles for a vacation. Just outside town, Hal and I saw a billboard advertising Benny Goodman playing at a place called Victor Hugo's.

Hal and I looked at each other and asked our parents if we could go to Victor Hugo's for dinner.

"Have you forgotten?" Dad asked. "We're having dinner tonight with Edna and Lonnie." (Edna and Lonnie Farrow were our folks' oldest friends.)

But when we got to the Farrows' house, Edna, bless her, asked, "Where would the boys like to go for dinner?"

> # "*When she came back, she had Benny Goodman with her!*"

"Victor Hugo's!" we blurted.

I'll never forget the scene as we walked into that supper club. The room was dark, but the bandstand was brightly lit, and the band, in the middle of a broadcast, was on its feet belting out the *King Porter Stomp.*

Lights reflected from the saxophones in the front row as they turned to the left while the trombones above turned right. Then they'd reverse directions like bands in those days would do.

Hal and I just stood there, open-mouthed and bug-eyed, until we were dragged to a table. For the next 2 hours, we reveled in every note as the band worked its way through favorites like *Don't Be That Way, Avalon, Stompin' at the Savoy* and that classic all-time barn burner, *Sing, Sing, Sing.*

It was a glorious, incomparable experience. But the best was yet to come. Edna disappeared for a few minutes, and when she came back to the table, she had Benny Goodman with her! The King of Swing at our table!

He sat and chatted pleasantly with us for 15 or 20 minutes, but neither Hal nor I can recall a single word. In fact, we can't remember what we had to eat.

That was many years ago, and I've stored up many wonderful memories since. But few compare with the memory of entering Victor Hugo's that summer night in 1938 and seeing Benny Goodman's band on its feet, going full-bore, blasting, driving, pounding out the *King Porter Stomp.*

Now, *that* was swing! ☎

DAPPER DUCKS. At 18, Tom Swafford looks very much the "hepcat".

❧ I Knew Them When ❧

Wrestled with Some Real Talent

EACH SUMMER from 1929 to 1935, a lanky blond fellow would arrive at our family's resort hotel in Livingston Manor, New York. He'd stay there from Decoration Day through Labor Day.

He was a young singer and aspiring comic, and from his first appearance on the stage as an inexperienced teenager, he showed the talent that would make him one of the world's great entertainers.

I looked forward to those summers he'd be there—and whenever he performed, he would inevitably stop the show.

I also still carry the scar on my ear I got when Danny Kaye taught me how to wrestle. —*Johnny Weiner*
White Plains, New York

Found Happy Trails

GROWING UP in Duck Run, Ohio, I got to know Leonard Sly, who was a buddy of my brother, Lawrence. Leonard shared many a bowl of breakfast oatmeal at our home, and Father sold Leonard his first horse, "Ol' Babe".

Leonard later bought another horse named "Trigger"...and became Roy Rogers, King of the Cowboys.
—*Helen Wiseman Thatcher*
Byron, Georgia

Had a Feeling She'd Be a Star

WHILE attending UCLA in the early 1950s, I was Hi-Jinx chairman for the Associated Women's Student Body and needed performers for our program.

I was watching a theatre arts department program one night and was captivated by a young woman who did a comic version of the song *That Old Feeling.*

I later looked her up and asked if she would perform in the Hi-Jinx. She was delighted but didn't know what she could do. I suggested she just repeat her song act, and she agreed.

She was natural, enthusiastic, eager to please and fun to be around. She kept the audience in stitches with her act.

In my own way, I feel I discovered Carol Burnett. —*Ann Trapnell*
Los Angeles, California

Lesson from Future First Lady

WHEN I was attending Whittier (California) High School, I had a very good teacher my junior and senior years. She was also in charge of the school's Pep Committee and visited assemblies at several other schools for ideas.

I was absolutely thrilled one day when she asked me to come along. Afterward, we went to lunch and were discussing the assembly, when out of the blue she said, "Betty, you don't feel very good about yourself, do you?"

I was stunned but admitted she was right. We had a long talk, and by the time we finished lunch, I had an entirely different feeling about myself. I never again put myself down.

I'll never forget that wonderful teacher, Pat Ryan, who later married Richard Nixon. —*Betty Johnson*
Valley Center, California

Ambition Drove Him

IN 1938, I was driving truck for the Union Oil Co. at the main plant in San Diego, California. I was also the relief driver for several of the other drivers on their days off.

I remember one of the young drivers I relieved. But he decided that driving truck was not for him. He quit to go back to school and later moved to New York City.

The young truck driver found another job. In 1944, Gregory Peck debuted in *Days of Glory.*
—*Elvyn Reeves, Hesperia, California*

All About Eve

I GREW UP in a suburb of San Francisco called Mill Valley in the 1920s. There was a girl in my high school named Eunice Quedens, and I remember loaning her a green beret of mine when she was cast in a play being staged in the city.

One day Eunice was advised to choose a stage name. On her dressing table was a bottle of Evening in Paris perfume and a jar of Elizabeth Arden facial cream. She put them together, and that's how Eunice Quedens became Eve Arden!

"Eve" was successful on Broadway and later in the TV show *Our Miss Brooks.* We were all so proud of her. I recall that the first big gift she gave to her mother was a real fur stole.
—*Donna Shepherd*
Redding, California

Before He Moved To "Mayberry"

BACK IN 1952, I was just out of school and working for Allison-Erwin, a wholesale distributor in Charlotte, North Carolina.

I especially enjoyed my first company Christmas party. The entertainment was provided by a young man from Mt. Airy who did funny monologues, one he called "What It Was, Was Football".

The highlight of the night for me was when he started up a dance called the "bunny hop". Being one of the youngest in attendance and the newest employee, I got to be first in line, behind this wonderful entertainer. What a thrill!

He wasn't that well-known then, but today, Andy Griffith is a star we all love. —*Betty Reeves*
Charleston, South Carolina

By Rita Haban
Reynoldsburg, Ohio

EVERY FALL our family piled into Father's green Model A Ford and headed for the Hocking Hills to go nutting, one of the many ways we supplemented our food supply during the Depression.

We watched the weather carefully, knowing a stiff frost would open the clustered burrs around chestnuts, while warm dry weather was needed to break the heavy upholstery on the outside of hickory nuts.

But black walnuts were something else! Some 2 inches in diameter, those gems were encased in a tough green hull almost impossible to breach.

We'd bring home a basket of black walnuts and store them in the garage until someone was hungry enough to tackle the horrendous hulling job—a process that left your hands stained black.

Dad Got Hungry

I recall one fall Saturday in 1936 when my father asked why he hadn't seen a black walnut cake—after all, we'd collected a load of those delicious nuts, and they were just sitting in the garage, waiting to be used.

"I refuse to stain my hands cracking them this year," Mother informed him.

"Get the kids to do it," he said.

"The girls are getting older. They don't want their hands stained either," Mother said firmly.

"Then give Billy a hammer and tell him to get busy," Father said.

"He's too little," Mom countered.

Defeated, Father stalked off, mumbling something about "kids". Then he went outside and began to tinker.

A couple hours later, he burst into the house shouting, "Come out in the backyard—I've got something to show you!"

Our backyard in Columbus, Ohio was an average city lot, with carefully trimmed hedges on either side and a

Hulling Walnuts 'Tired' Us Out

Michael P. Gadomski

GOING NUTTING. Gathering wild nuts was a family activity in the good old days.

Julie Habel

two-car garage and a garden in back. On the other side of one hedge were the Millers. We kids didn't dare venture into their yard, and Mrs. Miller kept any baseballs that accidentally landed there.

"If it gets into Mrs. Miller's yard, it's gone," Mother always told us, refusing to intercede.

Following Father into the backyard that Saturday, we caught our breath—there, in the middle of Mother's garden, was the Model A. Its rear end was jacked up, and a wooden trough was positioned an inch or so under one back wheel.

"My garden!" Mother screeched.

Father brushed it aside and instructed Mother to get behind the wheel and race the engine.

"I'll feed the walnuts into the trough," he explained. "When the nuts hit the wheel, the skins'll come right off! You kids stand back and watch.

"Go ahead—rev it up!" Father called from behind the car.

Run for Cover!

Father whistled as he spilled walnuts into the trough. Within seconds, green hulls were flying everywhere—and black nuts shot out from under the wheel and ricocheted off the Millers' garage next door like bullets from a Gatling gun!

"Turn it off! Turn it off!" Father shouted.

But Mother couldn't hear and the engine continued to race.

As more walnuts fell into the trough, the whirling tire continued to fire them into the garage—*Pow! Pow! Pow!* When the last walnut was fired, we kids crawled out from hiding, Father knocked on the car window and Mother let up on the accelerator.

Climbing out of the car, Mother surveyed the mess in our yard. In the Millers' yard, a pile of hulled walnuts lay next to the garage…and Tillie Miller came bustling down the back walk with a basket on her arm.

Mother scowled and shook her head. "Like I always said: If it gets into Mrs. Miller's yard, it's gone." ☎

Dad in 1963

Fare Is Fair

By Carolyn Skotnicki, Greensburg, Pennsylvania

TO AVOID ANY MISTAKES, my dad, a trolley car conductor in McKeesport, Pennsylvania in the 1950s, held his hand out flat when he counted change for his passengers.

Each person had his change counted, and he never missed one. The shiny silver "changer" sat snugly to his right and held coins in tube-shaped columns—pennies, nickels, dimes and quarters.

In those days, it cost anywhere from a dime to a quarter to ride on the streetcar—unless your father was the conductor.

Any time there was nothing to do, I'd walk down to "the loop" where the streetcars turned around. Dad would open the door and suddenly smile because there I was...surprise!

And what fun it was riding from McKeesport to Glassport. The best part of the trip was the long stretch of road with no stops that Dad called "the straightaway". We really flew in that big, old red streetcar. It shook and swayed so much you'd think you were on one of the rides at Kennywood Park!

I still remember one drizzly autumn afternoon when the last passenger was making her way down the aisle before going through the door and stepping off into the darkness. It was a little bent-over old lady toting a brown Balsamo's shopping bag. When she reached the front of the car, she demanded another quarter from my dad, claiming he'd shortchanged her.

He told her politely that he knew he'd given her the correct change, but she insisted.

"Okay," Dad said, a bit disgusted. "But look. I'll have to give you the quarter from my own pocket. Otherwise, I'll be shortchanged when I count my money at the end of the night."

Reaching into the side pocket of his blue uniform, Dad handed her a quarter. Then she stepped off and disappeared into the mist.

While the streetcar continued on to Glassport, I sat there quietly. At the loop in Glassport, Dad got to take a break. He opened his black metal lunch box, pulled out a sandwich and offered me half.

Good Ride? Nun Better!

As we shared lunch, he told me the story of the nun he'd given a ride to only a few days before.

It had been a beautiful sunny day, and Dad was a few minutes behind schedule. Of course, the place to make up lost time was "the straightaway". Dad thought everyone had gotten off, so he powered up the streetcar and away he went.

In the midst of all the swaying and shaking, he looked in his mirror and, to his horror, saw the black-clad figure of a nun hanging on for dear life as she tried to make her way to the front of the streetcar.

Oh, brother! Would she report him?

Dad was getting ready to apologize when he looked up to see an angelic smile on her face. "What a ride!" she said as she departed. "That was the best I ever had. Thanks!"

Lunchtime was now over, so Dad started back on his route again. He even let me push the brown button on the control panel that made the bell ring.

On our way back to McKeesport, the rain fell harder and the streetcar windows fogged up. Then, through sweeping windshield wipers, I barely made out a shadowy shape—a figure huddled under an umbrella.

When the streetcar came to a stop, a familiar little old lady approached the open door. Holding out her hand, she gave my dad a coin, explaining, "When I got home, I found the quarter on the bottom of my shopping bag."

As she turned away and headed back home in the rain, Dad turned to me and smiled. I guess that night we shared more than a sandwich and a humorous story—we shared a lesson in honesty. ☎

CONDUCTED A PARTY. "The Pittsburgh Railroad hosted fun employee Christmas parties," remembers Carolyn, seated on Santa's lap. "This photo, taken over 50 years ago, shows my father, Steven Yaga (in his conductor's uniform), my mother, Eleanor (wearing the tam), and my sisters, Rosemarie (on left) and Annette."

A Great Time on A Great Lake

By Dean Thornton, Salt Lake City, Utah

I WAS about 5 years old the first time my parents took me to Utah's Great Salt Lake in the early 1930s.

On the east side of the lake was a long white sandy beach where, during Depression-era weekends, cars full of families and friends parked in long rows facing the lake. There was even a train with three or four open cars that made regular round-trips from Salt Lake City, where most of us lived.

I remember my mother sitting on a blanket with the picnic basket, while my father took me out into the lake. He'd put me on my back and assure me that I wouldn't sink as he slowly lowered his hands. Sure enough, I'd float just like a cork!

I also learned *not* to splash water into my eyes because the salt would sting and make them tear up. The only way to get your sight back was to put your finger in your mouth, suck all the salt off, then rub the salty water out of your eyes—along with your tears.

Reading Was Suspenseful—Literally!

The best thing to do was lie on your back and float —some people even read books. It was so easy and fun that if you didn't watch it, you might stay in the water so long that when you got out, you'd be brightly sunburned on the front and salty white on your back.

Along the beach where the Salt Palace once stood (part of a huge resort complex called "Saltair" that burned down in 1925), there were two small resorts called Black Rock and Sunset Beach. They sold sandwiches, cold drinks and an assortment of snacks and candy.

There were also overhead water pipes with cold running water so swimmers could wash off the thick white layer of salt that accumulated on their bodies as it dried.

My mother passed away in 1941, when I was 12. By then, I had a good neighbor friend named Chris Argentos. His family *always* went someplace on Sundays and took me along.

Whenever we went to Great Salt Lake, we'd leave in the morning to get a good place to park in the front line of cars facing the beach. On weekends, the beach got so crowded that sometimes there were cars from one resort to the other, three or four rows deep.

By 1944, when I was in high school, people didn't frequent the lake as much. During the middle of the week, it was almost vacant. That's when my girlfriend, Marie (now my wife), and I would bicycle the 16 miles to the lake with a little picnic basket and spend the whole day.

Sunsets Haven't Changed

We didn't venture into the water much then, because on weekdays, the showers were usually off. If we did go into the lake, the salt dried on us, and our clothes rubbed it like sandpaper on the ride home!

Maybe someday, someone will build another resort or attraction to bring people back, but for now, when we drive by the old Salt Lake beach, it's no longer lined with cars and happy people. There's only a small marina with colorful sailboats tied to a pier and a few boats out on the water.

The sunsets haven't changed, though. They're still just as spectacular as when Great Salt Lake was the biggest recreation area in all of Utah. ☎

SUN, SAND, SALT. Droves of beach lovers visited Great Salt Lake during the 1920s, '30s and '40s. Author's aunt, Deana Thornton (top center), and a friend or two were there, as was the author (above) in 1944 with future wife Marie Trimming enjoying Black Rock Beach.

The Automat Was a Diner's Wonderland

By L C Van Savage, Brunswick, Maine

AS A CHILD in the '40s, I was lucky enough to eat at Horn and Hardart Automats in New York City. Those glass-brick, yellow-granite and gleaming-steel restaurants offered good, hearty fare at low prices.

My grandmother would take me there after we'd gone to a double feature. A large woman with a personality all her own, Grandmother usually sailed into the restaurant wearing gobs of vivid makeup, immense gaudy hats and long ropes of rhinestones or pearls. Though she could afford to eat anywhere, she chose Horn and Hardart's.

Clutching Grandmother's hand, I felt fear and fascination as we entered the large, noisy restaurant. The first thing you did there was to exchange dollars for nickels from a harried woman at a high desk in the room's center. I'd hand her a bill and she'd return 20 nickels, enough to buy dinner.

The next order of business was for Grandmother to stand in the center of the restaurant and glare at any diners who appeared to be nearly finished. They'd glance nervously at her, and when they finally put down their forks and prepared to leave, she'd descend on their table.

Beaming triumphantly, Grandmother would slap her huge purse on the table. Then, with the attitude of a great empress, she'd turn and grant me permission to select my foods. This was always my favorite part.

There was a long steam table where servers with enormous spoons loaded meat loaf, corn, mashed potatoes and gravy and Harvard beets onto thick white plates. I never wanted that stuff —my favorite foods were behind the Automat "windows".

Not unlike postal boxes, they formed a huge wall of small, heavy glass squares framed in stainless steel. Behind those windows reposed a wonderland of food choices.

There were sandwiches on soft white bread, centers bulging with ham, corned beef, egg salad or chicken. Other windows displayed fat glistening hot dogs, bowls of soup and red-umber baked beans dripping from dark-green porcelain bowls.

Back and forth I'd walk, the nickels growing damp in my fist. Finally, Grandmother would give me a stern "hurry up" nod, her big hat wobbling.

I had to decide…the egg salad sandwich? No. Tuna? No. Soup…maybe the beans…

When I'd made my choice, I put the required number of nickels into the slot. With a snap, the window popped open. I'd reach in, grab the white plate and slide the treasure onto my tray.

Just like magic, that window slammed shut and, as the empty space where my food had been whirled away, an exact duplicate appeared.

Balancing my tray, I weaved my way back to Grandmother and carefully slid it onto the heavy, Bakelite table. It was yellow with wide, pale-green borders,

"My favorite foods were behind the windows…"

and I loved its smooth, worn feel.

Grandmother ordered milk from a waitress, who poured it from a sweating metal pitcher. I always savored the contrasting sensation of cold milk from a glass still hot from the dishwasher.

However, there is one Horn and Hardart memory that still causes me to wince. Grandmother was a world traveler who'd been to the Far East, where she'd learned a greeting she maintained was recognized by all Oriental people.

Back in New York City, of course, the Automat was filled with people of all nationalities. Whenever Grandmother spotted an innocent, unsuspecting Asian, she'd try out her greeting.

"Hong Yong Dissie Mew-ee!" she'd caterwaul across the enormous cafeteria. Everyone would turn and stare.

It was dreadful, but in spite of those embarrassing moments, my memories of the Automats are happy ones. And, while I wish they still existed, I know the food couldn't possibly be as good as it was back then. Never again will 20 nickels buy so much pleasure! ☎

Lace Curtains Stretched Our Patience

By Vincenza Clayton, Trenton, New Jersey

During the Depression, lace curtains in the windows—the sign of a stable comfortable home—were a luxury my mother could only dream about.

For 8 long years, our family lived like gypsies, moving from town to town and house to house as Father looked for work. Every time he lost his job and couldn't pay the rent, we had to move.

For 2 years, we lived in a house so far out in the country that we didn't really need curtains. We five kids loved living there, but Mother was unhappy.

Father was a laborer with the WPA, but Mother could see no future in this. She scrimped and saved all she could from Father's wages, plus what we earned picking and selling berries, and convinced Father to move back near a city and open a business.

Finally, we did just that, moving to the suburbs and renting a large house with a storefront. Mother and Father's $50 in savings was enough to open a grocery store.

Behind the store was our large living room with its 10-foot-high ceiling and two long windows on one side. As the business got off the ground, Mother continued to set aside a little money. Eventually, she had enough to order lace curtains from Sears.

Starched and Stretched

Oh, how lovely they looked in our windows! But the first time we washed our curtains and put them back up, they were limp and shapeless and hung in lopsided folds.

Our neighbors, who also had lace curtains, laughed and explained, "You have to starch them before you put them up. They're made of cotton."

We boiled starch, added a little blue wax bar of Satina to keep the iron from sticking and hung the curtains on the line to dry. But even after we ironed our curtains, we still couldn't get them to hang straight, no matter how we tried.

Our neighbors *then* informed us that the secret to hanging clean lace curtains was something called a "curtain stretcher". We ordered one from Sears and assembled it according to the directions.

After this wooden frame was set up, we carefully stretched the curtains out over it. The edges of the frame contained rows of little headless nails, evenly spaced about a half inch apart, onto which the edges of the curtains were hooked.

The Fun Faded

We kids, teenagers then, thought it was fun to stretch the curtains. There were only four panels to stretch, so we'd wait for one to dry before removing it and putting on another. Soon the novelty wore off, and curtain stretching became a tedious, time-consuming task. In the summer, when the curtains were put outside to dry, the wind invariably knocked

over the frame, dropping our clean curtains to the ground.

During the winter months, we'd dry the curtains indoors and try to hook more than one panel on the stretcher. This sometimes resulted in two panels sticking together because of the starch. It was quite a challenge to pry them apart without ripping them.

Those lace curtains proved to be a lot of work. But to Mother, they would always represent a return to a more gracious way of living.

Luckily, our store turned into a profitable venture, so we didn't need to move again. And in the living room, our lace curtains continued to hang proudly. ☎

Logging Camp Life Was a Cut Above

By Ernest Leaf, Seattle, Washington

THIS LOGGING CAMP was my home in the 1920s, when I was 5 to 9 years old. Through a child's eyes, it was the most wonderful place in the world!

Known as Camp 7, it was located near the Wynoochee River in the foothills of the Olympic Mountains, and owned and operated by the Simpson Logging Company of Shelton, Washington. My dad worked for the company for 25 years.

Our home is in the foreground and can be identified by the litter on the woodshed roof. About 10 houses of our neigh-

bors are seen along the railroad tracks. It must have been laundry day, since there are sparkling white diapers hanging outside four of the houses.

In the background, on a spur, are the bunkhouses where the single men lived. A cookhouse was part of the complex, and it's where the workers ate Paul Bunyan-sized meals.

The loggers were heavy eaters. They'd rush in at 50 miles an hour and eat fast and furious. They were big meat eaters, so there were always hams and stews, bacon and eggs plus pastries, cakes and cookies. They also ate a lot of hardtack. They'd leave the cookhouse with their hands full of

sandwiches that they'd take back to the bunkhouse and eat at night.

The cook served breakfast and an evening meal. They packed lunches for the men to take out to the work area.

I recall hanging around the cookhouse, hoping to get a cookie or some other treat. The cook or "bull cook" (jack-of-all-trades helper) often made friends with the children by such offerings.

Families like ours never ate at the cookhouse. Our mothers made meals in our houses. My mother was a wonderful cook, and the house always smelled good.

My parents ordered foodstuffs once a week. The logging company filled the orders at the company store and had them brought up by train. They'd set the boxes of groceries outside the houses. I remember Mom and Dad bought 5-gallon containers of lard and 50- or 100-pound bags of flour that seemed as big as I was.

These logging camps stayed in an area for only a few years while nearby forests were logged. After the area had been clear-cut, the camp was moved to another location, closer to the next logging area.

Each of the rectangular houses was built on skids. At moving time, they could be placed on railroad flatbed cars and hauled to the next camp site.

The lean-to attachments, such as extra rooms, porches and woodsheds, were rebuilt at the next location. Hand-split cedar shakes and lumber were readily available, so it didn't take too long to expand the standard-size house.

When I lived in Camp 7, a bus took us to a small school about 15 miles down the Wynoochee Valley toward the town of Montesano.

After we moved to the next camp, there was no road access, so the school became part of the camp, with grades one through eight handled by a single teacher.

The teacher managed by asking the older students to do some of the teaching of the lower grades.

The best part of this camp was that I met my future wife there when we were teens, and we've been married 57 years.

To some, a logging camp may appear to be a dismal place, but I remember them as home. Being close to nature made for a marvelous way to start life. ☎

LOGGING DAYS. Ernest Leaf, at left with his parents and dog outside their home at Camp 7, grew up in that logging camp (far left) and others in Washington during the 1920s. His father, Andrew (seated below on a skid with legs dangling), and other logging crew members used the donkey engine they're gathered around to haul huge logs to the railroad landing.

How I Impressed Girls

By Lester Brookshire
Rome, Georgia

I HAVE ALWAYS been able to impress girls, which you will plainly see as you read my memories.

One morning in 1957, when I was 12, a pretty girl named Sue Ellen got on my bus in Calhoun, Georgia. All day long, I thought about her.

In the afternoon, I was to get off the bus just before she did and wondered how I could impress her.

I decided to leave the bus in a "manly" way, leaping to the ground instead of using the steps. I don't know why I thought this would be so spectacular, but I made sure she was watching before I made my big jump.

Unfortunately I had grown, if just a little, and miscalculated my trajectory. My head hit the top of the bus and I fell back down the aisle and rolled down the steps, landing in the gravel on the roadside.

The bus driver, jaded by long experience, looked at me without a smile, shut the door and drove off.

I did get Sue Ellen's attention, however. I could see her delicate white hands stretched out a window pointing at me, and I could hear her lovely voice peal with laughter.

Not Using His Head

By age 15, I'd learned to leap from a wooden board 8 or 10 feet in the air and perform a sort of jackknife without killing myself. I considered myself a high-diving expert and used this skill to my advantage one summer to impress Kay Anne. I saw that she and a few other girls from school were swimming in New Town Creek.

An old humpback bridge spanned the rippling water, and I climbed to the road and prepared to jump. I decided this wasn't high enough for the effect I wanted, so I climbed to the top of the bridge and waved at the girls.

This didn't seem so high, but as I fell, my body took much longer to reach the water than it did off the wooden diving board. So I changed from a jackknife to a shallow dive. Still, the force of the fall pushed me all the way to the bottom.

If you know anything about creeks with fast-running water, you know the bottom changes all the time. The last time I had swum there, the bottom was sandy and about 4 feet deep.

Since then, a rainstorm had washed the sand away, leaving a sharp outcropping of layered shale.

I executed a perfect shallow dive, and as I curved upward, the rock caught me below the neck and slit my skin to the navel—not deep, but enough for the blood to run over me.

At first, I resisted any show of pain as the water stung me, but when I noticed how the little group of girls shrieked and squealed over me, I started moaning.

They placed me on the bank, and lovely Kay Anne leaned over me as she dabbed at the blood. I got a good 20 minutes of attention out of that.

At 19, I met a gorgeous little lady on the Berry College campus in Mt. Berry, Georgia. When Wanda and I spoke, sparks flew, but we were not ready for anything serious, so we backed off.

By the time I was 20, I was an old hand at impressing girls. This came in handy when I attended a Christian fellowship conference in 1966.

A thoughtful young lady offered me a ride in her car. She had arranged for another student to drive, so she sat in the middle, and I was to sit by the window. As I started to get in, I saw Wanda in the backseat. I knew this was my chance, so I got in the back with her and we talked, laughed and giggled over nothing all the way to the conference.

Who's Chasing Who?

I chased her all weekend—she always ran, but not too fast. I almost kissed her coming back from a hike and was looking forward to the ride back. Imagine my surprise when Wanda was not in the car. Our driver told me she had specifically requested the Berry bus. I slid in the front seat, with the other young lady in the middle.

On the way back, we passed the bus.

Illustrations: Burt Gross

HAPPY ENDING.
Although Wanda missed Lester's big trick, she married him anyway in 1966 (right). They renewed their vows in the same wedding chapel in '91 (above).

118

hand just as the driver would make a U-turn in front of some little country store with people out front.

I'd lean out, almost touching my head to the pavement as if I were about to fall out of the car, and scream loudly. The people would jump up in a panic, then I would sit up, slam the door and we'd speed off laughing.

Now as we pulled in front of the bus, I did what I had always done, except I had to put my left hand behind the girl in the middle. I shoved the door open, leaned out and screamed.

Trick Caused Bedlam

Several things went wrong. First, the bus driver swerved to miss what he thought was soon to be a body and almost turned the bus over. Also, I had always performed this trick at a low speed, but this time we were going about 60 mph, so the wind slammed the door on my temple. (Oh, and before, everybody knew I was going to do this

That's when I got my big idea on how to impress Wanda. It was a tactic I had originated back in high school. I would sit next to the passenger window, place my left hand in the center slit of the bench seat and open the door with my right

trick. This time, no one did, resulting in bedlam.) The girl in the middle clawed red stripes in my chest, tearing my shirt as she tried to pull me back in and save my life.

When I finally sat up and slammed the door, I had a splitting headache and the girl passed out in my arms. The driver had wild eyes.

When the girl came around, both she and the driver wanted explanations. I've always been an honest person, if not a wise one, so I told the whole story. The girl was furious and the driver didn't speak to me for the rest of the trip.

Later, I found out Wanda had missed the whole thing! Other people told her about it. I had a 3-day headache for nothing.

It didn't end so badly. Wanda and I started dating, and 7 months later we were married. That was years ago, and people still ask how I first impressed my wife. ☎

In the Mood for a Musical Quiz on Love Songs?

AS THE SONG SAYS, "Love, like youth, is wasted on the young." Who doesn't have a story or two about how they tried to impress a girl. Sometimes it worked, sometimes it didn't. And sometimes, as with Lester Brookshire's hilarious story, the door hit you in the head. Songs have a way of telling the story of love lost, love gained and all the other wonderful foolishness that goes along with that age-old game. Here are some lines from love songs. See if you can match the lyrics on the left with the titles on the right. If you get stumped, the answers are printed upside down below.

1. "Someday, when you grow lonely, your heart will break like mine and you'll want me only…"
2. "She didn't even say she was leavin'…"
3. "I can be happy, I can be sad, I can be good or I can be bad…"
4. "I'd rather be lonely than happy with somebody else…"
5. "The sky was blue, and high above, the moon was new, and so was love…"
6. "I took one look at you, that's all I meant to do; and then…"
7. "She's got eyes of blue, I never cared for eyes of blue, but she's got eyes of blue…"
8. "Why don't we get along? Everything I do is wrong…"
9. "They asked me how I knew my true love was true?"
10. "Each night I ask the stars up above, why must I be…"
11. "Say that everything is still okay, that's all I want to know…"
12. "Today I passed you on the street, and my heart fell at your feet…"
13. "I tried so not to give in, I said to myself, 'This affair never will go so well'…"
14. "I hear singing and there's no one there…"
15. "…because I feel so well, no sobs, no sorrows, no sighs…"

a. *This Can't Be Love*
b. *That's My Weakness Now*
c. *I Can't Help It (If I'm Still In Love With You)*
d. *It All Depends On You*
e. *What's The Reason (I'm Not Pleasin' You)*
f. *After You've Gone*
g. *I've Got You Under My Skin*
h. *Somebody Stole My Gal*
i. *Love Me Or Leave Me*
j. *You're Just In Love (I Wonder Why?)*
k. *A Teenager In Love*
l. *My Heart Stood Still*
m. *Smoke Gets In Your Eyes*
n. *Say It Isn't So*
o. *Lover, Come Back To Me*

Answers: 1-f, 2-h, 3-d, 4-i, 5-o, 6-l, 7-b, 8-e, 9-m, 10-k, 11-n, 12-c, 13-g, 14-j, 15-a.

Here Comes the Jewel Tea Man!

For decades, housewives relied on the Jewel Tea man to deliver quality products.

MY HUSBAND and his mother thought there was nothing like Jewel Tea pine oil to get rid of flu germs, odors, dirt—whatever. My husband would go through the house twirling a rag with pine oil on it.

One Christmas, Jewel Tea came out with a silver tinsel tree and a revolving, colored light wheel to shine on it. For years to come, we didn't have to buy a tree or decorate it.

—Frances Yates
Bridgewater, Virginia

WE ENJOYED buying from the Jewel Tea man in Denver in the 1960s. As a young mother with two small children, I found it very helpful to have home delivery.

Jewel had many products other than food. I remember buying a new gown and robe when I got home from the hospital with our second son. It made me feel so good to have something new and comfy that I didn't have to shop for with the new baby.

—Rosalie Rippie
Albuquerque, New Mexico

MY GRANDMA, Georianna Truttier, frequently ordered from Jewel Tea. Her regular Jewel Tea man was training a good-looking young man I had a crush on. One delivery day, I was talking to him (really flirting more than talking), when he suddenly turned red.

I thought I had made quite an impression on him, until I noticed I was ironing my unmentionables.

—Mary Anne Musgrave
Newport, North Carolina

MY FUTURE HUSBAND, Charlie, always smelled so good when we first met and started dating in the late '50s. I later found out he bathed with Jewel Tea's Gold Bar Soap.

Soon after we married, Jewel Tea stopped serving our area, and I was

HE DELIVERED. "My husband, Orville (top), was a Jewel Tea man who worked out of the St. Louis branch in the '30s," relates JoAnn Kinion of Raytown, Missouri. "The other photo shows the Jewel Tea products I ordered in 1936 (front: mayonnaise, peanut butter, vanilla, mustard, baking powder; back: coffee, soap, spaghetti) and the Autumn Leaf teapot I received as a premium."

unable to get the soap. I'd love to find it again to see if it still smells the same.
—Dawn Shaw, Leesburg, Virginia

MY DAD, Harry Ericksen, started working for Jewel Tea in 1915. Jewel Tea coffee was the main product. It took a good salesman to convince the customers that the coffee was worth the higher price.

Dad would tell his customers, "You only need to use half as much of Jewel Tea coffee as you do the other brands, so it's not expensive, and the taste is so much better."

As a baby, I had blond hair with thick curly ringlets. When my mother would take me out, and people would stop her to inquire about my beautiful hair, she was quick to tell them that she washed it with Jewel Tea shampoo.

Dad sold a lot of shampoo as a result. *—Kay Ericksen*
Naples, Florida

I REMEMBER the Jewel Tea man coming to our house in 1938. Those were hard times for my parents, and sometimes my mother just couldn't afford to buy anything. But she hated to tell the Jewel Tea man that.

So on those days, when the Jewel Tea man knocked on the door, Mother would say, "Girls, come quick and get into the closet under the stairs," and we'd hide until he left.
—Myrna Myers, Eaton, Ohio

BRING BACK the old Jewel Tea popcorn! It was large, plump, tender, hull-less and so tasty. Our family enjoyed it for many years. I purchased other Jewel products, but nothing compares to Jewel popcorn. *—Rosemary Stradal*
Albuquerque, New Mexico

ONE EVENING in the '50s, I was driving with my nephews and nieces in our little community of Hutto, Texas when nephew Bub said, "Oh, Aunt Lois, look! There's money on the ground!"

I stopped, and we found money scattered all over the road. We also found an open billfold that belonged to the Jewel Tea man.

The man had already left town. So I left word with my brother-in-law at his gas station. When the Jewel Tea man came back looking for his billfold, I returned it to him, along with his $125.

He wanted to reward me, but I said I didn't want anything. Later, I found a box on my porch containing a four-place breakfast set and a note that said, "God bless you." *—Lois Gainer*
Hutto, Texas

MY FATHER worked for Jewel Tea for 37 years. His most embarrassing moment occurred one day when he came into a kitchen and set his basket of products on a chair while the lady of the house decided on her order for his next delivery.

All the time he was there, the children of the house were looking for their parakeet but couldn't find it. When the order was complete, my father picked up his basket to leave—and under it was the parakeet.

—*Carolyn Staples Walters*
Davenport, Iowa

ONE OF MY fondest memories was the trip our family took to the Jewel Tea headquarters and test kitchen in Barrington, Illinois in the early '30s.

My father, Laurence Murray, was a Jewel Tea man for many years. He started working for the company in 1927 and had routes in southwest Michigan.

In the test kitchen, the "Mary Dunbar" cook sat my little brother on the table and gave him a cookie.

Mary Dunbar was the name on many of the Jewel Tea Company's kitchen products.

—*Ramona Wright*
Vicksburg, Michigan

LIVING IN Redwood City, California in the '60s, I anxiously awaited the delivery of blueberry bars, which were similar to Fig Newtons, by the Jewel Tea man.

—*Linda Byrd*
Litchfield Park, Arizona

JEWEL TEA *WOMAN*. "It wasn't always a man! Alta DonLevy had a Jewel Tea route for a dozen years in the Green Bay, Wisconsin area," writes Mary Olsen of Spooner. "She enjoyed visiting the farm wives, who were isolated in those days. The wives anticipated with pleasure a visit from a female salesperson. Alta drove many miles during her time with Jewel Tea and did very well. She now lives in Moline, Illinois."

Courtesy Jewel-Osco

How It All Began

WHEN Frank Skiff and his brother-in-law, Frank Ross, started selling coffee and tea from their wagon in 1899, their sales for that year were $11,000.

When they earned enough money, they bought another horse and wagon and added another route. By 1909, they had 100 routes; by 1912, 400. And by 1915, their Jewel Tea Company operated 850 routes, with sales over $8 million!

The men kept their customers by offering fresh coffee and premiums, available with the purchase of so much coffee or tea. Jewel Tea china, especially in the Autumn Leaf pattern, was a premium selected by most, and millions of pieces were chosen by housewives over the years.

By 1919, however, the company was in debt because of increasing costs and manpower shortages caused by World War I. The two founders were forced out by their creditors.

Throughout the 1920s, expenses were controlled, and purchasing and distribution methods were improved. By 1930, the company had a surplus of

about $1.5 million.

When the Loblaw Groceterias in Chicago came up for sale in 1932, Jewel bought the company and its 77 stores. It took years for the stores to become profitable. The routes still made the most money.

But by 1939, Jewel had 119 stores. Ten years later, there were 154 stores and 1,876 routes in 43 states! In the succeeding decades, there were more acquisitions and mergers.

People still remember Jewel stores today, and their slogan—"Fresh to your family from Jewel for 100 years"—traces its roots back to Frank Skiff and Frank Ross, who ground and roasted the coffee that started it all.

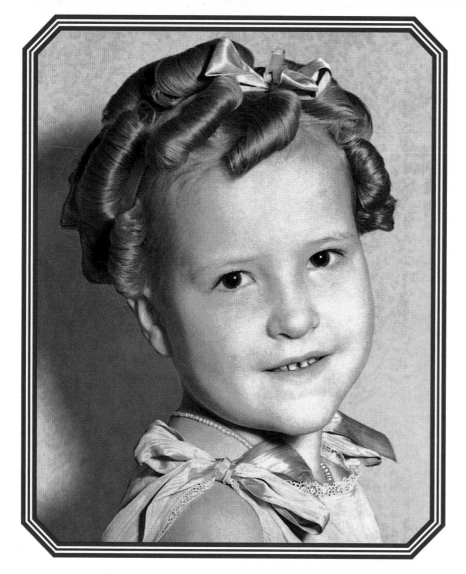

Shirley Temple Made 'Permanent' Memories

By Marilyn Jensen, La Habra, California

The day that Junior O'Malley dipped my braids into the inkwell at school was the day my mother vowed no daughter of hers would ever wear braids again.

From then on, her instructions to the barber were concise. "To the tips of the ears and shingle the back!" she'd say each time I was marched to his chair in my hometown of Ferndale, Michigan.

It took a national craze to change Mother's mind about keeping me in short hair. I was in the second grade during the '30s when Shirley Temple dimpled her way across America's silver screens.

Her golden curls (52 of them, according to fan magazines) tumbled rakishly from her little head and captured the heart of an entire country.

Mothers everywhere—mine included—took up the challenge of transforming their own offspring into reasonable facsimiles of Shirley.

Mom maintained it had nothing to do with Hollywood, but not long after that child star twinkle-toed her way through her second picture, my hair was long enough to curl for special occasions.

Before every birthday party or piano recital, I'd be herded into the kitchen, where Mother would have the curling iron heating on the gas stove.

She'd lick her finger and touch it to the iron. A sizzling sound indicated it was ready. "For heaven's sake, stand still," she would say, brandishing the iron and waving away the first whiff of singed hair.

The result of her efforts was nothing short of a miracle. My well-cowlicked mane was still straight as ever, but I was certain the frizzled border around my ears admitted me to some magic kingdom where only curly haired movie stars belonged.

Those sessions around the stove finally ended when a retired beautician

---

"It was nearly dinner when I arrived home in all my frizzled glory..."

---

moved into the neighborhood. She agreed to give me a professional permanent in exchange for Mother's making her a dress from some silk she'd brought home from China.

Visions of Shirley danced in my head! On the appointed day I was awake before dawn, eager to meet the beautician. Alas, I hadn't realized the price I'd pay for curls that would "outlast a party". Acrid fumes from the permanent lotion brought tears to my eyes, and if I wiggled, I got rapped on the head with a comb!

When each strand of hair was tightly wound and secured, I was clamped to a machine that pulled at my hair and sent heat surging through to my scalp.

How long I was trapped there I don't recall. All I know is that I'd gone to the beautician's right after breakfast, and it was nearly dinnertime when I arrived back home in all my frizzled glory.

No little dumpling curls like Shirley's covered my head, but the machine's work was indeed permanent. I know, because the moment I got home, I stuck my head under the faucet as a test. The frizz remained, but the set was gone before Mother ever saw it.

"I spent all that time sewing for you to look like *this*?" Mother shrieked when she caught sight of me.

Just recently I read an article by some Hollywood know-it-all claiming that Shirley's curls weren't really hers at all—that she simply wore a wig.

Say it ain't so! I'd hate to think so many of us girls went through so much to look like something that never was!

Scott E. Zimek

A Bloom to Last Forever

By Clinton Griffith, Charleroi, Pennsylvania

IN 1929, Wall Street gamblers lost their shirts and the awful Depression began. It was a year of change for me, too. I'd taken my first job that spring, at age 10. From 6 to 11 on Saturday nights, I sold the Sunday edition of the *Pittsburgh Sun-Telegraph* from a street corner.

The first Saturday I worked was one of those early spring nights that couldn't decide whether it wanted to rain or snow.

I went to the news store, picked up my papers and took them up to my corner on Second and Main in Monongahela, Pennsylvania, south of Pittsburgh. I had to make three trips because the Sunday edition was big and I was small.

First I stacked my papers in the entrance of a restaurant to keep them dry (no one will buy a wet newspaper). But a man came out and told me to move them because someone might trip.

So I got a pasteboard box from the alley, set it on its side by the lamppost and put my papers inside.

Before long, I was wet to the skin and couldn't stop shaking. An old lady getting off the streetcar looked at me and asked, "Little boy, aren't you cold?"

"Paperboys don't get cold," I told her proudly.

After waiting on customers from the last streetcar, I gathered up my extras and returned them to the news store. It

was 10:20. Marge, the lady at the counter, smiled and shook her head. I must have looked awful, all wet like that.

Next I hurried across the street to the flower shop just as Mr. Rocco was locking the door. "Please, Mr. Rocco," I pleaded. "Will you open up? I just *have* to have a flower. Mother's Day is tomorrow."

Out of Luck?

"Yes, I know." He stood there for the longest time, looking at me and rubbing his chin. "Well, all right, come in."

He opened the door and turned on the light. "Now, what is it you want?"

"I want the most beautiful flower you have," I replied.

"And just how much do you have to pay for this most beautiful flower?"

I held out a wet hand showing a quarter and dime. He nodded, then showed me a plant on the counter. "I can give you this one for 35¢," he said.

"Aw, gee," I protested, "it looks like a weed!" About 18 inches high, the plant was in a small crock covered with faded red crepe paper.

"You asked for my most beautiful flower," said Mr. Rocco. "Now trust me, boy—I promise that tomorrow morning when you get up, you will find your most beautiful flower."

I knew him to be a good honest man, so I agreed to take it. Mr. Rocco put a paper bag over the plant and told me to hurry home.

"You don't want your plant to get a chill," he cautioned.

No Time to Lose

Thanking him, I ran the rest of the way home. It was almost midnight when I arrived. Kicking off my wet shoes, I hung my wet coat and tassel cap over a nail on the back of our cellar door.

Mom was sick with tuberculosis and using the front bedroom. I peeked in to see if she was asleep, then quietly tiptoed in and set the plant on the table beside her bed. I wanted her to be surprised when she woke on Mother's Day.

The next morning, I dressed and hurried downstairs. The sun was shining through the kitchen window as I looked into Mom's room. She motioned for me to come in, then glanced over at the table where the plant was.

Holy mackerel! There were three big yellow trumpet-shaped blooms. It was just like Mr. Rocco said—the most beautiful flower I ever saw!

When I looked at Mom, she was smiling as tears streamed down her cheeks. She held out her hand for me to come near, then pulled me close and hugged till it hurt.

Then, remembering her contagious condition and that she wasn't supposed to touch me, she quickly let go.

My dear mom died the next night. That moment she hugged me turned out to be the most wonderful moment of my life. Not only had that beautiful plant helped show just how much I loved her, but I'd always know how much she loved me. ☎

NEWSBOY. Clinton Griffith was a working 10-year-old when he discovered just the right gift for Mother's Day.

⋙ Short ⋘ Memories

Beaned in the Helmet

MOTORCYCLING has always been my passion, so when I was offered the opportunity to ride for pay, I took the job.

It was after World War II. The Pittsburg, Kansas police department had acquired a new 1949 Harley-Davidson motorcycle, and I was assigned to ride it (see the photo below).

"You are the traffic department," Chief Tom Stowers said to me. "Look for and apprehend traffic violators."

That's just what I was doing one day when I stopped a very attractive young lady for speeding near the university. As she was signing the citation, a carload of teenage boys went by, and one of them threw out a beer can. The can hit my helmet just as I was handing the lady her ticket.

It took me two blocks, but I caught the car. I told the boy who tossed the can he would be charged as a litterbug and could likely spend time in jail for having an open can of beer in the car.

I knew the empty can was not much in the way of evidence. So I told the boy that if he could walk all the way back and pick up the can, and show me by his walk that he wasn't under the influence, I wouldn't charge him.

He walked like a very sober boy.

The incident remains fresh in my memory mainly because of how hard the young lady laughed when that can bounced off my shiny new helmet. I guess I would have laughed, too.

—*John Chester, Pittsburg, Kansas*

JOY RIDERS. The children at left were riding in a big red vehicle that was known around Rochester, New York as the "Joy Car". Fred Beach of South Elgin, Illinois says his father, George, a member of the Church Extension Society, raised $3,000 in small donations back in the early '20s to have this vehicle specially built. It held up to 36 children, and on warm evenings and Sunday afternoons in the summer, Mr. Beach took groups of orphans and shut-ins for drives in the countryside.

Minnie Got Her Teeth into It

"MINNIE" the mink, for a time, had free run of the house when I was growing up on our mink ranch near Pearl Beach, Michigan.

Minnie had lost her mother and was only a thumb-sized, hairless kit when Dad brought her in.

Mink are very clean, and Minnie often tried to bathe in the bathroom if we'd forget to close the door. Once she bathed in a pitcher of grape Kool-Aid and came out all purple. Another time, she got into Mom's flour bin and looked like a little white spook.

Mink are pack rats, and we often lost items such as keys and bottle openers. But the funniest example of Minnie's pack rat penchant came one time when Grandpa was visiting.

Grandpa kept his false teeth in a glass of water on the dresser. Minnie loved to climb around and in the dresser looking for things to take. So naturally, she took Grandpa's teeth.

Grandpa jumped out of bed yelling, "My teeth! My teeth!", and ran after Minnie.

We dashed out to see what was happening and about fell down laughing when we saw Minnie running with Grandpa's teeth.

We got the teeth back, and Grandpa calmed down. But those two never did become good friends.   —*Ellie Mruzek Monroe, Michigan*

Doggone Bad Hair Day

"KING", a little, black curly-haired dog, was my constant companion when I was a girl of 7, some 73 years ago.

This was when bobbed and permed hair was the rage, and my mother decided to join the fashion parade. When I first saw her new "do", I thought, *Gee, she looks just like King.*

The next day, as dawn was barely breaking, Dad awoke in the dim light and saw a black mop of curly hair on Mom's pillow. He swung his arm out and clouted Mom on the head, sending her sprawling to the floor.

Mom sat up, dazed, and said, "Have you lost your mind, Al?"

"Sorry," Dad replied. "I thought you were the dog." He then made the big mistake of chuckling.

Mother thought it definitely was not funny, and I think Dad paid for the mishap for some time to come.

But as time passed, Mom was able to look back on the incident and laugh, and she permed her hair for the rest of her life.

—*Virginia Fitzgerald Quincy, Massachusetts*

The Shot Heard 'Round the Barn

MY FAMILY lived on a farm in upstate New York in 1920. I was 6 years old that year when my cousin moved away and left me his single-shot .22 rifle. One day, I was sitting with my rifle on the shady side of the old farmhouse, which was reportedly built before the Revolutionary War.

I took careful aim and put a few bullet holes in the clay chimney on the barn. When my father discovered what I was up to, he relieved me of the rifle and ordered me to bed.

Seventy-two years later, I was visiting the area and met the new owners of the farm. They'd beautifully restored the old house and barn, and I told them that back in 1920, there'd been a clay chimney on the barn.

"Oh yes," said the woman, "we still have the chimney, but we've put it inside the house to preserve it. During the Revolutionary War, there was a skirmish here and the chimney was full of bullet holes."

When I was sent to bed at age 6, I had no idea that I'd one day become a war hero. —*Alfred Nilsson, Humboldt, Tennessee*

Coming Clean with Mom

MY MOTHER used to round up my four brothers and me and take us to the creek about a quarter mile from our house to wash up before bed.

She scrubbed us with Ivory soap in the ice-cold water. She would laugh and tell us our cousins in the town downstream would be drinking our bathwater the next day.

My mother was quite a jokester, but everyone loved her. —*Linda Murphy Northborough, Massachusetts*

Guarantee Shattered

ONE DAY in the '40s, Father came home from nearby Cedar City, Utah with a large package and a mischievous grin.

In the kitchen, he opened the package and pulled out a glass tumbler. Scanning the room to make sure everyone was watching, he drew back his arm and flung the glass against the wall!

When it shattered to pieces, Dad's jaw dropped in bewilderment. We all gasped!

It turned out a salesman in the city had sold Dad a set of "unbreakable" glasses. In the store, the salesman had hurled one glass after another against a wall, and each had stood the test, much to the admiration of a crowd of onlookers.

Poor Dad's set was obviously defective. And after all these years, it's still fun to recall the look on his face! —*Irene Pollock, St. George, Utah*

Rude Awakening

IN 1936, when he retired after many years as a barber, my uncle Bert Woltz sold his chairs, clippers and other tools of his trade. But he couldn't part with the fine marble countertops that had surrounded his two sinks.

With the sinks removed, each beautiful marble slab had a hole in the middle. Bert had a wonderful idea—he'd use them as marble privy seats!

He took those smooth slabs home and, sure enough, they fit perfectly in his outhouse. Bert was so proud... until he discovered a major shortcoming when cold weather arrived.

Bert summed it up this way: "Anyone who thinks *ice* is cold should try sitting on a freezing slab of marble on a winter night in Ohio!" —*Robert Cassill, Loudonville, Ohio*

By Wooda Carr, Fort Wayne, Indiana

Did You Read the Pulps?

DOC SAVAGE…The Shadow…The Spider…some of those early "superheroes" are still around today. But do you recall their humble beginnings?

Those characters—and many more—first came to life during the 1930s in 10-cent adventure magazines called "pulps". Through the Depression era, they dominated magazine racks everywhere!

Pulps, named for the cheap paper on which they were printed, entertained *millions* of youngsters back then…and served as a launching pad for many a famous author.

Loaded with mystery and charged with action, the pulps were nothing short of pure escapism during the drab years of the Great Depression. Set in exotic locales, stories had eerie, dramatic titles like "The Master of Murder River", "The Army of the Dead" and "The City That Dared Not Eat".

They weren't exactly great literature…but as a kid, I *loved* them!

Back before television, all you needed was a pulp and a good imagination to share the adventures of Doc Savage, "The Man of Bronze"…or ride along the Western trails with saddle buddies like The Lone Ranger, The Masked Rider, Pete Rice and The Pecos Kid.

Just one magazine was good for a whole afternoon's entertainment! We fought crime alongside The Phantom Detective, The Ghost and The Whisperer…or we roamed the jungle with royalty, escorted by Sheena, Queen of the Jungle, and Ki-Gor, King of the Jungle.

We walked the dark and dangerous streets of Chinatown with The Mysterious Wu Fang and Doctor Yen Sin—and enjoyed every gripping, suspenseful second we spent there!

"Undercover" Reading

The very act of reading the pulps was often an adventure. Since many parents didn't approve of those lurid books, kids had to smuggle them home and read them at night, under the bed covers with a flashlight. I know I did!

I vividly recall carrying a copy of *The Spider* home from school in my violin case. It was the March 1936 issue and was titled "The Green Globes of Death". Mother would have been horrified had she known!

HIGH ACTION was a mainstay in the pages of the pulps. The 1930s covers shown here are from pulp mysteries, battle stories and Westerns.

In 1936, one schoolteacher wrote: "The pulp magazines constitute a menace to pupils' morals, their English and their minds."

I didn't believe it then, and I still don't today!

My friends and I were avid readers of pulp magazines, and we all grew up happy, healthy and well-adjusted. Fact is, we just loved the suspense and action the magazines provided.

Doom Was Imminent

By today's standards, stories in the pulps may seem tame. The common theme running through them all was of good triumphing over evil.

The story lines were rather similar, and they all seemed to run (and sound) something like this:

Threatened by a mad genius, the forces of law and order have collapsed! This threat is too gigantic to be handled by ordinary means! Against the weak resistance of good men, criminal hordes are striding ever forward and...

At the climax of the story, the pulp hero would enter with fists flying and guns blazing and somehow manage to save the day. Next month, he'd have to do it all over again.

Where are these great old magazines today? Most remaining copies are in the hands of collectors, who believe pulps are a part of America's literary heritage and should be preserved for future generations.

If you should be so lucky as to find an old pulp magazine in your attic, hang on to it—pulps are highly collectible. But, please, don't just store that wonderful old magazine away!

Instead, open its pages and let it give you a chuckle or two as you read your way back into the past. And, just for fun, why not do your reading at night, under the covers, by flashlight? ☏

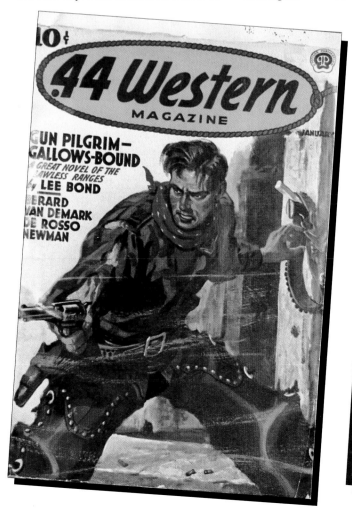

Route 66 Was a Highway of Sideshows

RABBIT RIDER. Author (left) enjoyed a fun stop at Jackrabbit, Arizona. This was one of many tourist haunts, like the one above, along Route 66.

By Delores Jones Dennis, Lexington, Kentucky

Today's highways bypass most towns and cities, and there's usually no stopping except for gas or emergencies. In our fast-paced world, that seems to be what most people want.

Not me, though! I miss those old roads that led you through every small town and offered plenty of places to stop and rest. Most of all, I miss the colorful roadside attractions.

When I was young, we traveled Route 66 from Standard, California to Heavener, Oklahoma. We made that round-trip at least once a year, and I'll always cherish the memories.

Dad drove our old Ford as fast as he could so we'd have a little extra time to stop at the attractions.

Hopping Along

One of the best was the trading post in Jackrabbit, Arizona. Near that store stood several large statues. One was a huge jackrabbit. I have pictures of three generations of my family posing with that rabbit!

Trading posts beckoned all along Route 66, so there was keen competition for motorists' money. What developed, therefore, was a highway lined with freak shows, playgrounds and miniature amusement parks.

Near the Painted Desert, you could buy colored sand in glass containers, and at the Petrified Forest, you might purchase small chips of petrified wood. The Indian reservations offered handmade jewelry and rugs.

Then there were the small places touting two-headed cows and other mistakes of nature. I recall one such enterprise that boasted a "rare" horned rattlesnake. Most travelers didn't know *all* sidewinder rattlesnakes have horns.

My favorite roadside stops featured covered wagons, stagecoaches and statues of horses. You could sit in the wagons or on the horses and have your picture taken.

Another part of traveling Route 66 were the border-crossing stations at each state line. Officials would check vehicles for fruits, vegetables, plants and other contraband that weren't allowed into a particular state.

LET 'ER BUCK! Author's father, Raymond Terry (left), got his kicks on Route 66 by riding a fake bucking bronco. Yahoo!

One time, Dad wanted to transport some night crawlers and catfish he'd caught back home to northern California. He took two tin washtubs, put the fish in one and covered them with ice, then filled the other with dirt and night crawlers.

Mom told him he'd never get them home, but Dad just *had* to try. In the meantime, she took a small bucket and filled it with dirt and night crawlers.

Mom Baited Border Officials

We managed to pass through both Texas and New Mexico without being checked, but things changed at the Arizona/California line. Dad was told he couldn't carry the fish or the worms into California.

After arguing with the officer to no avail, he finally had to dump both the washtubs. Mom, however, got to keep the worms *she* had by placing some dirty diapers on top of the bucket. When asked what was inside, she told the officer it was full of dirty diapers and he was welcome to check if he wished. He thanked her but didn't bother.

Dad was so mad, he wouldn't even talk the rest of the way home. I never knew whether it was because he didn't get to keep his fish and worms—or because Mom got to keep hers!

Most likely it was both, and for years afterward, Dad told us he was convinced the border guards gathered up those fish after we left and had themselves a big fish fry.

There'll never be another road like Route 66. In some ways that's good, but in others it's a pity, because travel will never again be quite so much fun. ☎

Jack Westhead

We've Got to Find Dad's Secret Melon Patch!

By Mildred Heck, Dayton, Ohio

EVERY AUGUST back in the '20s, watermelons would mysteriously appear in the icehouse on our farm in Wayne Township, Ohio. I never knew where they came from until my older brother, Bob, said he thought Dad had a watermelon patch hidden in the cornfield.

Our cornfield was home to another plant that wasn't hidden—corn beans. They were really just brown pole beans that were planted next to the young field corn and trained to vine up the stalks.

It was my job to plant the beans in the spring, using an old cutoff broomstick. Each week after that, I'd go to the bean patch with a hoe to make sure they attached themselves to the corn, then dust the leaves for bugs.

One August evening when I was about 7, I saw Dad go into the tall corn with our tin hand-duster. When I told Bob I had just dusted the beans, he said Dad was probably going to hoe and dust his secret watermelon patch. I kept an eye out, and sure enough—Dad came back out of the cornfield at the same spot he'd gone in.

A couple of days later, I watched Dad go back into the tall corn. Again, he came out in the same spot. *I bet I can find his secret melon patch*, I told myself.

The next day, I told Mom I was going to hoe the corn beans. But as soon as I got into the bean patch, I threw down the hoe and headed straight into the corn where I'd seen Dad go. I walked and walked. I went right and left, back and forth. I walked some more. The corn was high above my head, making it impossible to tell where I was.

Suddenly, there it was—I could hardly believe my eyes! It was a space about the size of our kitchen, filled with vines and big green watermelons sticking out from under the leaves.

I was so excited! I went from melon to melon, knocking on each one with my knuckles. I didn't know why, but I'd always seen the adults do it.

Wanting to rush home and tell Bob what I'd found, I plunged back into the corn…but I had no idea which way to go. I ran, turned and ran some more, but I was lost. Hot, dusty and tired, I sat on the ground.

After a time, I was missed at home, and my folks found my discarded hoe. Dad was clever not to let anyone else get lost in the tall corn looking for me. He stood by the bean patch

"We had no idea where we were in that big cornfield…"

and fired his shotgun into the air, hoping I was bright enough to move toward the sound. It took eight shots, but I finally found my way out.

I was dripping wet and dirty, and my face was red and hot. Mom had me stick my head in a bucket of cold water.

Why had I gone into the cornfield, Dad quizzed. What on earth was I looking for? I said nothing, but I couldn't wait to tell Bob what I'd found!

Dad sat the both of us down and said that if we were ever so foolish as to get lost in a cornfield, we should use our heads and simply follow one row all the way to the end. I'm sure he knew this would happen again.

A few days later, when Dad was gone, Bob and I took off into the corn to find the melon patch. We walked and walked but never could find it. We had no idea where we were in that big cornfield, then we remembered Dad's advice and followed one row out, ending up on our neighbor's farm. We went through his field to the Old Troy Pike road and walked home.

We never did see Dad carrying a melon—he must have gone to his secret patch at night. As soon as one was eaten, another showed up in the icehouse.

Long after the melons were gone, the field corn was dry and ripe and the corn beans were hanging ripe in dry pods, picked and stored in the attic. Later, on a winter evening, a dishpan full of corn beans was brought down, and we all sat around the kitchen table hulling them. They were soaked overnight and cooked the next day with a big ham bone and onions. That was good eating.

Many years later, I asked Dad how he was able to find his hidden patch so quickly. "Easy," he said. "I'd just enter at the same place each time, count a certain number of steps, make a right turn and go a few more steps, and there it was."

When I asked why he'd made it such a big secret, Dad laughed and said, "How else could I keep you kids and all the neighbor kids out of my melon patch?" ☎

129

I Lived the High Life

By Anna Mae Craig-Stregger, Saratoga, Cali-

I WORKED as a stewardess with TWA in 1943, back when that job was considered one of the most glamorous jobs a young woman could have.

After growing up in Gary, Indiana and attending Purdue University for a year, I'd decided I wanted to do something for the war effort, so I applied for a job with TWA as a hostess or ground agent.

When I got the telegram inviting me to interview for hostess training, I was excited. But when I saw the other applicants in the waiting room looking so poised and sophisticated, I didn't think I stood a chance.

To my surprise, I was the only one chosen from the bunch. I later found out it was because I looked "wholesome".

My parents didn't think it was safe for me to live in Chicago, so I stayed with them near Gary. This meant a 3-hour commute each way. I had to walk seven blocks lugging a suitcase—often in the middle of the night—to catch the South Shore train to Chicago, then ride the streetcar to Midway Airport.

Ugly Shoes and Nylon Blues

Our uniforms consisted of a sky-blue skirt and jacket with a navy camisole and an over-seas-style hat. Nylons were so scarce, I'd cry if I got a run. I can recall my roommate coming home from a flight and taking her nylons off—just in time for me to put them on!

Our shoes were plain brown oxfords—ugly but practical during turbulence, when we were buffeted back and forth while passing out "burp cups" to airsick passengers.

Our aircraft was the trusty DC-3, and our crew of three consisted of pilot, copilot and me, the hostess. The passengers were mostly military personnel, who had priority with the airlines. We often had to "bump" civilian passengers.

I empathized with the soldiers and airmen who were either going to war or coming home, but I was sometimes emotionally drained by their stories.

Flights then were longer, more turbulent and less pre-

HAPPY HOSTESS. That's what Anna Mae Craig (left) was when she got her job with TWA flying in the old reliable DC-3 as the only stewardess.

dictable...but they were much more exciting! Besides burp cups, I'd pass out chewing gum to help ease the pressure of stopped-up ears.

Served Food on Cardboard

The galley was drafty and cramped and had a strong "metallic" smell. Sometimes the food (especially scrambled eggs) tasted metallic, too—and nothing looked very appetizing on those cardboard trays.

I was responsible for the flatware kit. Every night I'd have to take it off the plane to my hotel room to wash it in the basin!

My suitcase had a divider inside, and only half was for my personal luggage. The other half contained flight reports and forms to be turned in when we landed.

In those days of smaller planes and fewer passengers, stewardesses could give more personalized service than they do now. I visited with passengers, and they sometimes showed their appreciation with letters of commendation. I still recall a Christmas flight when I took little wreaths and pinned them above each seat.

Those years were truly the time of my life. I flew the first delegates to the United Nations and occasionally saw celebrities like Howard Hughes. Though bad weather often stranded us in dull places, having a long layover in an exciting big city was adequate compensation.

One stormy night, a tall handsome naval officer boarded my flight. From then on, my flying days were numbered—a few months later, I married that good-looking Navy pilot.

In the years since, I've seen airliners increase greatly in size and sophistication. Still, the jumbo jets with their luxurious accommodations and super power just don't thrill me like that modest little DC-3 once did as it quivered at the end of the runway, ready for takeoff. ☎

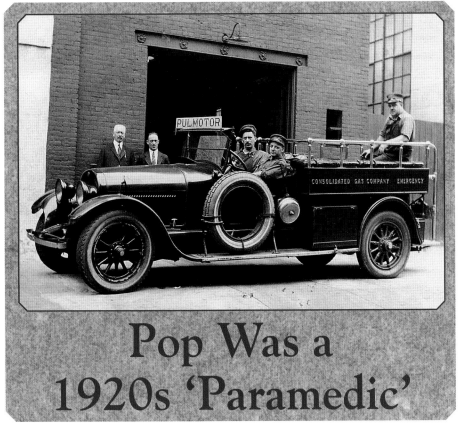

Pop Was a 1920s 'Paramedic'

By Edward Dziowgo, O'Neill, Nebraska

MY FATHER didn't look much like a Hollywood hero in the brown bib overalls he usually wore to work. But to me and to the families of the hundreds of people whose lives he saved, he was hero material indeed.

During the mid-1920s, Pop was the ranking man on one of the emergency vehicles operated by the Consolidated Gas Company in New York City.

Painted brilliant red, with shiny brass rails in the back, those vehicles resembled fire trucks but had no sirens or flashing lights. Instead, there was a beautiful brass gong on the side that was operated by pulling a rope.

The Consolidated Gas Company had five trucks, each with a three-man crew, that responded to such emergencies as gas leaks and explosions, fires and floods caused by broken water mains.

Pop was trained by a doctor who'd developed a form of artificial respiration that preceded by decades today's CPR.

Back in those days, the victim would be placed face-down, head turned to one side and resting on an arm.

Pop would place the palms of his hands on the victim's lower back and press in and release, maintaining proper rhythm by repeating, "Out goes the bad air...in comes the good air..."

Sometimes Pop used the "Pulmotor" (the latest resuscitator of that time) to help accident victims breathe. The device was carried in a large suitcase and consisted of tanks and masks that would put a mixture of oxygen into a victim's lungs.

Suitcase Saved Lives

Firefighters of that day were called "smoke-eaters" because they didn't have self-contained air packs and often breathed smoke to the point of being sick or unconscious.

Pop would enter a burning building and help rescue and revive victims with the Pulmotor or an improved apparatus called an Inhalator. As I recall, the gas company paid the crew a $5 bonus every time they had to use the machine.

In those days, some people tried to steal gas using a rubber hose to bypass the meter. That would cause a drop in pressure, and the pilot lights would go out. After the meter was reattached, the pilot lights would leak, and Pop and his crew had to make a run when anxious neighbors smelled gas.

Another type of emergency run would be made to repair a broken or cracked gas pipe. A temporary repair was made by kneading several bars of soap into one big glob that was slapped on the crack and held in place with heavy gauze and tape. It was crude, but it worked till the gas could be shut off and a permanent repair made.

He Rang the Bell

I loved visiting Pop's station on 111th Street in Manhattan. I'd put on his heavy eagle-adorned fire helmet, climb on the truck and play "fireman". When it was time to go home, the men would search through their pockets and give me a nickel to buy ice cream.

I was visiting Pop at the station one memorable day when an emergency call came in. Not only was I allowed to go along on the run (much to Mother's despair), but I got to pull the rope and ring the gong. Believe me, it got a workout!

While the men were in the burning building, I stayed on the truck, warning curious kids, "Stay away from my father's truck!"

On the ride back to the station, I continued ringing the bell all the way. The driver, Bud Clarke, probably had a temporary loss of hearing in his left ear!

But Bud, like my father and the other dedicated men he worked with, wasn't one to complain about minor hardships. In my book, those kind and courageous early "paramedics" will always be true heroes. ☎

TO THE RESCUE came the crew at right, responding to emergency calls. From left are Tom Dowd, Bud Clarke and author's father. That's the same trio above.

We Marveled At the '39 WORLD'S FAIR

By Sid Abrams
Cleveland Heights, Ohio

THE 1939 New York World's Fair in Flushing Meadows was three subway rides and a bus trip away from Brooklyn, so my teenage buddies and I had to start the trip at sunrise.

Looking back on that trip, I'm amazed at all the things we take for granted today that were considered "impossible dreams" back then...like television.

The fair was opened by President Franklin D. Roosevelt, and the ceremonies were televised. But very few people had television sets then, or even believed they'd work!

At the fair, television was being promoted in the RCA pavilion, which was shaped like a huge vacuum tube. You went into a small booth, sat in a chair and—*Presto!*—you could see yourself on a small screen.

"It's a toy," scoffed one friend. We moved on.

Look Out Below!

In the Du Pont building, a man held up what looked like a windowpane and announced, "Now I'm going to drop a 5-pound steel ball from the ceiling onto this window."

The crowd drew back as the ball dropped. But instead of the window being smashed to bits, the ball bounced off! "It's made of a new material called plastic," the man explained.

"It's a gimmick," a 15-year-old pal told us. We moved on.

In another part of the Du Pont building, a model demonstrated the durability of her stockings as she tore at them

with her fingernails and pins. She then turned around slowly for all to see and explained, "It's a new fabric developed by Du Pont called nylon."

"Did you see those legs?" asked another companion, oblivious to the scientific wonder we'd just witnessed.

The future uses of refrigeration were demonstrated when a man dipped two frankfurters into a canister of liquid nitrogen, then used them to play a small snare drum! "One day soon, entire meals will be frozen," the man said.

"I'm hungry," said another friend.

Hunger was easily satisfied at the fair, where we got doughnuts at the Wonder Bread pavilion, pickles at H.J. Heinz, milk at Borden's and Coca-Cola at that pavilion. Most of it was free.

Famous names provided the entertainment—Bill Robinson danced, Eleanor Holm swam along with Johnny Weissmuller and Buster Crabbe. Salvador Dali exhibited his painting *A Dream of Venus*.

A gigantic National Cash Register topped the entrance building to the fair, ringing up the attendance continually. Although the fair drew almost 45 mil-

lion visitors during its 354-day run, it lost over $18 million.

Ironically, many of the 63 nations that participated in the largest fair in history would soon be involved in World War II. But it was also the dawn of a new era—one of television, plastic, nylon and frozen food. ☎

I Worked at the Fair

By Louis Allen, Sarasota, Florida

MY FIRST JOB was as a demonstrator and guide in the Westinghouse pavilion at the 1939 New York World's Fair. How exciting for a shy boy of 16!

After a statewide exam was administered, the top science student from each New York high school was awarded a part-time summer job at the fair. Sponsored by Westinghouse Corporation, we demonstrated science exhibits.

Ironically, a tie was announced at New Utrecht High School in Brooklyn ...between me and my best friend, Sigurd. He and I were elated to find out that we'd *both* get to work at the fair!

It was an hour's subway ride each

KODAK · NEW YORK WO

PHOTOGRAPHED AT 1/100,000 SECOND!
EASTMAN KODAK EXHIBIT

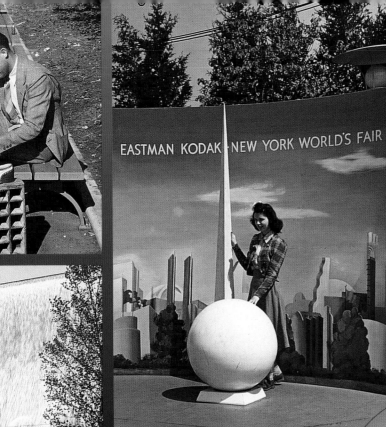

EASTMAN KODAK · NEW YORK WORLD'S FAIR 1

"magic" and were designed to astound the visitors to the pavilion. It was gratifying to see amazed reactions—particularly on the faces of the pretty girls. Some of them even hung around afterward to talk…an extra bonus!

For one of the experiments, I poured two colorless liquids into a beaker. Nothing happened at first…but then, after a predetermined time, I'd snap my fingers and the clear solution would turn jet-black. Everyone gasped in wonder, and I felt like a wizard!

Trick *Almost* Fail-Proof

This trick required practice and careful preparation of the liquids beforehand—and it worked about 95% of the time. When it didn't, I'd blush and go on to another trick.

When we weren't working, Sig and I took in the fair's attractions for free. Our favorite was Billy Rose's Aquacade, most likely because of all those pretty girls who made such artful entries into the water.

After watching one show, we stayed for a second…but soon found we were allowed to see it only once for free. The ushers led us out unceremoniously. It was a little embarrassing, but we got over it.

I also indulged my new hobby of photography that summer, snapping pictures with my brother's old reflex camera.

When I was drafted into World War II, I was trained as an aerial photographer. Soon after the Battle of the Bulge began, I was transferred to the 106th infantry division and shipped overseas as a replacement.

There I learned that Sig, who'd been in the same outfit, was captured by the Germans. He was later released, and after the war, we got together again.

Yes, we grew up fast after the war—but the summer of '39 is a priceless memory of my youth, hopes and dreams.

The New York World's Fair was a magical experience—a place where each day ended in grand fireworks and a musical fountain booming Tchaikovsky's *Fourth*. I still have the memories and photos to prove it. ☎

A FAIRLY GOOD TIME was had by all at the 1939 World's Fair. In the photos (at left) from Katherine Williams, Lumberton, North Carolina, her husband, Rufus, seems to be sitting on top of the world—actually the Perisphere, one of the fair's symbols—and also is bothered by aching feet. Louis Allen (below, seated second from left, and his pal Sig, standing on left) demonstrated science exhibits.

way, but our pay of $3.85 a day more than covered transportation and lunch costs. On top of that, we got unlimited admission to the fair and several of the entertainment attractions.

Demonstrated Chemistry

The other students were as nervous and excited as Sig and I, but we all felt like big shots walking around the Westinghouse exhibit with our lab coats on.

My assignment was to gather about 25 people, give a brief talk, then demonstrate four or five chemistry experiments. I ran through my routine two or three times an hour for 3 hours a day. Because I was so shy, this was a real effort for me, but I think the experience paid off years later in my career as a chemist and in management at IBM.

My experiments involved chemical

A Home of Our Own

By Madeline Huss, Bowie, Maryland

"ANYONE who buys a house 30 miles from the city is out of his mind!"

I'll never forget when my father-in-law made this statement, because that's just what my husband, George, and I were about to do.

It was 1956, and tract homes were springing up all over our part of New Jersey. They were for people just like us—couples with kids, not much money and a longing for a place of their own.

Many stories written about the '50s portray people building bomb shelters or living like the characters on *Leave It to Beaver* or *Ozzie and Harriet*.

In my memory, the '50s weren't like that at all. They were a time of great change, with moving vans crossing the country as veterans of World War II and

Korea looked for affordable homes for growing families.

We lived on the third floor of an ancient building on the outskirts of Newark. We'd been thrilled to get this rent-controlled apartment within walking distance of Branchbrook Park, home of cherry trees identical to those made famous in Washington, D.C.

Stairs Reduced Appeal

After our second child was born, though, the charm of that apartment was gone. It was 19 steps up to the terrace …eight more to the entrance, then two more flights to our door.

It was work enough with a toddler and the baby, but grocery day meant several trips down to the car. It was all too much.

"That's it," George said one day after a grocery store trip. "We're going to buy a house."

I shrugged. "That's easy to say…but how can we afford a house when we can barely scrape up the rent each month?"

WINTER IN THE 'BURBS. The Huss kids and friends enjoyed a big snow pile in 1961 (above left), while the author got her exercise by taking the "reins" for a snow sled caravan (left).

DRESS UP, DRESS WARM. When it was time for church, the kids wore their Sunday best (far left). But when Dad George pulled the sled (left), they donned much warmer gear.

We scoured the countryside every weekend and finally found a modest development of Cape Cods and ranch houses in the town of Old Bridge. There, for only $250 down, we could purchase a brand-spanking-new two-bedroom home just the right size.

Our parents were less enthusiastic—this meant they'd have to drive 40 miles to see us instead of 5. But we couldn't resist the lure of owning our own home.

Had Second Thoughts

When moving day arrived, I did have second thoughts. From our apartment, the grocery store and library were only two blocks away…but in our new home, the nearest A&P was 9 miles off!

In our old neighborhood, huge oak trees shaded our street…in our new one, the twigs planted in front of our model home wouldn't provide shade 'til the 30-year mortgage was paid off.

However, I soon discovered our new home was in a real neighborhood—and the clothesline was a wonderful place to meet neighbors. As we pinned diapers and underwear, we exchanged our vital statistics—little money, many children, one car.

It really didn't matter how many cars we had, since none of us women could drive, anyway. We were marooned amid the mud and crabgrass!

Septic Tank Parties

Another gathering place was the septic tank. Someone's was always overflowing, so the men of the neighborhood would pitch in on a Saturday for a communal septic tank repair. That night, the family with the bad septic tank usually hosted an impromptu party.

We didn't need nursery schools or day care. The little-traveled street served as a giant playground, and the milkman and bread man knew to wend their way carefully through the maze of children.

We lived there for 10 years and still go back to visit. The mortgages are paid off…the trees have grown…and most houses now have *two* cars parked out front.

We really didn't have much going for us in the '50s—just a lot of hard work, a lack of luxuries and lots of kids to take care of. Yet, looking back, we enjoyed every minute. ☎

Mother-and-Son Ensemble Was a Twist

By Mary Louise Hinton, Kansas City, Missouri

IN THE SPRING of 1960, I went to my doctor because I had been feeling lethargic. On May 12, I found out I wasn't sick—I was pregnant!

I was in a state of shock. Our daughter, Sharon, was 20 years old! Nevertheless, when our son, Gary, was born on December 7, I assumed the role of second-time mom with gusto.

After my nearly 21-year hiatus from baby caring, I was a little rusty, but Gary survived, and thrived. We looked on him as a sort of do-it-yourself grandchild.

In the spring of 1964, Macy's department store in Kansas City sponsored a sewing contest for children's wear. Entrants had to wear garments made from material and patterns purchased at Macy's.

I'd been sewing for many years. When Sharon was a little girl, I had made several mother-and-daughter ensembles. So, I decided to make a mother-and-son ensemble for Gary and me.

I bought the patterns and material from Macy's so I could enter Gary in the contest. Then I made a shirt, jacket and pants for Gary, and a skirt, jacket and beret for me (see photo above).

Gary marched in the fashion parade, but he didn't win. In fact, none of the boys did. The girls won all the prizes.

That didn't stop us from wearing our outfits, though, and thoroughly enjoying all the attention. Fortunately, Gary was too young to object!

I never did make any more clothes for Gary, but I still smile when I look at this picture. ☎

Motoring Memories

One day in 1923, those folks showed their appreciation for 15 years of service by honoring Dad with gifts of produce from their gardens.

When Dad drove into our yard that afternoon, his Ford was loaded down with vegetables. My brother proudly snapped a picture (below left) with his new box camera.

That "loot" filled our cellar, smokehouse and pantry. Our family enjoyed it all winter long!   —Clayton Martin
Harrodsburg, Kentucky

Won a Galaxie of Prizes

IN 1959, my wife and I visited the Harry Groussman Ford dealership in Englewood, Colorado. At the time, we were unaware of a contest being held there to celebrate the dealership's 20th anniversary. We told the salesman we wanted a new 1959 Ford Galaxie 500.

We'd visited other dealers in the Denver area, gathering price quotes to trade in our 1956 station wagon.

He looked at the highest offer for our wagon and said he didn't think he could match it, but he'd ask his manager.

Soon the manager walked out, extended his hand and said, "Congratulations, you've just purchased the 20,000th car sold by our dealership.

ALL ABOARD! "On a summer day in 1938, following our graduation from the University of Colorado, a friend borrowed his dad's new DeSoto Airflow," says Myra Hile of San Juan Capistrano, California. "He slightly deflated the tires, then took us for a ride along the Union Pacific tracks east of Boulder, Colorado—after checking the schedule at the depot to assure we wouldn't share the tracks with a train!"

You've won a host of valuable prizes."

One of the prizes was a free vacation stay at the Hotel Colorado in Glenwood Springs.

That new Galaxie (below) eventually carried us to Alaska, and friends laughed because we'd ordered air-conditioning. It proved invaluable on the long drive back home on the dusty Alcan Highway.   —Edward Curtis
Arlington, Texas

PROUD POSTMAN. Rural mail carrier Carl Martin did such a good job that the folks on his route showered him with produce (see story below).

Postman Got Special Delivery

IN THE early part of the 20th century, rural mail carriers were more than just "mailmen"—they were a main link to the outside world for the people they served.

My father, Carl Martin, became the mail carrier for Brumfield, Kentucky in 1908. He started his deliveries with a horse and buggy, but soon retired that rig and bought a Ford. After that, Dad never delivered the mail in anything but a Ford, and he owned a long line of them.

Whenever he'd buy a new Ford, which only came in black, he'd paint it battleship gray so the dust and mud from the roads weren't so noticeable to the folks on his route.

TURN OFF THE AIR! Sharon and Vickie Curtis posed near Dad's 1959 Ford Galaxie in Alaska.

THE BUG IS BIGGER? "In 1949, Arliss Sluder started work on this tiny car in his basement and finally completed it in 1956, only to discover he had to cut it in half to get it outside," relates Jeff Gibson from Bellingham, Washington. "I have been the owner of the Arbet, named after Arliss and his wife, Beth, since 1989. The car has a twin-cylinder, air-cooled 13-horsepower engine and a top speed of 45 miles per hour. It's just 7-1/2 feet long and weighs only 1,006 pounds. The Arbet is fully equipped, right down to windshield wipers and washers and a cigarette lighter. Arliss put 14,000 miles on the car commuting to his job at the Sylvania Company in Montana. The top comes off for easy entry."

Only in America

YEARS AGO, you never knew what you might encounter at a roadside gas station.

After completing my Navy duty, I decided to see some of America before returning home. I was crossing Montana one day when my car ran out of gas at the top of a hill. I coasted down to stop in front of an old house with a gas pump outside.

When I got out of my car, an old woman called down from a second-floor window, "Pump your own."

I did just that, and my total came to $3. Then a metal cup was lowered down the side of the house on a string.

"Put the money in the cup," the voice commanded. I put the money in, she pulled the cup up to the window and I continued on my way.

—Robert Legel, Livonia, Michigan

The Spark of Knowledge

I WAS 11 years old, in 1929, when my father bought a new Ford Model A touring car. He took my mother, two sisters and me for a ride almost every evening around Spirit Lake, Iowa.

We also used the car to go berry picking. One time, when the car was loaded with baskets of gooseberries, Dad drove too fast over a set of railroad tracks.

We had to "repick" pretty near all the gooseberries. But it was fun.

Dad always parked the car in the backyard. One day, when nobody was looking, I got the keys and decided to start the car and pretend that I was driving.

I got the car started but then had a better idea. I used to watch my dad and his friend work on the Model T we had, so I figured I would play mechanic.

With the engine running, I opened the hood and started to take out a spark plug. The next thing I knew, I was flat on my back, some distance from the car.

That's the last time I worked on a car engine, running or not.

—Carl Carlson
Glendale, California

LOOK OF SUCCESS. "When my husband got a new job with an insurance company in 1959 in Midland, Michigan, he was told he should look successful," writes Lois Crites of Punta Gorda, Florida. "So he bought new clothes and this baby-blue 1957 Chevrolet convertible our daughters Nancy and Debra are posing in. Wow! We really felt special driving that car around town. But the car leaked when it rained and was cold in the winter. After 2 years, we got rid of it."

I Grew Up Around the Ford Rotunda

ROTUNDA READY. Ed Kerr (on right in photo at left) posed before a visit to the Rotunda in '37 with his dad, brother and sister. That building (above) and its interior (far left) were amazing.

By Ed Kerr, Dearborn Heights, Michigan

There has never been anything like it. Decades ahead of its time, the Ford Rotunda, an Albert Kahn architectural masterpiece, was part of my life for the entire 28 years of its existence.

This building was created for the 1934 Chicago World's Fair. After the fair's run, it was dismantled, hauled to Michigan and rebuilt on 13-1/2 acres on Schaefer Road in Dearborn, facing Ford's world headquarters.

We lived a quarter mile from the Rotunda. Every summer day in 1935, I took a bike ride to the construction site. The structure rose 110 feet and looked like a giant birthday cake. The center was originally open to the elements but was later enclosed with a dome. The building had a limestone exterior and terrazzo and walnut interior.

The landscaping was breathtaking for a kid raised on a 40-foot lot in Dearborn. Expansive lawns, huge trees, flowering shrubs and fern-edged waterfalls made the site exquisite.

Behind the building were 21 "Roads of the World", duplications of pavement in other countries, including cobblestone, brick, gravel, log and asphalt. Visitors were driven over these roads and through the lush gardens in the latest model cars.

"Rainbow" in the Round

After sunset, the three rings on top of the Rotunda were floodlighted, each with a different color. Every 8 seconds, the color on each ring changed. From our front porch, this was a beautiful sight year-round.

The Rotunda was air-conditioned, a luxury in those days. Inside the building were mural-lined walls and, of course, the latest Fords, Lincolns and Mercurys. In the center stood a 45-foot-diameter rotating globe.

One wing contained the company's archives, and the other housed a comfortable modern movie theater and stage. The "Ford Sunday Evening Hour" concerts were often broadcast nationwide from this stage.

During the day, films were shown continuously—industrial newsreels, cartoons and fabulous travel adventures. As a frequent visitor, I learned more about industry, geography and current events than I did in grade school. The Rotunda was open to all at no cost, even to kids like me in shorts and dirty tennis shoes…as long as we behaved. The only time I was reprimanded was when I hooked up the battery cable on a Lincoln so I could sit inside and listen to the radio.

Tours of the nearby Rouge Plant, the biggest industrial complex in the world at that time, left from the Rotunda every hour. The tour included the steel mill, glass plant and engine building, always ending at the final assembly line, which to me was the most interesting.

War Brought Changes

The Rotunda closed during World War II and was used as an office to run Ford Motor Company's war production. But after the war, the Rotunda reopened in all its glory, and the popular annual Christmas show was held once again.

Long lines formed outside to see Santa's World. Santa, animated nursery rhyme displays, dolls and miniature Christmas lights (rare then) were all viewed with awe. By the '50s, I was married and introduced my own children to the wonders I'd known as a child. They still talk about it.

But it was the Christmas decorations and the added roof that led to the Rotunda's demise. On November 9, 1962, roofers were repairing the roofing deck when somehow their hot tar kettles ignited the cork insulation. The flames spread to the combustible Christmas decorations being unpacked for the approaching holiday season. In only 45 minutes, the historic showplace was reduced to a heap of ashes.

The next day I walked through the rubble in disbelief, overwhelmed by the memories of my happy childhood hours there, and of my wife and children's visits to Santa.

The Rotunda was never rebuilt, but to us, it will always be the most beautiful building in the world. ☎

I Wore a Shower Curtain To the Prom

*By Verdene Langford
Bettendorf, Iowa*

WHEN SENIOR PROM rolled around in the spring of 1945, finding a date, dress and shoes became a unique challenge. World War II wasn't quite over, and many of the boys who would have been eligible seniors had been drafted. (Uncle Sam gave them credit for their last semester of high school.)

Rationing was still in effect, too, and that meant three pairs of shoes a year was the limit, so no one was going to use their stamps for dancing shoes. There were a few plastic shoes available—they didn't require ration stamps, but they were expensive and not very durable. Of course, they only had to last 1 night.

For me, the choice of dresses was also limited. I was 5-foot-2 and weighed 97 pounds! After talking it over with Mom, she agreed to make my dress, so off I went to buy a pattern and fabric.

The war had also narrowed the selection of fabrics, since manufacturers were still supplying the armed forces. I made an exhaustive search of the yard goods departments at all the local stores in Rock Island, Illinois and couldn't find anything I wanted. They had dotted Swiss...but I'd worn a dotted Swiss dress to my junior prom. As a senior, I wanted something more sophisticated.

Then I saw it—a pale yellow taffeta, almost the color of fresh corn silk. The texture was perfect, and there was just enough for a dress. The only thing was, the material was a shower curtain!

I didn't care, though...I bought it and took it home, prepared to convince Mom that she could make a prom dress from a shower curtain.

She readily agreed. After all, she'd been "making do" for years, sewing our underpants out of flour sacks and our coats out of hand-me-down men's suits.

Great Job, Mom!

When Mom finished sewing, the dress was perfect. It had a sweetheart neckline, cap sleeves, a nipped-in waist and a billowing skirt that swished when I walked or danced.

But it was a bit too plain...it needed a little something more. That's when a dear neighbor came up with yards of black velvet ribbon for a beautiful sash. We made a big double bow with long streamers in back that gave a bustle effect. The look was completed with long, over-the-elbow black gloves.

All I needed then was some jewelry. My best friend, Pat, suggested I wear her mother's antique cameo on a black ribbon around my neck. It was the perfect accent. (I'm not sure Pat's mother *knew* her daughter had loaned out a family heirloom, but it was returned safely.)

On the night of the prom, I was certain I had the most beautiful dress there...and the most unique. I doubt anyone else there was dressed in a shower curtain. ☎

OUT OF THE SHOWER. Author (top left) had other dresses, but there was nothing like that pale yellow number that got her to the prom.

I Was a Messenger To the Stars

By Patricia Martin, La Quinta, California

CAN ANY GIRL ever be the same after she's been asked by Tyrone Power to run down to the corner drugstore to buy him some cigarettes?

I'm certainly not. I worked at Columbia Pictures for 5 years in the '50s, and I came away with numerous memories of people I would *never* have met under any circumstances.

It started in 1955, when I moved from Long Beach, California to Hollywood. Like just about every other 19-year-old then, I wanted a job with a movie studio.

I made the usual rounds but saved Columbia Pictures for last, because it was only a few blocks from where I lived at the Hollywood Studio Club.

The Studio Club was founded in the '20s as a haven for aspiring young women who came to Hollywood. I figured the girls there had all applied long before I'd arrived, but I filled out an application anyway.

As I was leaving, the personnel director told me, "Just forget you ever came in. I may call you tomorrow, or then again, I may *never* call you." Three days later, he called asking if I'd like to be a messenger girl. *Would I!*

I discovered there were strict rules for studio employees. Harry Cohn, who owned Columbia Pictures, insisted no employee could be photographed on the lot with anyone. And we were *never* to ask actors for autographs.

This was cause for instant dismissal. Also, no employee could accept a part in any film…they'd have to quit their job before that.

The first sound stage I walked onto was the set for *Queen Bee*, starring Joan Crawford. I had a telegram to deliver, but as I edged my way up to where she was standing, an assistant grabbed it out of my hand, saying, "Is that for Miss Crawford? *I'll* give it to her for you."

Thrilled by Joan

I was crushed. But there were to be many more deliveries. One day on the back lot, Miss Crawford smiled at me and said, "I'm certainly keeping you busy these days." I was thrilled!

One of the most stunning sets I ever saw was the ballroom set for *The Eddy Duchin Story*, starring Tyrone Power and Kim Novak. It was the hottest day of the summer, and all the extras were sweltering in their fancy evening wear and mink coats. (If you saw the picture, you'd have never known it.)

Columbia was a small studio, and everyone knew one another. Back then, employees still worked on Saturdays, and a lot of us kids in the message center would go over to the makeup department and get made up if we were going out.

Many also volunteered as guinea pigs for the apprentice makeup artists, who'd practice putting the most gory-looking scars on us with lots of fake blood.

If I had to pick a favorite personality, it would be Dick Powell, who was a joy to be around.

His office was on the second floor, and every morning I'd hear him get off the elevator singing at the top of his lungs. At the time, he was directing his wife, June Allyson, and Jack Lemmon in *You Can't Run Away From It*.

One day June said to me, "All my life I've wanted red hair like yours."

"You'd have to take all these freckles with it," I quipped.

"I wouldn't mind that one bit!" she laughed.

Once I delivered a script to Cornel Wilde, who talked me into holding it while he practiced retrieving it with a

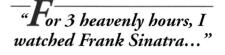

"*For 3 heavenly hours, I watched Frank Sinatra…*"

bullwhip for a picture he was doing with Jane Russell!

But my biggest thrill was when some stage hands sneaked me into a booth overlooking a recording stage. For 3 heavenly hours, I watched Frank Sinatra record *The Lady Is a Tramp*, *I Didn't Know What Time It Was* and *I Could Write a Book* for the soundtrack of *Pal Joey*.

I didn't know it at the time, but those would be the last years of the "old" Hollywood studios as we knew them. Before too long, Columbia's sound stages would be filming television commercials, and one by one, studios were being taken over by corporations.

The Hollywood of today can't compare with the studio system I knew. But it was certainly wonderful while it lasted! ☎

PART OF THE JOB. Patricia Martin (left) met stars like Tyrone Power (top, at the piano in *The Eddy Duchin Story*) while working.

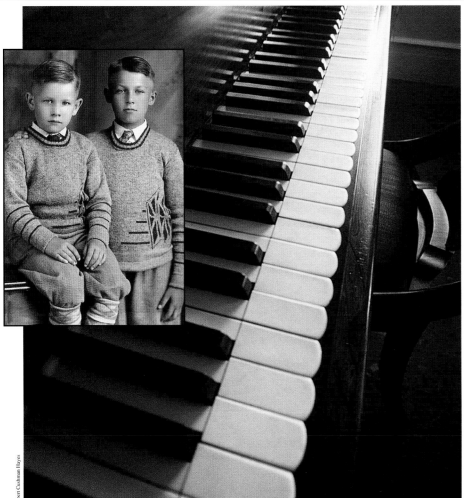

Robert Cushman Hayes

BUDDING VIRTUOSOS Wally Zahn and big brother Raymond posed for the photo at far left in 1930, when they were 7 and 10. Today, Wally admits Ray was the better piano player, saying, "It always amazed me that he could play *Manhattan Serenade* by heart."

Dreaded Piano Lessons
Finally Paid Off

By Wally Zahn, Rancho Viejo, Texas

WHEN I WAS a boy in West Bend, Wisconsin in the '20s and '30s, Mother made me take piano lessons. I'll tell you one thing—Liberace I wasn't!

My lessons were at 7 o'clock on Wednesday mornings. I told Mother this was too early, but she left for work at 6:30 and wanted me out of the house by the time she was gone. That gave me half an hour to walk the mile to my lesson, half an hour for my lesson and another half hour to walk the mile to school.

Boy, I remember that walk as if it were yesterday! I started across a field and through the cattails along the Milwaukee River, then up an embankment to some railroad tracks, over the river on the railroad trestle, then about eight more blocks to my lesson.

Before I left, Mother would give me 50¢ for the lesson, and I'd put it in my back pocket—the one with a button. The first thing I did when I got to the piano teacher's house was to give her the money. Mother always wanted to make sure everyone got paid.

My brother, Ray, went through the same routine, but his lessons were on Thursday mornings. An awful lot of quarters and 50-cent pieces went into our back pockets during those years.

Recitals Were Vital

One requirement, of course, was that we had to play in the recitals the teacher put on every once in a while. I guess it was to show that all those quarters and 50-cent pieces were paying off.

They were usually held in the parlor of one of the local churches. On the day of the big event, our teacher would get all gussied up in a flouncy dress with a corsage made up of every kind of flower that grew in her backyard.

She'd stand next to the piano like a chanteuse, waving a big lace kerchief around and introducing each of us as if the audience was really going to hear something.

Some kids didn't do too badly, I guess—especially the girls in their fancy dresses. A few of the boys, though, wearing their best knickers and their hair all slicked down with Vaseline, had trouble—*lots* of trouble!

The parents sat there with smiles on their faces, but deep down, they were hoping against hope that their kids wouldn't sound like they had at home.

Although they all clapped after each selection, I think many were counting the kids and seeing how many more renditions they'd have to sit through.

Mother Knew Best

Mothers put a lot more faith in their kids than we ever realize—and usually it's not misplaced.

My mother knew darn well I'd never be a concert pianist, but she also knew the training would provide me with a source of personal enjoyment for the rest of my life. And it has.

Last summer, my wife and I were visiting Mother in her retirement home. Everyone had gathered in the dayroom for a community sing, but the piano player was nowhere to be found.

Since I was the only one there who knew the black keys from the white keys, I was elected. I played and played and played, klinkers and all, and everyone sang and sang and sang.

I'll tell you, for however long it was, I felt like Eddy Duchin, Liberace and Van Cliburn all rolled up into one.

Marilyn and I looked at my mother and saw that her eyes were full of tears. She had a "mother's" look on her face and she kept whispering, "That's my son. That's my son."

All of a sudden, those quarters and 50-cent pieces I'd carried to my piano teacher were worth more than a million dollars. ☎

NUMBER, PLEASE. Mary Gould was chief operator of the telephone exchange in Englishtown, New Jersey in the '30s. Here she's seated at the board in 1939, ready to plug in the next call.

Mom Was The Friendly 'Hello Girl'

By Sally Smith Lewis, Freehold, New Jersey

THERE'S A MAGIC we've lost with technology. It just isn't the same when you can press *one* button programmed on your phone to dial a friend and no voice intervenes.

To get a call through back in the '30s, you had to turn a crank on the box in your home, which triggered a little shutter in the telephone office. Then—no matter how many times you turned—you had to wait for the operator to notice the call and plug in, asking, "Number, please!"

Often there was only one operator on duty, and many a customer lost patience during very busy times. But the *magic* was the personal attention and care with which the "hello girls" performed their duties.

My earliest memories are of sitting in a big brown leather chair in the telephone office in Englishtown, New Jersey, where Mom was the chief operator.

Father had died when I was 3 and my sister was 9. In order to make a living and keep her family close, Mom, Mary Gould, became a telephone operator. The switchboard office was the front room of our house, which meant Mom served as night operator. I grew up with "Number, please…" and "Operator…" resounding in my ears.

Some nights she'd roll a cot into the office near the switch-board, but more often she slept with me. My room had a big bell that clanged when there was a call and kept clanging until Mom ran downstairs to answer it.

I also learned how to operate the switchboard—a skill that would later help finance my college education. I memorized all the numbers and still recall many of them—#1 was the firehouse, #2 was Al Young's garage, #3 was the Hamilton's Drugstore coin box. And on it went as far as #199.

There were four party lines with the letters J, R, M and W. Some of the rural lines had as many as eight parties, so there was lots of eavesdropping and many arguments.

The telephone office was also the clearinghouse for community news. If the fire siren sounded, the shutters on the

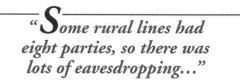

> "*S*ome rural lines had eight parties, so there was lots of eavesdropping…"

switchboard started falling furiously as folks called in to see where the fire was. One afternoon there was a grass fire behind the basket factory—try saying *that* tongue twister 40 times! Operators convulsed with laughter as they reported a fire "in the bass behind the gasket factory" or "in the gas behind the grass bactory".

Englishtown operators knew their customers well. The local doctor, for example, was famous for his temper if awakened in the night or called away from his Wednesday evening prayer meeting. I recall Mom pulling the plug, then calmly reconnecting him with his patient when he'd finished his tirade.

The light in the telephone office burned all night. People in need felt free to drop in and ask for help. Linemen out troubleshooting would stop to get warm and have a cup of coffee.

Because Mom had a sympathetic ear, lonely hearts found a friend in her, both by telephone and in person. Grateful subscribers often sent gifts, usually candy or fruit and occasionally a live goose.

Mom was also the kind of person who moved to help when she saw a need, so she was surprised when recognition was given for a "heroic" adventure in the summer of 1933.

When a severe thunderstorm crippled telephone services, Mom put my sister and me in charge of the switchboard, then took off in our little yellow "flivver" to report the damage between Englishtown and Freehold.

We later learned that she'd been in considerable danger from fallen trees, live wires and broken telephone poles.

I didn't realize Mom was a "heroine" until telephone officials announced she'd receive a silver medal and $250 at a testimonial dinner in Asbury Park. I got out of school *and* had a new dress with a matching lace hat Mom made me.

The calls Mom made weren't the cordless or conference calls of today. But they had the magic of a person who was interested in each call, knew everyone in town, would call you back when the line was free…and could keep a secret. After the local office in Englishtown changed to a dial system, the "hello girl" became just a pleasant memory. ☎

My Years with 'Truth or Consequences'

By William Burch
Sacramento, California

Sometimes good luck and timing alter the course of our lives. Such was the case with me one day in 1945. My new bride and I were returning to Hollywood from our wedding in her hometown of Rushville, Indiana.

We stopped in Las Vegas for the night, and I called my office at NBC. It was lucky that I called in—my boss, Howard Wiley, wanted me to handle an assignment for *Truth or Consequences*, one of the most popular radio programs in the country.

Back in California, I met Ralph Edwards at his home in Beverly Hills. Ralph told me about an idea for a special broadcast to honor a wounded Marine at a hospital in Honolulu.

The Marine's hometown was Salem, Oregon. Ralph's idea was to have the young serviceman, through the magic of radio, "walk" down the main street of Salem. On his walk, the Marine would greet the mayor, druggist, barber who cut his hair, a buddy from high school and, finally, his parents.

My job was to go to Salem and line up all the people for this remote broadcast, then record background sounds to add realism and bring the Marine as "close to home" as possible.

The magic worked—that show won awards. A month later, I went to work for Ralph Edwards Productions as writer/director for *Truth of Consequences*. The next few years were a ball!

There were four of us "idea men" who met once a week at Ralph's house to come up with the gags and stunts that made the show so popular.

Of *thousands* of stunts we did, the two funniest and probably best-remembered were those we called "Amateur Comedian" and "Thump Melons".

The Amateur Comedian stunt required a woman to read a very bad joke from a card. It was a joke *no one* would laugh at…but when the woman read the

WHAT A LIFE! Ralph Edwards' *This is Your Life* began in '48, giving him two popular radio shows that became TV hits.

punch line, the audience howled.

What she didn't know was that every time she read the punch line, we'd dunk her husband in a tank of water just out of her sight! She'd tell the joke over and over without the slightest idea of why the audience was laughing so hard.

The Thump Melons stunt started with Ralph asking for a woman volunteer from the audience who thought she was a good shopper.

After being shown a table with five smooth-skinned melons, she was blindfolded and told to pick out the ripest of the melons by thumping them.

What the woman didn't know was that after she was blindfolded, we substituted her husband's bald head for one of the melons. Believe me, no matter what the woman said, she got a laugh!

As funny as those stunts were, the most talked-about and publicized of all was one we called "Mr. Hush".

The March of Dimes had asked Ralph to come up with a fund-raising promotion. Rather than "just another stunt", Ralph got the idea of having a well-known personality record a jingle that would contain a clue to his identity. Each week the clue would change, getting easier, as more prizes were added.

But who would be Mr. Hush? We didn't want to disguise his voice, so most familiar radio and movie personalities were eliminated. It wasn't until the night before the show was broadcast that Ralph and I finally decided on boxer Jack Dempsey.

The two of us were the only ones who knew the identity of Mr. Hush. For the next 8 weeks, hundreds of thousands of people sent in donations along with their guesses. I don't remember who finally figured it out, but the March of Dimes was the big winner.

Later, there was a Miss Hush (actress Clara Bow) and The Walking Man (Jack Benny, so named because of his hometown, Waukegan, Illinois).

In those days, working for Ralph was a family affair. But a few years later when television came along, one show a week became five. Seven employees grew to 50…and the office over Ralph's garage became an entire building.

After that, at least for me, it was never quite the same. ☎

WARMIN' UP THE CROWD. "This picture shows the warm-up before airtime on *Truth or Consequences*," explains William Burch (far right with host Ralph Edwards and co-worker Jay). "We had a routine—Ralph pretended to throw a cup of water into the audience from the stage, then we rushed down the aisle and started 'mopping' some poor woman with our handkerchiefs. Meantime, another staffer, Al, went farther back in the theater and chose a pretty girl to mop…he even sat on her lap 'til Ralph yelled, 'Hey, Al—the water's over here!' "

A Sip From The Dipper

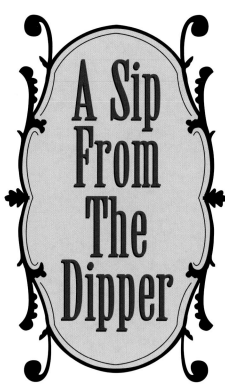

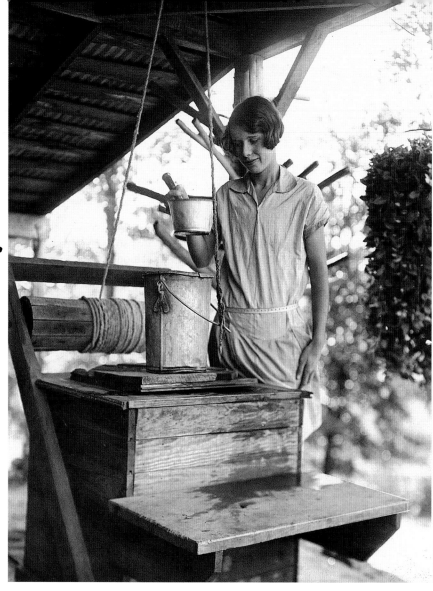

J.C. Allen and Son

By Monica Winston, Eliot, Maine

AT THE END of a hot summer day, it was such a treat to follow Grandpa to the well outside his and Grandma's Kensington, New Hampshire home. It overlooked a peaceful meadow that the cows had cropped until it resembled a manicured lawn.

While I peered over the edge at the damp rock walls and the dark, gleaming water below, Grandpa would attach the pail to the windlass. Down…down… down, the pail was slowly lowered. When it reached the water, it would float there for a second, then begin to sink out of sight.

"Don't lean too far—you might fall in!" Grandpa would warn. I was careful, because it was too easy to picture myself disappearing like that bucket.

Nonetheless, I was fascinated by this cave-like world with its underground stream and curious about something my brother had told me. He said that from the bottom of a well, you could see stars even in the daytime. Curious as I was, I wasn't about to go down there and try.

Up…up…up would come the tin pail as Grandpa cranked slowly and steadily. There was a real knack to doing this, because if you cranked too fast or jerkily, the pail came up half-empty.

There was a trick to carrying the water back to the house, too. That full pail demanded a smooth and easy gait or you'd slosh water on your legs and feet.

All the water used in my grandparents' house had to be carried inside. Two pails were always sitting by the kitchen sink—a fresh one for drinking and another for chores. Though all hot water had to be heated on the woodstove, Grandma's floors shone like china plates, and there wasn't a speck of dust to be found—not even on the dustpan!

On warm summer evenings, my brother, sister, cousins and I played hide-and-seek on the lawn while the grown-ups sat talking on chairs moved outside from the kitchen.

Eventually we kids got so thirsty we'd have to stop and get a drink of

> "*There was a trick to carrying the water back to the house…*"

that cold, crystal-clear water from the well. I can still remember the slightly metallic taste from the single dipper we took turns using.

Yes, it was only a drink of water… but somehow we went home refreshed and satisfied in ways hard to explain now. Curiously enough, at family reunions nowadays, we all agree that one of the most pleasurable memories from those days is the taste of cold well water straight from that dipper.

My grandparents felt blessed to have a well that provided an unfailing source of water even in the dustiest, driest summers. Even so, I'm sure that Grandma, with her passion for cleanliness, would have rejoiced in the modern convenience of hot-and-cold running water.

Still, there really was something special about that old well that can never be re-created. After all, I can't imagine my grandchildren ever saying with nostalgia, "Remember what it was like to get a drink from Grandma's faucet?"

I Was a Maid For the Mayo Family

By Sally Bunge Keithley
San Jose, California

FARM LIFE on our 160 acres in southeastern Minnesota was hard. Besides the endless chores Dad gave us, we helped our mother with the canning in summer and fall.

So, when my girlfriend Alice Smith and I graduated from Austin High School in 1932, we decided to travel north to the big city of Rochester and seek work as housekeeping maids.

It was my good fortune to be hired to work in the largest and most impressive mansion in town, the stone fortress of Dr. William James Mayo and his beloved wife, Hattie.

In 1914, Dr. Will, as he was called, and his younger brother, Dr. Charles Mayo, established the famous Mayo Clinic in downtown Rochester, just a few blocks from the mansion on College Avenue.

Exciting Place to Be

I was a first-floor maid at the mansion. My duties included cleaning the reception rooms, polishing all the silver in the family's extensive vault and serving meals to the Mayos.

It was an exciting place to be in those days. The clinic attracted many world leaders to Rochester, and the Mayos en-

tertained in lavish style. Dinner for fewer than 50 was considered informal.

The highlight of my 4 years working for the Mayos was decorating and serving at their 50th wedding anniversary on November 10, 1934.

Another exciting event for me was seeing President Franklin D. Roosevelt in his motorcade when he visited Rochester in 1934 to bestow humani-

tarian honors on the two Mayo brothers.

But the best part of my domestic duties was working on *North Star*, Dr. Will's river yacht, which cost $50,000 to build in the early '30s. It could sleep 12 and had a staff of three officers, a cook and a maid.

Took Yacht Trips

The yacht was kept in New Orleans in the winter. After he retired, Dr. Will and Hattie took guests up and down the Mississippi in summer. My favorite trip was the one we took down to the Missouri River and then to Kansas City.

Dr. Will sold the yacht in 1938, when the contrast between poverty and luxury in the country became more than he could stand. He donated the money to his clinic's social services to help the poor.

It was also in 1938 that I decided to leave the Mayos and enter nursing school. When I told Dr. Will of my ambition, he immediately picked up the telephone and made sure I got into the Kahler School of Nursing in Rochester.

I graduated in 1941 as a registered nurse and retired 30 years later after a career as a surgical nurse.

It was quite a life...especially for a farm girl who was the only one of my parents' four children to be born in a hospital. ☎

MAYO MANSION. For 4 years, the author (top) worked in the mansion of Dr. William Mayo (above). Dr. Will (far right) and his brother, Charles, were honored by President Roosevelt (on left) in 1934.

Brown Brothers

Itchy Knickers Came Up Short

By J.M. Henry, Newalla, Oklahoma

I GREW UP a country boy and went directly from diapers to overalls. I wore no other kind of clothing until my eighth-grade graduation in Wister, Oklahoma.

I would have worn overalls then, too, but the occasion was just too important. Mama went to town with some eggs and cream and traded them for a white shirt and the fanciest pair of robin's egg-blue pants I ever saw. That was the only time I was *proud* to change from my overalls.

But I'll never forget the day when I was 6 and Mama's insistence on a change in wardrobe caused a small family rebellion. I can still hear her voice:

"Jim, I'm warning you for the last time! Get in your room and let Elsie help you dress. Those are real fine clothes your Aunt Vickie brought you, and you ought to be proud to wear them to church."

I suppose just about everyone who's grown up poor has had better-off relatives pass along clothing their own kids no longer wore. In my case, that was Aunt Vickie.

"These are perfectly good clothes," she would say, "al-

KNICKERLESS. Jim Henry was wearing his favored overalls in the photo below, but if his mama had had her way, he'd have looked like the dapper chaps at left.

though they're no longer in style in the city. But you can get some real good wear out of them."

Oh, how I dreaded visits from Aunt Vickie...especially after the "perfectly good clothes" she brought me included a pair of knickerbockers.

It wasn't just that the pants were a cross between girls' bloomers and too-short boys' pants. The whole suit was made of pure wool and scratched like the dickens!

Stopping just below the knees, the pants bloused out over an elastic band. Long wool stockings came up under the band. I don't even want to talk about the dumb cap that completed the outfit!

To my mind, a boy needed overalls that hung loose so he could run free and have all the pockets he needed. For me, that meant my slingshot (or "bean flip", as we called it) was always handy in the right rear pocket and the ammunition in the left rear. The left front pocket was for miscellaneous stuff like fishing corks and hooks, string and my precious Hike-O-Meter, which was a prize for selling Cloverine salve.

The right front pocket was reserved for my trusty Barlow knife. On the bib, a thin pocket on the left side held a pencil. Next to that was a pocket for my hand-me-down Big Ben dollar watch. Sometimes I used that pocket to carry baby snakes

---

"A boy needed overalls so he could run free..."

---

to scare the teacher and those silly girls in school. But there would be no snakes in my new knickerbocker suit.

"Mama, I'm not gonna wear them stupid old clothes to church," I whined. "Everybody will laugh and make fun of me."

"Jim Henry, if you know what's good for you, you'll get those clothes on right now!" Mama was Dutch-Irish, and Dutch-Irish folks just don't lose arguments...at least in our house.

"Aw, Mom," my sister, Elsie, pleaded, "why don't you let him wear his overalls? All the other boys do."

Bless her heart. My problems with Mama would have been much worse if it weren't for Elsie. But even she was powerless to help me just then.

Yes, I did wear "them stupid old clothes" to church—jacket, cap and all. But I didn't wear them *into* church!

When Mama and Papa walked inside, Elsie held me back. Taking me by the hand, she quickly led me home, where she pulled off the stupid clothes, put my overalls back on, brushed my hair and returned me to church.

All this time, not a word passed between us. But, oh, how I adored my big sister that day. It would be nice if every little boy had a big sister who understood that even a 6-year-old is subject to peer pressure.

I can't recall the consequences of our little rebellion. But I do know that those hated knickerbockers were never mentioned at our house ever again! ☎

When Knickers Brought No Snickers

By Ken Randall, Tucson, Arizona

ONE AFTERNOON I settled into my lounge chair to watch a golf match on TV and noticed that one of the competitors was wearing knickers. *Oh my,* I thought, *they're coming back!*

The illusion was shattered when the announcer identified the man as Payne Stewart—dressed in his "plus fours". These sports knickers, worn by golfers and English gentlemen, are longer than what I remember wearing as a boy …and if any kid of my day wore knickers this baggy, they were probably hand-me-downs from a relative.

No, in the '30s we wore *real* knickers made of corduroy as durable as Bessemer steel—although the knees could blow out at the first tackle during a sandlot football game.

To counter this tendency, mothers sewed patches of leather or corduroy onto the knees of their sons' knickers. Fortunately, this wasn't looked upon as a sign of poverty—even the richest kid in my hometown of Morristown, Pennsylvania wore patches on his knees.

Pockets Sprung Leaks

The pockets in knickers also seemed to tear out quickly. We liked to stuff our pockets far beyond their capacity—especially the back pockets, which held leather pouches of marbles with the drawstring hanging stylishly out.

If you played "for keeps" and Dame Fortune had smiled on you, the pouch began to swell beyond the limits of the pocket's endurance, and *presto!*—an-

other hole. If you just played for "funsies", the shape of the pouch never changed.

Every adolescent boy had to have a pair of "high tops" to go with his knickers. These leather boots laced up to the knee and had a leather pocket sewn onto the side containing a small pocketknife. As soon as the boots were brought home, fathers rubbed neetsfoot oil onto the surface to preserve and waterproof the leather.

High tops were in vogue from October through April. During other times of the year, we wore long wool stockings to cover our calves. These stockings had an elastic band at the knee to keep them up. The stockings and woolen knee bands of the knickers often initiated unbearable itching. It was normal to see a student doing "times tables" with a pencil in one hand and scratching at his leg with the other.

I used to think my mother had the X-ray vision of Superman, because when I'd walk through the front door, she'd call from the back bedroom upstairs, "Pull up your socks!"

I wore knick-

FASHION PLATE. When Ken Randall was a boy (right), knickers were the style.

ers until the eighth grade, when I received my first pair of long pants in the form of a pale blue "slack suit". I couldn't resist parading up and down the alley behind our house to show off my new pants and sports shirt to envious playmates.

Had 'Em Pegged

In my teen years, I graduated to pants that were "pegged". The normal circumference of long trousers at the top of the shoe was 18 inches. Pegging reduced this anywhere from 17 to 14 inches, and "Whatcha peggin'?" was a common question among youths.

"Peggin' 17" was a mere acknowledgment of the style, while "peggin' 14" might cut off circulation to the foot.

This was also the era of the zoot suit, though none of my friends had the money for such an extreme fashion statement.

We *did* affect another form of jitterbug fashion, though—a long chain that hung in an arc from belt loop to knee and back up into the side pocket. The chain never held more than a house key—but it showed you were "hip".

When I see young people tucking and rolling their jeans to hug the ankle, I'm tempted to tell them they're emulating the styles of *my* youth…but that would probably bring the practice to a screeching halt.

Besides, I doubt any of them would understand if I walked up and asked, "Hey, whatcha peggin'?"

Grocer's Son Has Shelves of Memories

By John Deden, Missouri City, Texas

MY FATHER was a prosperous young grocer. He started his own store, complete with an attached pharmacy and soda fountain, before entering the Marines and World War I.

When he came back from the war, he again owned and operated his store, Deden's Grocery & Market, in Fort Smith, Arkansas. I entered the picture a little later, working in my dad's store in the mid- to late '30s.

"Grocery" was really a misnomer. Dad also presided over a full-service meat counter and bakery. He offered top-quality beef, pork, chicken and turkey, and his cakes, pies and breads always sold out before Saturday was over.

It was a small independent store and provided very personal service with Dad, me or another employee waiting on each customer. There was free delivery to anywhere in town or its outskirts, sometimes a distance of 20 miles —regardless of the order size.

> *"Dad and I were the only ones to cut meats or cheeses..."*

Dad especially catered to the elderly, poor and pensioners. One little old lady, when she wasn't feeling up to the two-block walk to the store, had a neighbor phone in her order.

It usually was a 5-cent pint of milk, six eggs, a quarter pound of bacon or salt pork and a 5-cent loaf of bread—her week's food for about $2. Then the other grocery/delivery boy or I drove the order to her on our shiny green and chrome bicycles.

Our customers were special, and we got to know them well.

Customers Were Friends

"Aunt Mandy" Tinsley (not a relative) lived in a tiny house at a "V" in the main railroad tracks at the edge of town. I'd guess she was at least 90, but she and a young helper would trudge the 5 to 7 miles to our store to place her order. Phones were a "pure waste", she said.

Her tiny house and property were a gift from the railroad to her and her husband, who had been a Pullman porter or conductor for about 50 years, never missing a single run. The property was theirs, free, until they died.

Mom, Dad and I looked forward to her visits, because she and her husband had known several important people, including a President, congressmen and railroad executives. She was so dignified, well-read and well-spoken that she was one of our favorites. We took her a big basket of food at Christmas and, perhaps, Thanksgiving.

Engineer Loved Speed

Then there was Old Man Miller, a retired railroad engineer of local fame. He and a few other engineers raced their passenger train engines to see who could take certain curves at the fastest speed without derailing. He enjoyed telling Dad that he took one curve at the highest speed of any of them.

On occasion, he appeared at the store in bandages after an attempt when the train jumped the tracks. He often ended up in hot water for his escapades. I think the railroad breathed a sigh of relief when he retired.

During busy times, work at the store could be hairy and fun. One of us grocery boys would man the mechanical adding machine while Dad and the other boy retrieved articles from the shelves for customers.

They'd yell out the name of the item and throw it over the head of the customer to the person at the adding machine. It was pure joy. We made one-handed catches, two-handed catches and catches high in the air or off to one side, but we *never missed.*

We even tossed meat packages from behind the meat counter. Dad and I were the only ones to cut meats or cheeses. It was a cardinal sin to cut these items more than 2 or 3 ounces off the requested

two of bread for his lunch. Because Mr. Pitts was usually in a hurry, Dad tried to have these items ready. Sometimes Mr. Pitts agonized over his choices, and Dad and he would talk about what sort of day they expected to have.

A bit later, other workers and often teachers came in to hurriedly buy lunch items. So, you see, the store *had* to be open and available.

Our store usually closed about 7 p.m. on weekdays because, again, working people on their way home might stop by for dinner items.

Saturdays Were Long

Saturdays were very long days. We started at 6 a.m., when we did our daily dusting and straightening before opening, and we didn't close until 10 p.m. or maybe midnight, if business was brisk.

Through it all, I thought it was a joyous but tiring time, especially when I turned 12 and could learn proper meat cutting, weighing, running the adding machine, pricing items in the store and—best of all—eventually learn to drive the delivery car.

Sometime after Thanksgiving, Mom, Dad, a friend or two of mine and I would go to the Ozark Mountains and cut down a few cedar Christmas trees on free land. Some were for sale or gifts and one big tree was designated for our home.

We'd also pick up stray branches that Dad would place on a hot plate in the store so they'd heat up and give off the sweet, pungent pine aroma.

Nothing Fishy

Dad allowed no fish in the store because their odor polluted the otherwise enticing aromas of candy, cheese, pickles, kraut and baked goods.

The end of those very personalized independent stores, including grocery, clothing and dry goods stores, occurred slowly but surely as the marketing giants took over.

With increasing supply and demand, small stores couldn't compete. It became a lot easier and less costly to buy food by the carload than by the bicycle load, so an era passed.

Thanks, Dad, for memories of good times and bad, of good aromas, togetherness and of customers who were as much friends as customers. Thanks for giving me the pride and delights of being a grocer's son. ☏

DAD'S STORE. Otto Deden posed in his Fort Smith, Arkansas store (above), below one of his son John's model planes. The outside of the store is seen at left in a photo taken from across Towson Avenue. John worked in the store in the '30s.

On cold winter days and nights, Dad heated the store with a small, coal-fed potbellied stove in the back near the bakery. He'd installed a "Dutch oven", a round oven surrounding the chimney, and it was very hot—for warming, frying and baking.

Late at night, after the store closed, Dad sometimes brought out a pan of his excellent buttermilk biscuits and put them in the Dutch oven. Next he sliced off chunks of salt pork, washed them to remove the excess salt and popped them in the oven with the biscuits.

From the ice-cold meat counter, he'd bring out a big slab of real country butter, a bottle of fresh farm milk and, from his ever-ready cabinet, a jar of jam or jelly. Sometimes Mother joined us and we'd have a midnight party with family and friends.

Dad opened his store at 6:30 a.m. because of Mr. Pitts, a shoe salesman at Hunt's Dry Goods Store. He'd come by at about 6:30 to buy a piece of cheese, a slice of bologna and a piece or

quantity. We told the customer the weight and asked if that was okay. If the customer said no, we'd cut another piece to their satisfaction and hope someone else would buy that miscut piece.

However, if the miscut was cheese and needed a slender slice taken off, Dad and we grocery boys feasted on it together with some of Dad's great bread and sour pickles. Of course, that was after all the customers had left. That was a real treat!

149

Bring Back the Creature

THE GROVE THEATER in downtown Beech Grove, Indiana was the neighborhood theater I knew best. It was packed with kids on Friday and Saturday nights.

Every seat would be taken, at least temporarily. Often, there were two of us in one seat. The noise could drown out the sound from the screen.

The ushers never ushered us *to* our seats. But they did have flashlights and tried, mostly unsuccessfully, to keep order. A beam of light in your face was your only warning before being ushered *out*.

There was one picture, however, that commanded our full attention, *Creature From the Black Lagoon* in 1954. We were always on the alert during that movie, as one never knew when the monster might slither from the murky water and onto the row of seats in front of you, aided by that fad of the '50s—3-D and the accompanying cardboard glasses (below).

The Grove has been gone for almost 40 years. But all I have to do is close my eyes, and I'm back there on Friday night in the '50s.
—*James Johnson
Greenwood, Indiana*

THE MOVIES WERE MAGIC

What fun we had at the picture show!

people from the surrounding community. In fact, they became so popular that we added a second show.

One Saturday night in 1933, the featured film was *Adorable* starring Janet Gaynor. While the movie ran on one projector, I threaded the second one and kept an eye on the screen.

To my surprise, an image of flames shot across the screen—the first projector was burning the film! I quickly shut it off and started the second one. That cut 10 minutes off the end of the first reel, but no one complained.

As the movie's title promised, Janet Gaynor was adorable in that film…but its plot was so sketchy, the omission went unnoticed. —*Harvey Marks
Littleton, Colorado*

Fans Got Too Close to Star

IN 1941, when my buddy Billy Morris and I were both 12, our favorite cowboy movie star was Gene Autry.

Were we ever excited to learn he was coming to our town of Enid, Oklahoma to promote a new movie at the Cherokee Theater! Gene would arrive on a private plane at Woodring Airport, a few miles east of town.

On the big day, Billy and I skipped school and rode our bicycles out to the airport to await the plane.

When it arrived, local photographers gathered around and took pictures of Gene stepping out onto the runway.

They also got a picture of Billy and

me standing on either side of our hero with his hands on our shoulders. Billy and I were delighted beyond words.

The next day, Billy, Gene and I were on the front page of the *Enid Morning News*. Unfortunately, the paper came out *after* we'd both explained our previous day's absence was due to illness.

That newspaper photo earned us each a trip down the hall to see the principal. Even so, Gene Autry will always be my favorite cowboy.
—*Perry Choate, Pampa, Texas*

Dropped Rug and Ran

MY COUSIN Gertrude and I often went to the movies together in the '20s. One evening we did something so outrageous we've laughed about it ever since.

That was the era of the raccoon coat, and Gertrude's father had bought her one, which she proudly wore.

It was impossible to wrinkle or crush those coats, but Gertrude was extremely careful with hers and usually held it

ULTIMATE USHER. Harvey Boese "looked pretty sharp" in his head usher's uniform in the '20s, says his wife, Elsie, of West Allis, Wisconsin. He worked at the Modjeska Theatre on Milwaukee's Mitchell Street. Elsie recalls the aroma of hot buttered popcorn, adding, "The films were exciting and priced right."

Fire Didn't Hurt Film

IN HIGH SCHOOL during the late 1920s, I ran a 16mm silent movie projector. In 1930, when I went on to college in Naperville, Illinois, I volunteered to be campus projectionist.

There was no movie theater in town, so our Saturday night shows were popular not only with students, but with in her lap while watching the movie.

Pictures were shown continuously then, and we arrived in the middle of a feature film at the State Theater in Scranton, Pennsylvania. When we reached that portion of the movie where we'd come in, we got up to leave.

Gertrude had her bulky raccoon coat over her arm, and when we got to the lobby, she discovered that somehow, on our way out, she'd brushed off a man's toupee and it got caught in her sleeve!

Instead of telling an usher our story, which any sane person would do, we walked back down the aisle in the dark, plopped the toupee on the first bald head we saw, then ran for the exit!

Over the years, we've giggled many a time at the consternation that gentleman must have felt if we chose the wrong bald head. —*Josephine Dunn Newark Valley, New York*

Cisco's Most Loyal Sidekick
DURING the late '40s and early '50s, my sisters and I eagerly awaited Saturday afternoons at the Beacon Theater in Omaha, Nebraska.

An ardent fan of the Cisco Kid and Pancho, I often imagined myself riding side by side with them through the desert—always arriving just in time to save someone from danger.

My world changed when the actor who played Cisco was hospitalized. His illness wasn't life-threatening, but to me, it was disastrous—Pancho and I could not be effective without him.

While Cisco was healing, I sent a get-well card to him in the hospital. In return, he sent me a signed postcard (at right). The jubilation I felt upon its arrival cannot be described!

We continued going to the Beacon, but my exuberance was dampened until Cisco returned to action. Then (in my mind, anyway) Pancho and I went to the corral, mounted our horses and rode off into the sunset with our hero. —*Pauline Martin Eagle Rock, Missouri*

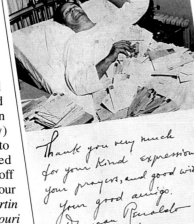

OH, CISCO! When actor Duncan Renaldo, better known as the Cisco Kid, was in the hospital (at left), Pauline Martin sent him a get-well card. The Kid answered Pauline's card as well as many others, and soon he, Pancho, Pauline and all the other Cisco Kid fans were back in the saddle again.

She Towered Over Other Fans
ONE DAY in 1946, my friends and I went to the old Gary Theatre in Gary, Indiana to see a Gene Autry picture. During the intermission, Gene's sidekick, Smiley Burnette, made a personal appearance.

Fans were invited backstage to have their picture taken with Smiley and get his autograph. I was 16 at the time, and my friends dared me to stand in line with all those little kids waiting to have their picture snapped with Smiley.

Taking them up on the dare, I felt both excited and embarrassed. I laugh now when I think of me standing in line, a good head taller than those little kids.

Still, I'm glad I took that dare—when I look at this picture of Smiley and me (at right), it reminds me of the unforgettable fun of old-time movies.

—*Hazel Miller, Terre Haute, Indiana*

Secret Pocket Came in Handy
WE LIVED in West Los Angeles when I was 10 years old. My fondest memory is of taking my weekly allowance and heading for Hollywood on an old red streetcar.

One block east of Hollywood and Vine was a small movie theater called The Hitching Post. For 2 bits, you could see two full-length Westerns, four serials and a whole bunch of cartoons. My heroes were the Lone Ranger, Lash LaRue, the Cisco Kid and Gene Autry.

The ushers always checked to see if we kids brought a six-shooter cap gun. If so, it got hung up on the wall until the show was over—otherwise, things just got too rowdy inside.

One Christmas my folks gave me a nice long jacket. I asked

SMILE, SMILEY. When Gene Autry's sidekick, Smiley "Frog" Burnette, made a personal appearance in 1946 (above), Hazel Miller was there. Read Hazel's magical movie memory above left.

Mom to sew a little pocket inside where I could hide a tiny derringer cap pistol!

I remember the anticipation (and the apprehension) the first time I smuggled my cap gun into the theater. At just the right moment, I let those bad guys have it between the eyes!

The ushers hunted high and low but never found out who had the gun. I was the envy of all my sidekicks. What a great way to spend a Saturday afternoon! —*Daniel Monahan Mission Viejo, California*

The Hills Were Alive, And Alive, and...
MY HUSBAND and I moved from Illinois to Santa Clara, California in 1966. The first time we went to San Jose, we noticed *The Sound of Music* was playing at the beautiful Circle Theater.

We didn't have much money, but we just *had* to see that movie before it left town.

What a joke. *The Sound of Music* played in that theater for over 2 years! In fact, the movie made so much money, they were able to build two more theaters. —*Janet Lusch Vandalia, Illinois*

The Day We 'Crashed' the Grand

By Bruce Ferguson, Lakeview, Arkansas

AS A 7-year-old in 1938, I spent my Saturdays at the American Theater in Evansville, Indiana. The American was a "second-run" movie house where my buddies and I enjoyed cowboy matinees.

"First-run" movies like *Snow White and the Seven Dwarfs* and *Gone with the Wind* were shown at other theaters located farther downtown, like the Grand. Those movie palaces also featured live Big Bands and popular singing groups like The Ink Spots.

Of course, the Grand was out of our price range, but we didn't care because it didn't show cowboy movies. Besides, the management wasn't too crazy about patrons who brought their own popcorn from home and sometimes stood on their seats to see better!

One Saturday afternoon, though, curiosity got the best of us. In spite of instructions from our mothers, my friends and I left the American matinee early, ran the three blocks down Main Street to the Grand and managed to sneak in the side door.

Once inside, we were awestruck! None of us had ever seen anything like it—the aisles were covered in carpet, not linoleum. It was just like the principal's office.

Not only was the Grand carpeted, but each row had a tiny aisle light near the floor so you wouldn't trip over the feet of someone in the end seat, dumping his popcorn and making him cry.

The domed ceiling, with its painted fleecy clouds and golden curlicues, was as high as I could throw a softball. In the center was a huge chandelier, which we all agreed came right out of the castle in the movie *Sinbad*.

No Cowboy Shows Here

There was a big balcony where you could sit like a king and watch Johnny Mac Brown or Bob Steele duke it out with the bad guys...if a snooty place like the Grand ever showed cowboy movies instead of films with skinny women like Bette Davis and Claudette Colbert.

On stage that day was the Ted Weems Band. We watched open-mouthed, after skulking into the first row nearest the side door. The band swung through *The Dipsy Doodle* and my mother's favorite song, *Harbor Lights*. I was sorry she wasn't there to hear it.

Then one of the band members walked up to the microphone, put on a cowboy hat and sang *I'm an Old Cowhand (From the Rio Grande)*. We simply couldn't believe it—an hour earlier, at the American, Gene Autry's sidekick, Smiley Burnette, sang the same song! I hated to admit it, but Ted Weems' singer, a guy named Perry Como, sang it better than Smiley.

We thought we'd seen just about everything when Ted Weems introduced Elmo Tanner. When Mr. Tanner began his act, we nearly fell off our upholstered seats—he was a whistler!

When Elmo Whistled, People Danced

He could whistle better than my friend J.C. Mayo did during the brief but notable period when he had only one front tooth. When Elmo whistled *Sweet Georgia Brown*, people danced in the aisles.

It was nearly 5:30 when I got home, and Mother was plenty mad at me for being late. But as I told her of the marvels we'd seen and how beautifully they had played *Harbor Lights*, her anger melted away and she hugged me. Then she made me promise never to sneak into a theater again.

Mother turned back to the kitchen, singing *Harbor Lights* in her pleasant voice. Now, when I hear that song on a "golden oldies" station, I can still feel her hug, and I wish she were here to enjoy it with me once more. ☎

MOVIE MANSION. When reader (top left) and his pals sneaked into the Grand, an elegant movie palace like this one, they saw wonders unknown at their neighborhood theater.

The Treasure of Hawk's Hill

By Harry Paige, Potsdam, New York

WHILE CLEANING my mother's attic not long ago, I found a faded sheet of notebook paper dated June 1933. On it was a treasure map drawn in a boyish scrawl and the words "The Treasure of Hawk's Hill".

After a moment, I recognized the handwriting as my own, and I remembered that Hawk's Hill was located about a mile from my boyhood home in Elsmere, New York. I'd given it that name because from there I had once released an injured hawk to freedom.

I'd forgotten all about whatever treasure I'd buried as a boy. What could it be—a few pennies in a tin box? A favorite marble or a rusty jackknife?

A treasure of memories at the very least, I thought. So I decided to "play pirate" and go back to another time to seek what I had planted.

My family moved away from my hometown when I was 14 and I'd never

"*I felt a moment of glory as it flew off...*"

been back. Now my old street seemed a miniature of what it had been, and our former home seemed somehow shrunken by the passing years.

I parked my car and headed across a field that lead to a valley below Hawk's Hill. As I climbed toward the hill, I let my mind wander back over the years….

When I had found the hawk, it was walking, its wing bent and trailing in the grass. Still, its fierce eyes expected no mercy. Those defiant eyes attracted me most, showing the naked courage of a creature that would not be victimized.

I knew the hawk was not safe on the ground, so I coaxed it to grab onto a stick with its talons and eased it upward into a tree branch. Then I went to fetch a pair of heavy leather gloves, an empty tin can and some raw meat.

I nailed the can to the tree and filled it with water from my canteen. Then I placed the food on a flat part of the branch and waited.

The hawk eyed me suspiciously, then moved to the food. It tore at the meat with its beak and talons and threw it down its throat. Occasionally, it looked at me and ruffled its feathers in a show of bravado.

When the meat was gone, I put on my gloves and made a slow approach to the bird…but it began flapping its wings. I didn't want to take a chance on further injury, so I pulled away.

The hawk showed no gratitude, just a wild remoteness that told me it belonged to the sky and would not be tamed.

After a few days, the bird began facing into the wind and flapping its wings. Sometimes it just stood there, its gaze fixed on the sky with a fierce yearning. (Years later, I saw a similar look in my father's eyes as he stared into the last sun of summer from a hospital window.)

I continued to feed the hawk, watching it grow stronger. And then one day, we both sensed it was ready. Diverting its attention with meat in one hand, I grabbed it with the other, raised it to the sky and let it go.

The hawk took off into the sun with a wild cry of freedom…then wheeled and dove at me, coming within inches of my head, before flying off forever.

At the time, I was convinced that the diving return had been a salute, and I felt a moment of glory that two so different spirits could be connected.

Now, approaching Hawk's Hill once more, I saw the tree was gone. Only a charred stump remained, a monument to what once had been a mighty oak.

Following the faded map, I walked 12 boy-sized paces west of the stump and started digging, feeling more than a little foolish. After a moment, I struck

Ron Holt/Unicorn Stock Photos

something metallic. I reached down and gently withdrew a rusted tin box. When I tried to life the lid, the box fell apart, sprinkling coins on the ground.

There were three nickels, three pennies and a St. Christopher medal. This, then, was the Treasure of Hawk's Hill.

Even as the past squeezed at my heart, I smiled at what I had planted as a boy. Six coins, a medal and a tree stump were the only relics of a time when a wild hawk and a tame boy had made a memory that stirred nearly 60 years later.

The boy was alive and well—I could feel him still inside the man, laughing and running knee-deep in the fields of June. The hawk, too, had survived—I have seen its look in the eyes of my father and all creatures that yearn to be free.

So, for the sake of those memories, I buried the coins again. But this time, I carried away a much more valuable treasure—in my heart. ☎

Her Career Started at The Top

perched on top of upswept hairdos like birds' nests.

After working in the shop for a while, I had the courage to buy a hat that looked like an upside-down ice-cream cone. It was aqua velvet with lace embroidery—fussy but fashionable.

Berets and duckbill or jockey hats also had their day. My favorite was a navy ribbon jockey hat, for which I took a lot of ribbing. Once I wore a green felt hat with a sprightly feather, and my date called me Robin Hood or Peter Pan!

From Stocking to Sales

One busy Saturday, a woman selected a hat and looked about for a clerk. They were all busy, so she approached me with hat and money in hand. I took both to my favorite saleslady, who helped me complete the sale. Soon, other customers began asking me to assist in making selections.

I tried to find the most flattering hat in the store for each customer. I'd study her features, complexion and general appearance, then search the drawers for the perfect hat.

I was on cloud nine when those customers later brought in their mothers and friends and asked *me* to wait on them. I kept on giving my sales to the one saleslady until the other clerks noticed and asked me to share my sales with them.

When the manager heard about this, she spent an evening observing my work. Then she handed me a sales book and said, "Here's your book—go ahead and sell hats." That's when I discov-

By Florine Cherwin, Milwaukee, Wisconsin

FIRST JOBS always make a lasting impression, and mine was no exception.

When I was 15, in the mid-'30s, a school friend told me that The Grand, a fashionable women's store in Milwaukee, Wisconsin, needed a stock girl. I jumped at the chance.

The woman in charge looked me over, asked a few questions and said I could start the next day. My hours were 6 to 9 p.m. Mondays and Fridays and noon to 9 on Saturdays.

My job was to put away hats left on counters and dressing tables by customers and sales clerks. Each hat had a white tissue inserted in the crown and was nested in a neat row in a very large pull-out bin.

Each bin held 10 or 12 hats across in six or seven rows front to back. The hats had to be carefully stacked, and it took some skill to keep the rows intact when searching for a certain hat at the bottom of the last row. Being only 5 feet tall and 90 pounds, I sometimes barely kept from tumbling into the bins!

It was exciting to handle the delicate pastel spring hats trimmed with grosgrain ribbon, clusters of flowers or veils. In fall, the hats were made of felt and trimmed with ribbon, feathers, pins and even pom-poms on the more daring models.

The velvet hats were stunning in turquoise and royal blue with sequins or jewels framing the face. Some were worn turban fashion; others

HELPFUL HAT LADY. Like this saleswoman, Florine Cherwin enjoyed helping customers select just the right hat and was thrilled when they sent their friends in.

ered that each sale recorded in a sales book earned a small commission. How naive I'd been!

For my work, I earned 12¢ an hour plus sales commissions. The pay was meager, but I stayed with the job for 10 years, which helped pay for my college courses.

I also got my hats at a discount. No well-dressed young lady went anywhere without some kind of hat, and my small assortment made me feel chic.

My first job taught me how to approach strangers with confidence and poise and inspired me to take a sincere interest in people's needs. When customers confided little problems or frustrations, I listened.

I'll never forget the pleasure I saw on the face of one young woman when I found a hat that made her eyes look as blue as an azure sky. She left the store excitedly promising to send her family, friends and neighbors to buy from me...and she did.

What could be more rewarding?   ☎

THE GIRLS. Sisters Verna, Ruby, Hilder, Mabel and Lillian Lunden (top) loved to play cards in 1920. At a 1950 family get-together (above), Verna, Ruby, Hilder and Mabel were joined by their brother Arthur. Canasta, anyone?

Playing with 'The Girls'

By Sue Leaster Hanson, Mentor, Ohio

WHEN I recently joined a senior center and was asked if I played canasta, a wide smile lit up my face.

My mother and her four sisters were born between 1884 and 1905 in Mt. Jewett, Pennsylvania. From birth until they passed away, they were known simply as "The Girls".

By the time I was born, they all lived within 20 miles of each other, and whenever three or more of them were together, canasta was the game of choice. Since none of "The Girls" drove, they either walked, had a spouse drive or took a cab to be together on Sat-urdays after lunch for their weekly canasta game.

They were an interesting group. Lillian was the adventuresome one who once went to Oregon to homestead. Mabel loved children but had none, so she spoiled me instead. Hilder was the family-oriented one. Ruby, my mother, was the peacekeeper, and Verna was the shy sister.

They'd each put a quarter in the pot as I'd dream of all the penny candy that money could buy.

I'll never forget the first time I was asked to play canasta with them. They never allowed me to put a quarter in, but there was always one there. Maybe Mom had something to do with that.

That first game was quite an experience. I knew about wild cards, but I soon learned that you *never* jump up and down or tell the whole world that you've been dealt six wild cards.

Another lesson: If your partner is your mom and asks if it's okay to go out, you'd better say no if you have enough wild cards to make several more canastas. But, since I had *never* before in my life said no to my mom, I told her to go out. Wrong!

These canasta games continued through the years until only two of the five sisters were left. It had been several years since I'd played.

Did I play canasta? You bet. I was taught by the best players in the world—The Girls!   ☎

155

By Jack Clifford
Bridgewater, Massachusetts

BORN AND RAISED in Brooklyn, New York, I was first caught up in the lure of Ebbets Field in 1933. That's when I went to work as a turnstile operator for 50¢ a day.

Once the crowd was inside and the gates were closed, I got to watch the games for free. What a joy!

Getting to see my beloved "Bums" for free wasn't the only benefit of working at Ebbets Field. When the action on the field was slow, I'd go help one of the hot dog vendors with his crowd of customers. Not only did I get a dollar or two for helping, I could eat my fill of the greatest hot dogs at any ballpark!

Plenty of Perks

There was no end to the advantages of working in Ebbets Field.

For example, I knew the secrets of getting onto the roof, where I could find plenty of baseballs that had been fouled up there.

Of course, with all of these "perks", I was the envy of many kids in my neighborhood.

After a couple of years on the job, my pay was reduced to 49¢ a day. Social Security came into existence in 1935, and one penny of each day's pay was sent to Washington to be credited to my account.

Little did I know that all those pennies would contribute to the retirement check I now receive. What a return on investment!

Promoted to Usher

It wasn't long, however, before my pay went up. After a few years on the turnstile, I advanced to the job of usher.

This was a big jump indeed. Not only did I get to wear a spiffy green uniform, but my pay was now $3 a day, plus tips!

One game I'll never forget was in 1938 when the Cincinnati Reds came to town with their red-hot pitcher Johnny Vander Meer. Vander Meer was coming off a no-hitter in his last game, and this was to be the first night game at Ebbets Field.

Working for 'My Bums' Was A Dream Job

What a thrill it was when those hundreds of lights went on to illuminate that beautiful field. And what a game when it became obvious that Vander Meer was working on a possible second-in-a-row no-hitter!

The Brooklyn fans had booed Vander Meer in the early innings, but as the game went on, they changed their loyalty and cheered "Johnny!" each time he came to the mound. And when Vander Meer struck out one of their beloved Bums, the crowd gave him a standing ovation!

Besides allowing me to see one of Vander Meer's back-to-back no-hitters and the first night game in Ebbets Field, this event also offered me financial opportunity.

The section I worked that night had a number of empty box seats that had been purchased by a group of Cincinnati businessmen whose flight had been canceled at the last minute.

Working all the right "angles", I filled those empty reserved seats with folks holding "standing room only" tickets…while graciously accepting their tips. I went home a rich teenager that night!

A Memorable Series

I'll never forget the 1941 World Series, but not because Micky Owen dropped the ball, costing the Dodgers dearly. It was because that series against the Yankees was the last time I worked at Ebbets Field. World War II interrupted all of our lives, and many of us moved to other states.

Ebbets Field, of course, is no more. A housing development now stands where I once worked. But I hope to go back to Brooklyn someday and visit the old neighborhood.

One of my stops will be that housing development. Ebbets Field might be gone, but I still have my memories, and I'd love to reminisce one more time where the Brooklyn Dodgers used to play. ☎

FLATBUSH FANATICS. The Brooklyn Dodgers inspired incredible fan loyalty—feelings shared by folks lucky enough to actually work at Ebbets Field.

Bumper Bag Was Laughable Luggage

By Sherrie Gibson
Tallassee, Tennessee

Shining like a new penny, Uncle Lou's 1957 Ford sat parked in his Boston driveway. Load after load of necessities were being packed into the 1-year-old station wagon for a long trip to Southern California.

Uncle Lou and Aunt Emma were going to see my grandmother, and she had given Lou a bit of travel advice: A canvas water bag would be essential for this trip.

Uncle Lou's little two-wheeled trailer was full of camping gear, and his car was filling up fast, but he figured he'd better take the water bag to keep Grandma happy. After all, it had been years since they'd seen each other.

So, when Aunt Emma held up the water bag and said, "Don't you forget this!", Lou chuckled and replied, "Wouldn't dream of it."

Took Route 66

Once they reached Chicago, Emma and Lou would travel along Route 66. They'd plotted their course on a map, picking out the best campgrounds, to the delight of their wide-eyed kids.

The trip went smoothly as they traveled through the Southwest and into Arizona, where they discovered the desert was flatter, drier and hotter than anything they'd experienced.

The heat was intense. It hit a blistering 118° as they pulled into a "last stop for gas" station. Uncle Lou pumped gas into his almost-empty tank, and Aunt Emma filled the water bag—just to be on the safe side.

When Emma tied the dripping water bag to the front bumper, Lou snickered. It looked ridiculous dangling

there, and besides, the car was only a year old and was running great.

As they drove on, the sun set. Even then, the temperature still hovered around 100°. This was nothing like the weather back in Boston!

The moon peeked over the Arizona mountains, casting dim light on the ribbon of road crossing the lonely

> *"Uncle Lou said he'd never cross the desert without one..."*

desert. It was almost midnight when the Ford's headlights caught some movement ahead on the road.

A man was waving his handkerchief as a distress signal. The hood was up on his car, and two small children were clinging to him in the darkness. Uncle Lou pulled up near the stranded family.

The man said his car had overheated and he couldn't drive on without water. He'd flagged down several motorists and asked for water, but no one could help.

One of the man's small children whimpered as he explained how long they'd been stranded in the sweltering heat without water.

That's when Uncle Lou pointed to the canvas water bag tied to the car's bumper.

Leave It to a Yank

"Hallelujah!" the man cried. "Leave it to a Yankee from Massachusetts to have a water bag! Who would've imagined it?"

Uncle Lou smiled and told the man that he'd never cross the desert without one.

The two men chatted as they poured the cool water into the radiator. Then they shook hands, wished each other good luck and drove off on their separate ways.

Continuing west on Route 66, Lou and Emma finally came to another gas station. This time it was Lou reminding Emma to fill the water bag!

The family made it across the desert and to Grandmother's house with no problems. And as they pulled into her driveway (when the accompanying photo was taken), Lou was quick to tell the story of how the stranded family was saved by the canvas water bag.

And Lou had to admit Grandma was right...this time! ☎

Remember The House Out Back?

I compiled a section of photos entitled "How Not to Do It". One example showed an outhouse I saw in eastern Kentucky some 50 years ago.

Actually, there had been several outhouses, each backed up to a bluff overlooking a river. Those folks might not have had running water in their homes, but they had it below their outhouses. They were kept continually flushed!

When I went back to take some pictures, there was only one outhouse left (below left). I wasn't about to go walking around in the backyard of strangers taking a picture of their outhouse, so I used a telephoto lens.

The outhouse shows its age and is leaning "downriver", but it appears to have been updated for its time. It looks like a wire is going into the house. Maybe it had a light for nighttime calls.

—McAdoo Bruington
Richmond, Virginia

Stitch in Time Froze Behind

I ATTENDED a one-room school in the late '30s and early '40s. Like nearly all the boys at that time, I wore bib overalls.

One winter day at school, I ripped the seat out of my overalls. The teacher asked my older sister to sew them up while I was still wearing them.

Later, I had to go to the privy. When I got out there, I discovered my sister had sewn my overalls to my long johns! I had to remove my coat, shirt and underwear. I nearly froze—it was about 10° below zero that day.

—Clarence Knouse
Huron, South Dakota

These Outhouses Had Running Water

WHEN I WORKED for General Electric, I liked to spice up my technical audiovisual presentations with a little feature to educate and entertain.

Climbing Society's Ladder

BACK IN THE little town where I grew up, you could tell what ring of society's ladder you were on by the appearance of your outhouse.

I guessed I knew what rung Granny and I were on. Our outhouse matched our little run-down house. It was ugly, with cracked wood and peeling paint and looked like a good wind would blow it over.

Inside it was dark and dank, and there was no toilet paper, just an old Sears catalog. Once in a while, Granny would get a box of fruit and we'd save the tissue paper the fruit was wrapped in.

Next door was the widow Simonson. *Her* outhouse was the envy of the neighborhood, with its sparkling paint job, shingled roof, marigolds planted all around and a real lock on the door. Plus, she cleaned it every week.

There was a roll of real toilet paper in there, too. When I thought nobody was looking, I used to sneak through the hedge and take advantage of Mrs. Simonson's outhouse.

Much later, I learned that both Mrs. Simonson and Granny knew what I was doing but never said a word.

—La Faye Packer
Cottonwood, Arizona

Not Your Garden Variety...

WHEN MY HUSBAND and I built our first house, in Jacksonville, North Carolina, we could only afford four rooms and a path to the "two-holer" that sat at the edge of the woods.

We had a huge garden and raised lots of pole butter beans. After I shelled the beans for canning, I tossed the shells behind the outhouse.

The next spring, there were butter bean vines all over the trees in back of the outhouse and beans galore.

But when I picked some and prepared them for dinner, the oldest of our four kids knew where they'd come from and would not touch them.

The children are adults now, but when we get together, we still laugh about my "toilet beans".

—Maria Whaley
Kernersville, North Carolina

SHINGLE SISTERS. "That's me (left) and my sister-in-law, Neva Raddatz Plourde, sitting atop the 'relief office', as Neva's folks called the outhouse on their farm near Fowlerville, Michigan," relates Marlyn Plourde Balogh from River Rouge. "I spent two wonderful summers on the farm during WWII while my brother was in the Marine Corps. We took this picture to send to him."

We Catered to the ★ Troop Trains ★

By Patricia Eggler, Naperville, Illinois

I KNEW there was a war on that summer of 1944, but I was 6 and didn't really understand the seriousness of what was happening all over the world.

I did, however, understand what was taking place in my small part of the world...the south side of Chicago known as "Back of the Yards".

There were victory gardens to be tended, even though I broke out in a rash each time I weeded our patch. There were lines at the grocery store for rationed items like coffee and sugar, and I went door-to-door with my sister selling war bonds.

We also had to pull the shades when the sirens sounded a blackout. But the most exciting event that summer was when the troop trains began stopping on the stretch of tracks about a half block from our house.

We often played in a field alongside those raised tracks. The tracks themselves had been declared a forbidden zone by our parents, but we often climbed up some nearby coal chutes and played on the tracks until the railroad men shooed us away from there.

When the troop trains stopped, it took hours for them to be switched to the right tracks. The soldiers would get out and stretch, but they weren't allowed to leave the vicinity of their train.

When they saw us down the hill in the field, the men began tossing money, asking us to fetch them items from the nearby stores.

Hoisted the Goods

Some of the soldiers even made a hoist out of a bag and a rope so they could pull their purchases up the hill. We couldn't climb up because the railroad men were always around when the trains were in.

We enjoyed running the soldiers' errands, especially after realizing we could almost always keep the change. And when the neighbors and local shopkeepers found out what was going on, they also got into the act.

Mr. Thomas owned a tavern on the corner, next to Charlie's grocery store. When he saw what we were doing, he began sending pails of beer back with us. Like most in the neighborhood, Mr. Thomas had sons in the service.

Then Mrs. Lewis and some other ladies who were in charge of the victory gardens began sending vegetables. Grandma and Mrs. Mahoney baked bread and pastries, and Charlie the grocer made sandwiches.

Some neighbors even got together and built a platform to make it easier to get the supplies to the soldiers.

Sang with the Soldiers

Nearly every day someone brought along a guitar, accordion or harmonica, and we sang songs like *Frere Jacques* and *Mairzy Doats*. We also learned the words to *Over There*, *Boogie Woogie Bugle Boy* and others before summer was over.

Everyone on the block pitched in to make the men as happy as possible while they were waiting to continue their journey to the war.

The next summer, the war ended. The trains kept coming, taking the men home, but they no longer stopped to switch. All we could do was wave as they went by.

Eventually, the platform and that stretch of track were dismantled, and our lives returned to normal. We soon resumed our forbidden treks up the coal chutes, but the old excitement was gone. Nothing could compare with the fun we had running for the troop trains. ☎

SERVING PROUDLY. Author (on right) with parents Jim and Lucile Hughes, and siblings Barb and Paul, around the time they ran errands for soldiers on trains passing through their city.

Dad's Willow Whistle Saved the Day

Anthony Beaverson

By Margaret Benton, Spokane, Washington

I'LL NEVER FORGET the Sunday in 1919 when Dad said he was going to show my sisters and me how to make a willow whistle—just as his father had shown him when he was a lad in Ireland!

I was one excited 8-year-old that morning, sitting on the front porch steps of our home in Omaha, Nebraska waiting for Dad to finish shaving. My sisters, Lizzie, Mary, Cecilia and Rose, were as eager as I was, because Dad stropped his razor *and* his pocketknife until both had a keen edge.

Then he turned to us with a big grin and said, "Now, let's go check the willows and see if the sap is running. If it's just right, we'll make some willow whistles!"

We girls gave out a whoop and ran down the lane, jumping, shouting and doing somersaults as we urged Dad to hurry to the willow patch.

The meadow glistened with dew like a carpet of diamonds in the warm sunshine. Meadowlarks and red-winged blackbirds sang to us from the willow trees, and we knew that they were telling us the sap was just right to make our whistles.

Dad inspected branch after branch, looking for one about the thickness of his middle finger. When he found a branch the right size, he cut off a 6-inch length, sliced one end on a slant and cut out a wedge about an inch from the slanted end.

With his sharpest blade, Dad made a circle all the way around the stick, careful to cut only the bark. "Now we'll find out if we can make a whistle," he explained, gently tapping the stick with his knife handle.

Dad tapped and slowly turned the willow stick until the green bark slipped off. He then cut the "wind channel" into the wedge end of the stick. "Next we'll make the sound chamber," he said. "The more I cut, the deeper the tone will be."

I wanted my whistle to have a deep, loud sound. Mary wanted a thin, shrill sound. Lizzie wanted hers sharp and loud, and Cecilia wanted hers soft and sweet like a bird.

Rose didn't care—all she wanted was a whistle made by

> ## "Rose wasn't in bed ...she was nowhere to be found!"

Dad to show the other kids what he'd done for us.

When our whistles were made, we raced back home, tooting and whistling exultingly. We whistled for Mama until she finally said, "Run along now and play 'til supper." I guess even with the best of whistles, enough is enough!

We played the rest of the day, being careful to wet our whistles in the horse tank from time to time to keep them from drying out and cracking.

After supper, the music continued as Mama played the piano and Cecilia yodeled. Then it was time for bed.

When Dad came in to kiss us good night and ask if we'd said our prayers, Rose wasn't in bed…she was nowhere to be found! We looked through the house, in the barn, the chicken coop and the corncrib. No luck.

Mama asked us girls if we knew any place Rose might want to go. We all said yes, Rose liked to go to the creek to wet her whistle. At that, Mama gasped and shouted to Dad, "Mike! Mike! The creek! Hurry, Mike! Hurry!"

Dad ran through the woods toward the creek, and we stumbled after him in the dark, following the sound of his calling, "Rose! Rose!"

Cecilia started to cry, but Mama told her, "Hush…God won't let anything happen to my baby."

Then Lizzie said, "Wait…I hear a pewee peeping." Mama said pewees never sing at night, but we all stood still and listened—it was Rose's whistle!

Following the sound, Dad found Rose curled up on the ground, tangled in an old coil of fence wire. She had gone to the creek to wet her whistle, gotten lost in the dark and caught in the wire. When she couldn't move, she'd started blowing her whistle, "'Cause Dad made it for me, and I knew he'd hear it and find me."

Dad said Rose did the right thing, and he told us we should all blow our whistles if we ever were in trouble or got lost. That way, he and Mama could always come to help us.

Now I'm a great-great-grandmother, but I still remember my father's wonderful willow whistle and how that simple homemade toy helped save our Rose so many years ago. ☎

Charles Atlas Taught Me a Lesson

By Richard Murphy, San Augustine, Texas

WHEN Charles Atlas was still Angelo Siciliano, a skinny immigrant boy living in a tough section of Brooklyn in the early 1900s, he was beaten by a neighborhood bully.

About a year later, Angelo was at the beach with his girlfriend when a husky lifeguard taunted him and kicked sand in his face. At age 15 and weighing about 97 pounds, Angelo was not in a position to do anything about the humiliation.

Then he discovered the secret that would soon make him stronger—at the New York Zoo!

Standing before the lion's cage, Angelo watched one of the big cats awake and stretch. "The muscles ran around like rabbits under a rug," he recalled. "I said to myself, 'This guy doesn't need barbells and exercisers—he's pitting one muscle against the other!'"

That's how Angelo discovered "Dynamic Tension", now known as isometrics. In the next few weeks, he worked up a system of fundamental exercises and began to do them every day. In a few years, he had put on 50 pounds of well-proportioned muscle.

Practiced What He Preached

Angelo became Charles Atlas, wrote a book on his discoveries and began marketing his system. By the 1950s, under the management of a brilliant adman, Atlas was enrolling students from all over the world.

Atlas practiced what he preached. He did his Dynamic Tension exercises twice a day, didn't smoke or drink and maintained a healthy diet. His advice: "Get to exercising. Get on a healthy basis. We were created in God's image, and God is no weakling."

I'm one of the millions of boys and men transformed by the Atlas method. I, too, was a skinny kid who got regular beatings in 1940 in San Augustine, Texas from the neighborhood bully, Jesse. I tried to fight back but got only black eyes, a split lip and assorted bruises for my efforts.

With the help of Grandma's egg money, I sent for Atlas' book. I began doing his exercises every day after school.

After 2 weeks, I looked at myself in the horse trough and was certain I was on my way to becoming another Atlas... although the penny scale in front of the drugstore said I weighed 89 pounds, just a pound more than when I started my regimen.

Still, I figured it wasn't pounds that counted, it was muscles. After 3 weeks, I decided to put my new muscles to the test. I took the direct route home from school past Jesse's house. He was outside getting a drink from the well, and his mean little eyes peered at me over the rim of the gourd dipper. I swelled my chest and flexed my arm muscles menacingly. Jesse was not impressed.

"Charles Atlas" © 2002 licensed from Charles Atlas, Ltd. (www.CharlesAtlas.com)

Hero of the Playground

With a banshee yell of "Yee haw! I'm gonna git you, sissyface—gonna make you eat dirt again!", Jesse came across the sandy yard like a runaway train.

My instincts told me to run. But I remembered Mac in the Atlas ads getting even with the beach bully. I braced myself, stuck out my right arm and doubled my fist. I also closed my eyes. Jesse, expecting me to run, came in too fast to dodge. His 140 pounds hurtled face-first into my fist. I felt the jar clear down to my toes.

When I opened my eyes, Jesse was flat on his back, twin streams of blood running from his nostrils. "You broke my node," he sputtered, tears on his freckled cheeks.

Word spread, and I became the hero of the playground. True, Charles Atlas' Dynamic Tension didn't make me a muscular hulk...but it did teach me not to run away from my problems—a lesson worth more than the cost of the course.

SKINNY KID. The author, shown in striped coveralls with fellow fifth graders, concentrated on a comic book project. A year later, he put his efforts into a stronger body with help from a book by Charles Atlas (above).

We Survived 'Old Shaky'

NOWADAYS, cars whiz along on Interstate Highway 8, a modern expressway near Yuma, Arizona. Back in the '20s, though, things were quite a bit different on the same desert route.

Motorists then were lucky to hit speeds much over 12 mph...and even at that pace, it was a tooth-rattling ride. That's because the original road was made of *wooden planks*. No wonder they nicknamed it "Old Shaky"!

In 1924, my family and I made a trip across the desert on Old Shaky, and I'll *never* forget the experience. Then called Route 27-B, this hardwood

By Lucille MacDonald, Reno, Nevada

highway helped travelers negotiate the shifting sand dunes known as "The American Sahara" between 1915 and 1926.

Old Shaky was made of portable 12- by 8-foot sections laid end to end. The sections consisted of 4- by 12-inch planks bolted across heavy timbers. Three strong metal bands held each section's planks tightly together.

After sandstorms, a maintenance crew with a four-horse team would dig up sand-covered sections and, if neces-

sary, reposition the road to fit the new lay of the land.

I was 10 years old when our family moved from California to Arizona. Dad drove us in his 1920 Dodge touring car, pulling a homemade trailer behind.

The two-lane, hard-surfaced highway we'd been traveling on ended in El Centro, California. Ahead of us loomed Old Shaky, snaking its way out into the desert.

We stopped at a service station for gas and water, and the attendant's tales of what to expect in the miles ahead frightened Mom, sis and me. We were especially worried when he brought up the possibility of bouncing off the road and getting stuck in the sand!

Dad tried to calm our fears. "We're lucky today," he soothed. "It's cloudy and cool, so the radiator won't boil... and there's no wind blowing,

BUMPY BYWAY known as "Old Shaky" (top) snaked its way across desert dunes. The wooden plank road was dismantled in the late '20s (left).

so flying sand won't be a bother."

Mom sighed. "I'm glad for that," she said. "It's such a nuisance to put up the side curtains!" Those were made of isinglass and heavy black leather. When weather threatened, we'd remove them from under the backseat to enclose the open touring car.

Away They Went!

Worried but determined, we set off. Dad's Dodge shook and rattled uncontrollably as its tires rumbled over Old Shaky's "washboard" surface.

Automobile springs just weren't designed to handle such a hammering. No matter how slowly Dad drove, the up-and-down motion of the Dodge seemed to accelerate. It was necessary to stop occasionally just to quell the bouncing.

Since the road was only 8 feet wide, oncoming cars could not pass one another. Turnouts at quarter-mile intervals allowed one vehicle to pull over and let another by.

"But what if we meet another car in the middle?" sis questioned in a worried voice when we passed the first turnout.

"One of us will have to back up," answered Dad. The fact that he had no experience backing a trailer didn't make us "Nervous Nellies" feel any better about the situation!

Trouble Up Ahead?

Later on, we did spot an approaching car. Luckily there was a turnout just ahead, so Dad pulled over and waited.

Finally, a chugging Model T pulled alongside. Dad and the other driver discussed road conditions and weather…but mostly they complained about the bone-jarring ride.

The day dragged on as we bumped our way across that desolate landscape, and it seemed as if the 10-mile trek to Yuma would never end.

When we finally reached town and stopped for the night, we discovered that a trunk filled with clothing had bounced out of the trailer somewhere along the way! We were so weary that no one even mentioned going back to look for it.

Not long after we settled in Arizona, Route 27-B was paved. Sections of the old plank road soon became historical relics—one was even displayed at the Chicago World's Fair in 1933!

Now "Old Shaky" is merely a curiosity in transportation history. But the memory of our bone-jarring journey still rattles around in my mind! ☎

"Let's Scare Up Some Snipe!"

*By Katie Hippert
Glenwood,
Minnesota*

IN THE SUMMER of 1957, my sister, Karen, and I had graduated from high school and wanted to escape from all the work on our family farm near Madelia, Minnesota.

We headed for the "big city", Minneapolis, and soon met Dorothy, who introduced us to three of her guy friends.

One summer evening, as we were cruising, the guys asked if we'd like to go snipe hunting. Never having heard of that, we agreed. We drove to a park about 2 miles outside of town. The guys got gunnysacks out of the trunk and gave them to us. They showed us where to sit and told us to be quiet. They'd go scare up the snipe, and when they came toward us, we should catch them quickly, as they moved very fast.

They went off and soon one shouted, "Here they come," but we saw nothing.

"Did you get one?" they asked. We didn't.

"All right, we'll scare up some more," they said as they left again.

Turnabout Was Fair Play

I thought his voice sounded fainter, but, after all, they had told us to be quiet. Dead silence. We waited and waited. After about 15 minutes, we called out but got no answers. We thought we'd better go look. The boys and the car were gone!

We walked back to our local hangout and there they were, laughing, along with everyone else who'd heard their story. We were so mad that we didn't get together for 3 whole weeks. Eventually we made up, and by fall, we were out cruising again. Now it was the season to go out looking for watermelons, if you knew where the farmers hid their patches. Since Karen and I came from farms, we pretended to know where there was a large watermelon patch.

The boys bought the story, so we took them 3 miles out in the country to a large cornfield. We told them to walk in 15 rows and they'd find the patch. We'd stay in the car to sound the horn if the farmer showed up.

The guys took their gunnysacks, climbed the fences into the field and started counting rows before we quietly drove away. Half an hour later, they had

hitched a ride and showed up at our hangout, but were they mad.

So much for cruising days! They found three new girls, although we did become friends again. I wonder if any of them remember snipe and watermelon hunts from the good old days. ☎

FUN-LOVING SISTERS. Author (on the right) reminisces about the adventures she and her sister, Karen, had during the summer of 1957, after they graduated from high school.

Selling Door-to-Door Had Its Rewards

By Walter Ribeiro Sr., Pennsauken, New Jersey

RECENTLY I was rummaging through some old boxes in my basement when I came across an old magazine carrying bag. It was the one I used for selling *Liberty* magazines when I was a boy. My mind flooded, recalling those days around 1930 in East Camden, New Jersey and how my first job came about.

A group of us kids had gathered on the street corner one day when a car pulled up and stopped. A man got out and approached us. He had a catalog in his hand and started rifling through pages, showing us all kinds of sporting equipment: baseball gloves and bats, footballs, Scouting equipment, roller skates—even bicycles.

Knew How to Get Their Attention

It looked like a miniature Sears catalog! Naturally, we became wide-eyed with excitement when the man told us we could earn these prizes. All we had to do was sell some of his magazines.

They cost 5¢ each, and we would get 1-1/2¢ profit on each sale, plus one green coupon for every five magazines sold. When we accumulated five "greenies", we could exchange them for one brown coupon. Each prize in the book was worth a certain number of "brownies".

It sounded easy, and there was nothing to lose. All I had to do was canvass the neighborhood and try to sell copies of *Liberty*, which was published weekly. The man took my name and address, then gave me 10 issues of the magazine and a bag to carry them in.

He said he'd stop by my house at a specific time the

"—an' a Sled—an' a Radio
—an' a Five-Dollar Gold Piece!"

next week to collect the money. I was excited and couldn't wait until I sold my first magazine.

Of course, Mom and Dad were my first prospects. Then I approached uncles and aunts and other relatives. When those opportunities ran out, I went door-to-door in the neighborhood. It wasn't as easy as I'd thought.

Collected Regular Customers

I used my bicycle to get around and eventually sold all 10 magazines. Most customers agreed to take the magazine weekly, so my dad helped me write their names and addresses in a notebook so I could keep a record of them.

When the man came by the following week, I settled up with him, keeping my share. He even gave me a few extra "greenies" for my hard work.

I took 15 magazines for the following week and sold them all. Eventually, I was selling 20 magazines per week. Anything that wasn't sold would be taken back by the man when I saw him.

Over a period of time, I earned a Scout hatchet (I was a Boy Scout), a baseball glove and a number of other prizes.

Today, at age 83, I still have that hatchet, which I painted gold, and will never part with it. It's the first item I ever earned on my own, making it one of my most prized possessions.

MAN WITH A GOLDEN HATCHET. Walter Ribeiro still has the bag he used to carry *Liberty* magazines in the '30s as he sold them to earn points for items like the prized Boy Scout hatchet he's holding in the photo at left.

Caddies Learned More Than Golf

By Robert Delaney, Cheswick, Pennsylvania

THE FOX CHAPEL Golf Club in Pittsburgh, Pennsylvania provided jobs for us kids from the coal-mining town of Harmarville in the late 1930s and early '40s.

The beautiful emerald-green and well-manicured course also provided a welcome change from our neighborhoods of densely packed row houses. Plus we got some exercise and a chance to breathe fresh air uncontaminated by coal dust from the aboveground processing operation in Harmarville.

The club was about 7 miles away by car. That's if we hitchhiked or took the caddie bus, which was a panel truck sent around if there was a special event or tournament.

When we got to the course, we reported to the caddie shack. At this point, caddying required great patience. It could be hours before the caddie master assigned you a golfer.

The club put up a basketball hoop and a horseshoe court to help the caddies pass the time. But we usually played cards, pitched pennies or played "baseball" with our pocketknives.

The caddie master also administered credit for caddies who needed to appease their teenage appetites at the pro shop, where food was for sale. Most of us ate our pay before it was earned.

If you were lucky enough to know someone who worked in the clubhouse kitchen, the occasional cookie, doughnut or cup of coffee was passed your way when the chef wasn't looking.

Day's Best Meal Was at No. 10 Tee

The best way to get food and drink was on the course, when players stopped at the "halfway house", a refreshment shack in an old springhouse at the No. 10 tee.

The golfers usually invited their caddies to "have whatever you want". We could get a Coke or a Pepsi, hot dogs, candy, potato chips and other treats not available at home.

There were also ways to make money while waiting to caddie. We could shag balls for members who used the first fairway for

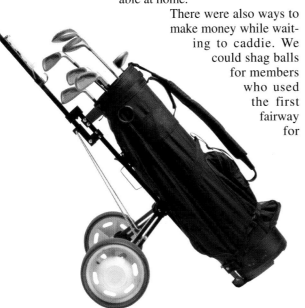

practice. That paid about 25¢ an hour.

Or we could "smash bags". That was the term used for carrying members' golf bags from their cars in the parking lot to the clubhouse. We hoped for a quarter tip.

Fox Chapel was an exclusive club, and the presidents and chairmen of the board of many Pittsburgh-based national corporations held memberships. Of course, that didn't stop us from giving them descriptive nicknames, such as "Hawker" for one who coughed and hacked during the round, or "Shanker" to describe one player's errant shots.

I remember the summer a college student named Scott worked as a caddie. He and I were out together one time when Scott's golfer couldn't hit a fairway. After five holes, he'd lost a half dozen balls.

"You must be the world's worst caddie," the golfer fumed at Scott.

Scott thought about that for a moment, then replied, "Hey, we must be a set!"

Our pay for 18 holes was 90¢. The players usually tipped us a dime to round it off to $1.

Caddies' Strike Paid Off

One time, just before the club invitational tournament, we went on strike for higher pay. We came to the course but refused to carry any bags. The members had to carry their own.

I remember one golfer, a doctor, who forgot to close the ball pocket on his bag while carrying it from his car to the first tee. We caddies enjoyed a few moments of muffled amusement as the doctor and his party tried to recover the dozen or so balls as they bounced along the sidewalk.

The day before the tournament, the strike was settled when the club professional came out to talk and agreed to raise the rate to $1.10. Since we could expect a 15-cent tip, that meant we'd get $1.25 a round—a substantial amount, considering admission to the movies then was 11¢.

On Mondays, the course was closed and caddies were permitted to play. We'd gather on the first tee when the fairways were still heavy with dew and keep playing until it was too dark to see the ball.

In addition to the money, caddying provided us with the basic attributes needed in life: self-respect, respect for those you serve and for your peers, responsibility and patience.

We also learned the value of a dollar, and the feeling of exhausted elation in knowing we'd earned it. Some of us learned how to play a decent game of golf, too. ☎

ON THE BAG. Author (top in the '30s) returned to the Fox Chapel Golf Club after retiring (right).

MY KIDS grew up with Mr. Rogers, but I'm convinced there's no televised teacher in the world to equal Miss Frances...and no classroom, real or imaginary, as fascinating as *Ding Dong School*.

An apple-cheeked woman with twinkling eyes, Miss Frances always had a friendly smile. Though she couldn't have been very old, her conservative clothing and matronly figure gave her a grandmotherly charm.

NBC television cameras brought Miss Frances (her real name was Frances Horwich) into my life in the mid-'50s, but the program had its debut in the Chicago area in October of 1952.

Within 6 months, it was such an overwhelming success that it was seen coast to coast, sponsored first by Scott Paper Company and later by General Mills.

Miss Frances had excellent credentials. She was, after all, a real teacher. She'd received a master's degree from Columbia University and a doctorate from Northwestern and was head of the education department at Chicago's Roosevelt College. Yet, despite her impressive academic background, she knew just how to talk to children.

Bend and Shape

When I was 6, living in Vancouver, Miss Frances taught me how to grow a sweet potato and turn it into a beautiful green plant. I remember feeling special when Mom displayed my plant on the coffee table.

Miss Frances encouraged kids to be creative. Although my artistic abilities were minimal, I was always eager to try a new *Ding Dong School* project. Once, Miss Frances showed us how to make something special out of pipe cleaners. She bent and twisted them into all sorts of cute animals.

At the end of the program, she encouraged us to run out to our local five-and-dime and purchase the inexpensive pipe cleaners. That's just what I did.

But I was devastated when the clerk said he was sold out—all the other boys and girls who'd been watching my favorite show had beaten me to the punch!

Remember Ding Dong School?

By Jan Parrott-Holden, Vancouver, Washington

TV SCHOOL DAYS. Author and brother Fred (inset) and lots of other kids seldom missed a class when Miss Frances (left) rang the bell for *Ding Dong School*.

Miss Frances received thousands of fan letters a week. At the height of her popularity, the show was watched by 95% of the nation's preschoolers. I didn't know what a fan letter was back then, but I wrote to Miss Frances and was delighted to receive a personal reply.

Years later, I discovered my mother (also a teacher) had written her own fan letter to Miss Frances. Mom appreciated Miss Frances' innovative approaches to teaching and liked the way she stressed respect and responsibility.

An Argyle Pony

My most fond recollections of the show come from the special times Mom and I spent together, trying out Miss Frances' ideas. I'll never forget the time Mom helped me make a stick horse out of an old broomstick and one of Dad's argyle socks.

I also recall how Mom tiptoed into the room during the last few minutes of the show to sit with me while Miss Frances told parents a few things about the program. Sometimes Miss Frances even told parents to send us kids outside to play.

I'm not exactly sure what she shared with parents during those times, but I imagine it had something to do with encouraging us kids to have good manners or learn how to be more independent.

Sometimes when I wasn't sharing or had lost my temper, Mom would remind me that "Miss Frances wouldn't approve". It may not have always worked, but it certainly gave Mom an ally.

I could almost hear the voice of Miss Frances asking, "Did you follow directions? Did you hang up your coat when you came indoors from play? Did you offer to help Mom set the dinner table? Good for you! Miss Frances is proud of her boys and girls!"

Those *Ding Dong School* days are long gone now. But I don't think I'll ever forget my television teacher, smiling and ringing her old-fashioned hand bell. That "cling-a-clang" was such a happy sound—a promise of good times to come with Miss Frances. ☎

With our first television in 1950 came some lifestyle changes at our Long Beach, California home. One rule held fast, though—an early bedtime for my brother, Treuman, and me on weeknights.

Occasionally I'd plead the case for extending my bedtime, but Dad was adamant. Worse yet, even though I couldn't see those evening programs, I could *hear* the tantalizing audio from my bedroom.

The show I wanted most to see was Milton Berle's *Texaco Star Theater*. When I heard the opening theme song, "Oh, we're the men from Texaco, we work from Maine to Mexico…", I was in sheer agony.

All that laughter—both from the audience and my parents—made me yearn to see what was so funny. I also wanted to know what Arnold Stang looked like.

One Tuesday night, I crept out of bed and tiptoed down the hall. After crouching in the doorway to the den, I crawled to a spot where a lamp table separated Dad's recliner and Mom's chair. I lay on my stomach so I could see the TV screen between the legs of the table.

As I remember, Danny Thomas was the guest that night, doing some kind of vaudeville skit.

When I thought the show was nearly over, I started crawling back to my

---

"*S*oon all three of us were howling…"

---

room. Unfortunately, I hit my head on the table, shaking the lamp and knocking a few magazines to the floor.

"What was that?" Mom said, swinging around in her chair.

Dad tilted his recliner all the way back and, turning his head, looked right into my face. "Seems we have a visitor."

"Maxine!" Mom got out of her chair. "What in the world?"

Tears welled up in my eyes, but I couldn't get a word out. After making sure I wasn't hurt, Mom sat down and hoisted me onto her lap. "Sit here with me and you'll feel better," she said.

Sitting on Mom's lap, I pretended not to watch the TV…but when Uncle

Who Could Sleep When 'Uncle Miltie' Came On?

By Maxine Averbuck, Sebastopol, California

Miltie did a sketch about Charlie Chan's No. 1 son, I started giggling. Soon all three of us were howling with laughter.

When the show was over, Mom tucked me into bed. "Don't say anything about this to your brother," she warned. "It'll be our secret."

"Can I watch Uncle Miltie again?" I asked.

"Dad and I will talk about it," she replied.

The next Tuesday as Mom tucked me in, she said, "Promise me that you won't sneak out again, Maxine."

I pouted. "Oh, Mama…why can't I watch Uncle Miltie? I'll be lying awake listening, anyway."

Mom smiled. "When the show starts, I'll come and see if you're awake. If you are, then you can come and watch."

I lay there repeating poems and telling myself stories, trying to stay awake. Suddenly I heard the Texaco Servicemen singing the show's opening theme song. Had I fallen asleep?

I quickly sat up in bed and saw Mom in the doorway, beckoning with her finger. "Shhh," she whispered. "We don't want to wake your brother."

It was wonderful. I got to see Arnold Stang, and I couldn't believe all the different facial expressions Uncle Miltie had.

Our little routine continued each week after that. If I was still awake when the show started, I got to watch in the den with Mom and Dad—although I had to keep my laughter down so I wouldn't wake my brother.

This went on until I was 13 and allowed to stay up later than my brother on school nights. Then, one Tuesday night, we were watching Uncle Miltie and heard a *thump*.

It was my brother, attempting to sneak back to bed—he'd just bumped *his* head on the table by Dad's recliner.

We Remember When TV Was New

Wunnerful, Awunnerful

BACK IN the early '50s, it seemed to our family of seven that everybody had a TV but us. There just wasn't any extra money to buy one.

Our mother, Mildred, played the accordion. In fact, she could make it dance. But one day Mom heard of a family who would trade a television for an accordion.

That's all Mom had to hear. We got our first TV. I don't remember what kind it was, but we sure did enjoy it.

Over 20 years later, Mom read an ad about an accordion for sale. It had the name "Mildred" on it. Yes, it was Mom's old accordion.

Of course, she bought it back and we again got to hear her make it dance.
—*Janet Blue, Walhonding, Ohio*

The Lone Shopper

ONE AFTERNOON in the early '50s, my parents and little brother went grocery shopping at the local supermarket in Lansing, Michigan. The store had a drawing for a new Raytheon TV, and my dad won it. He was so excited, he and my brother immediately took it home to try it out.

When my mother finished shopping, she couldn't find Dad. She had to walk home, carrying the groceries.

Mother walked into the house to find my dad and brother watching *The Lone Ranger*. Dad had completely forgotten about Mother.

They were together for 63 years, and that was the first—and last—time he forgot her. —*Betty Jo Sharp Hodges*
Blue Ridge, Georgia

Pioneer TV Repairman

MY FATHER only went through third grade, but he taught himself to fix radios and TVs and hoped his four sons would follow in his footsteps.

I was the only one interested and over the years, I worked on all kinds of TVs. My father and I used to assemble them from kits. They had screens from 7 to 12 inches.

The first related job I got was after World War II, with Dumont TV in Passaic, New Jersey. In those early days when I made "house calls", there were some amusing incidents.

One time, I was taking a chassis out of a cabinet. Attached to it was a large plastic bubble filled with oil. It was supposed to act as a magnifier for the 10-inch screen. The bubble was heavy, and when it slid out of its holder, one corner broke off and some of the oil spilled. The owner didn't seem to mind, though, and just wiped it up.

Another time I was working on an early color TV when the female owner said, "Please check the inkwells. The moving man told me he tipped the set and some of the ink might have spilled." I got a good laugh out of that one.
—*Edward Sidorski*
Susquehanna, Pennsylvania

My Dad, the TV Repairman

MY DAD, Ople Cheatham (above), started Cheatham's Radio and TV Service in Dover, Tennessee in 1951.

Dad was good at what he did, and people came from miles around for service "with a smile" or to buy. In the early days, Dad would pull a TV out onto the sidewalk in front of the store so passersby could enjoy a glimpse of this modern-day marvel.

The business had a downside for us kids. We never got to take a vacation because Dad had no one to watch the store. And there was many a night or Sunday afternoon when Dad would have to go on a "house call".

"You never know," he'd say. "Television just might be that person's only entertainment."

He was a great repairman and a wonderful person. —*Lisa Barrow*
Simpsonville, South Carolina

LITTLE BREADWINNER. "Our son, Donald, was just a toddler, but he never missed *Bandstand*, which is what the local Philadelphia show was called before it went national as *American Bandstand*," remembers Arline Quigley of Pipersville, Pennsylvania. "One February afternoon in 1955, I left the room to do some chores. When I came back, Donald was in the same position, but with an opened loaf of Bond bread, which at that time was delivered to our door. He'd eaten all the white portion of the bread and was so intent on the show that he didn't even move when I took this picture."

Go Fly an Antenna

LIVING ON the fifth floor of an apartment building in Manhattan gave me plenty of opportunities to fly a kite on the roof.

But little by little, our neighbors began buying TVs, and the antennas were installed on the roof. With 100 families living in the building, you can imagine what our roof looked like.

The kites kept getting tangled in the antennas, and within a year, the joyous hours of flying kites were replaced with watching television.

—*Blanche McIntosh*
Schenectady, New York

We Interrupt This Program

BACK IN 1958, I didn't think we could afford a television, but we watched one occasionally at a neighbor's. That's where we were one cold winter night, watching wrestling.

Some other people were there, too, so there wasn't an empty seat in the house. Just when the main wrestling event was about to start, the neighbor's son came home.

He looked around at all the people, then announced that the Catholic church up the street was on fire. When no one paid any attention to him, he said it again.

I guess everyone figured that he was just trying to get someone to jump up and look out the window so he could get their seat.

Finally his mother went to look, and the church *was* on fire! We all then went out to look and forgot about the TV, for the moment.

Yes, it had taken a fire to get us away from the television and out into the cold night. Two weeks later, we had our own set. —*Larry Brown*
Kirkland Lake, Ontario

Why They Invented VCRs

MOST EARLY television sets were made of wood, but the one my father purchased in the early '50s was wood grain-finished metal! It was *very* different.

I had trouble turning off the set and going to bed. I remember being disappointed the next morning, when I turned the set back on, that the same cartoon wasn't there where I'd left it the night before. —*Cheri Pearson*
Santa Clara, California

Those Were the 'Happy Days'

By Margie Roulette Romero, Altadena, California

I WAS 17 when I started working at Larry's Ice Cream Store in Pasadena, California in 1953. Most of the girls who worked as waitresses dated the neighborhood guys who hung out there. The guys had great motorcycles or cars, and were good dancers and fun to be with. They usually had a choice of four or five girls to date.

All the waitresses wore blue check blouses and skirts, and we hung the sale check books on our belts. I worked from 5 to 10 p.m. three times a week, plus Saturday nights, while going to high school and junior college.

As kids, we never had much money, although we could afford a cherry Coke or a burger now and then. The owner never seemed to mind all the kids who just hung out.

On weekends and in the summer, we would pile into about three cars and ride down Colorado Boulevard—the Rose Bowl Parade route on New Year's Day—to meet at a drive-in for burgers, fries, shakes and sodas.

Dick Ahrens drove a souped-up '48 Buick and was always looking for guys to race. We'd set up a time to meet late at night near the Rose Bowl, where there was a road, few cars and no police.

Just like in James Dean's movie *Rebel Without a Cause*, we girls started them off, and they would race for about 50 yards to see who could cross the finish line first.

Then some of us headed up to the hills on the west side of the Rose Bowl to dance. They were just starting to build houses there, so we would find an empty lot, park our cars in a circle, turn off the lights, tune our radios to the same station and dance the night away. When the DJ signed off at 2 a.m., we knew it was time to get home.

One by one, we got married. I married Ruben in 1955. Our bunch got together now and then, but eventually became busy with our own lives.

In 1980, one of the gang got cancer, but survived. I said, "That's it. From now on, we're getting together once a month."

Yes, the '50s were the "Happy Days"—filled with ice cream, sodas, dancing, young love, long summer nights and music, music, music.

Larry's Ice Cream Store is gone now, but not our memories. We all agree that the *Happy Days* TV show was inspired by Larry's and our group of kids.

COOL MEMORIES. The author serves a cone to one of the gang at the ice cream shop (above). Her husband-to-be, Ruben, shows off his boots (center) and gives buddies a ride (top). Margie and Ruben still gather with friends from the '50s.

Kresge's Was My 'Window of Opportunity'

By Ruth Heebner, Chadds Ford, Pennsylvania

ON MY 16th birthday, in 1928, I went to work at Kresge's 5-10-25¢ store on Market Street in downtown Philadelphia. My experiences there serving the public really made some memories.

My family had immigrated to this country from Denmark, and I first saw the statue of that impressive lady with the torch when I was 8. By the time I started at Kresge's, I had compassion for people because I knew the tough times they were up against. I was grateful for the opportunity to work.

I started out full of enthusiasm, making $12 a week. Each counter had two girls to help the customers, and all the girls were on their toes—no hanging on counters with folded arms, ignoring the customers in those days!

Working the "quick lunch counter", I juggled 12 waffle irons making waffle ice cream sandwiches. I could barely keep up and could have used 24 irons…but then, I would have had to clean them spotless every night.

I soon graduated to cake decorator. Kresge's had its own bakery in the rear of the store, and Mr. Hendricks, my hardworking

---

> ## *"I dressed as a chef and 'made' a giant cherry pie…"*

---

boss, would carry the layers up to me from the rear of the store, 24 at a time. I can see him yet, with arms stretched holding two big trays and yelling, "One side! One side!"

Mr. Hendricks was so loaded with energy, enthusiasm and ideas that the store manager gave him control of a display window facing the sidewalk.

She Did Windows

His job was to better inform the public of Kresge's new restaurant, which boasted 175 cushioned seats, 25 smiling waitresses and roast turkey blue plate dinners for a quarter. Mr. Hendricks told me I'd have some new duties—along with a 50-cent pay increase.

Not only was I to trim the display according to theme, I also had to dress in costume and appear in the window!

I was pretty nervous about my first appearance as a "live mannequin", but I eventually got used to being a spectacle on Market Street.

One week we had a special on cherry

pie—only 10¢ each. Plus, a cherry cupcake came free with all dinners. To highlight the special, I painted a big sign with the week's slogan, "Life Is Just a Bowl of Cherries".

I appeared in the window dressed as a chef, going through the motions of making a giant cherry pie and hoisting it high with a pulley.

Down the Aisle

There seemed no end to Mr. Hendricks' ideas, and the demonstrations in the corner window display—including

DOLLY IN THE WINDOW. When Ruth Heebner got the job of window dresser at the Kresge's store in downtown Philadelphia, she didn't figure that she'd be part of the dressing! That's Ruth on display for "Strawberry Festival" (left) and the "Bridal Banquet Specials" (above).

das with whipped cream.

Another time, the window carried the motto "The Devil Is Tempting You". I dressed in a red outfit with horns and a long tail, which I flung around my arm as I stalked around my window writing the tempting menus on a big blackboard.

Alarming Promotion

Once Mr. Hendricks collected 50 alarm clocks and kept me winding them all day long to remind the public that "It's Time to Eat!"

The clocks' ringing was piped to the street through a loudspeaker. It wasn't long before office girls from nearby Chestnut Street were coming over and telling me to knock it off!

One morning, Mr. Hendricks was standing in the window with a microphone. To my embarrassment, he handed me the mike and told me to broadcast this week's specials to the world. It was the first "talkie" on Market Street...with the city's first neon lights right there in my window.

"Someday you will see neon everywhere!" Mr. Hendricks predicted.

Fake Cakes

One time I'll never forget was our "Strawberry Festival". We displayed layer cakes in the window, decorated with lard instead of whipped cream so they'd hold up through the day. The berries were real, though, and the cakes looked absolutely delicious.

One customer was so taken with the display cakes that she insisted on buying one. I tried my best to tell her it was made with lard and even asked her to sample it. No use...I finally gave in and wrapped it up for her!

Sadly, the day finally arrived when "my window" (and the whole 10-story Kresge building) was torn down to make room for "the new". Today, a modern shopping mall occupies 931 Market Street.

But they can't tear down memories. Even now I sometimes imagine the old store the way it used to be...with *That Old Gang of Mine* playing from the record counter and plenty of smiling clerks, ever eager to help a customer.

me—soon became a big attraction on Market Street.

I put on a long white gown to sell passersby on the "Bridal Banquet Specials". One was a 25-cent dinner that featured stewed spring chicken and a bride's biscuit. Waitresses dressed as bridesmaids served the meal and used big fans to cool diners.

To push Kresge's Southern dishes, my boss managed to locate a Southern belle getup for me to wear, complete with pantaloons.

Outfitted as a Dutch boy, I stood in that window for hours making "chocolate dainties"—10-cent double-dip so-

By Gerry Serra
Mt. Morris, Michigan

Saturdays at S.S. Kresge's

MY COUSIN and I didn't have malls to go to in the '30s, but we had just as much fun when we spent a Saturday at Kresge's.

We always took the streetcar to downtown Flint, Michigan. It ran down the center of Saginaw Street. We'd drop our nickels into the glass-sided container as the driver watched to make sure that we didn't try to use slugs.

When our destination was in sight, we'd pull the cord over the window next to our seat. The streetcar usually stopped right at the corner where our fun place, the S.S. Kresge store, was located.

Often on the street near the store there would be a man playing a guitar and harmonica. He had a tin cup nearby in case anyone wanted to make a donation.

In the store window was a small man doing fancy tricks with a yo-yo. Of course, the yo-yos were on sale in the store.

Once in the store, we were serenaded by piano music from

"*I*t was such fun to see that strip of snapshots..."

a lady in the back who sold the sheet music of the tunes she played. Passing the counters of needlework, hair nets, candies and other items, we headed for our first stop—the photo booth in the lower level.

Once in the booth, we giggled as we decided how to pose. Then we put a quarter in the slot, looked at the spot marked on the wall and waited.

It was such fun to see that strip of snapshots. Usually one was blurred because of all our fidgeting, but no matter. They would be handed out later to special friends.

Kresge's was also the place where we bought our autograph books and those diaries with the tiny lock and key

where we could write all our secret thoughts.

We might also splurge on a wee bottle of Park and Tillford perfume, or something more practical like bobby pins. We just *knew* either would enhance our social lives.

Our final purchase was a bag of popcorn from the machine by the door, as the clock downtown let us know it was time to catch the streetcar home.

Those were always great Saturdays for us! ☎

TWO IN A BOOTH. Author (on the right) and cousin Myrel had big smiles when they posed in the photo booth at Kresge's.

The K in Kmart Came from Kresge

WHEN THE FIRST S.S. Kresge store opened in 1899, it was a variety store that featured low-priced merchandise in relatively small stores with sparse furnishings. This was a concept pioneered by F.W. Woolworth in 1879.

The concept worked, and by 1917, when Kresge incorporated, there were 150 stores, and the company was second only to Woolworth's as the largest variety store chain in the world.

Over the next 40 years, the company experimented with mail-order catalogs, self-service and opening stores in shopping centers. By 1959, it was decided that Kresge should go beyond the original variety store and get into the discount store market, offering a wider merchandise mix.

In 1962, the first Kmart store, the outgrowth of S.S. Kresge, opened in Garden City, Michigan. ☎

By Charles Neugebauer
Spring Hill, Florida

DURING THE Depression, people had to think up different ways to make money.

For example, a photographer in our Chicago neighborhood walked the streets with a tripod on one shoulder and a pony behind him. He sought parents wanting a picture of their children on horseback.

Because of those hard times in 1933, he passed a lot of homes without having anyone call out to him.

My loving mother, Constance, agreed to have my sister, Connie, age 5, and me, 4, pose together in our tank-top bathing suits on the horse.

For many years, that 8x10 photo (right) sat majestically on a long table in our living room. For that instant, as I held firmly on to the saddle horn, I was a cowboy, a jockey and Royal Canadian Mounted Policeman all rolled into one.

About 4 years later, another photographer with a pony came around and set up in a "prairie", actually three vacant lots. If you had your picture taken on the pony, the photographer would give you a long ride by walking you around the "prairie".

For kids whose mothers were at home but couldn't make it to the photo site, you could have your picture taken and get a horseback ride if your mother gave her approval.

This Was an Emergency

Without a moment's hesitation, I took off for home, which was some 600 feet away. I found my mother wasn't at home, but I just *had* to get a pony ride.

I raced up to the bathroom and washed my face, then climbed on the toilet seat to look into the medicine chest mirror so I could comb my hair.

After changing my shirt, I raced back to the photographer for my photo and ride.

When the photographer asked if my mom said it was all right, I mumbled a quiet yes. I have always made it part of my character never to lie, and in retrospect, I believe I have

He Couldn't Say Whoa to a Free Horseback Ride

done pretty well for 69 years. However, this was an emergency, and the big prize was a pony ride.

The photographer sized me up, and I'm sure the razor-sharp part in my hair (in those days when I *had* hair) removed all doubt that I had obtained approval.

Within moments, the picture-taking was over, and I once again felt the leather of the saddle slapping against my legs as the pony and I, with the photographer alongside, rounded the perimeter of the "prairie".

Several weeks later, I looked out the living room window and saw my mother talking with a man holding a folder and some envelopes. He looked somewhat familiar, even though he wasn't carrying a tripod or dragging a pony.

When I was called out to the front steps by my mother, I tried to answer her questions about the photos the man had shown her. After I stammered for a period of time, they eventually put together the fact that I had lied to get a pony ride.

Because family funds were a little tight, my mother did not buy the picture of me on the pony. Looking back, I think she would have thought it a criminal act to display a photograph of a pony rider who lied.

A Learning Experience

The photographer realized *he* was the one who got taken for a ride by a very young boy and chalked up his loss to experience.

My mother didn't spank me and neither did my father when he came home that evening. I guess they felt my getting caught in an embarrassing lie was punishment enough.

Maybe my being truthful in later years is a result of that early incident.

As I told my granddaughter, Maggie, when you get real old, your mind doesn't remember things too well and it becomes very important to tell the truth. Once a person starts drifting from the truth, it becomes increasingly difficult to remember what "story" they told. So everyone should play it safe and practice telling the truth while they are young.

Having said that, it *was* a great pony ride on the "prairie" that summer day in 1937. ☎

Pets From Our Past

Pooch Was Major Trooper

IN 1943, when I was 16, I enlisted my Chesapeake Bay retriever, "Major", into the Army. He was trained for 8 months in Nebraska, then sent to the Solomon Islands, where he was a sentry dog.

Major (at right) served from May 1943 to July 1944. His service star was proudly displayed in the window of our home in Ogden, Utah.

During the war, I was watching a newsreel at a local theater about the war in the South Pacific and war dogs in action. And there was Major, big as life! It was quite a thrill to see him on film.

Major was returned to us after his honorable discharge on July 27, 1944.

The records we have state that he was wounded in action.

When Major came home, he remembered me and the rest of the family. We continued to use him as a hunting dog, as he never lost those skills.

And what a watchdog! He met my sister at the school bus every day and carried home her violin. Major was gentle, but always alert. He was our protector. —*Owen Barnett Farr West, Utah*

Petey the Pasta-Loving Canary

OUR LOVELY yellow canary, "Petey", delighted us with his singing back in the '50s. He also enjoyed freedom from his cage during the day but was closed in at mealtime.

One evening I forgot to close the cage door before supper. The family had just been seated to a meal of spaghetti when Petey swooped down without warning and skidded across our son's full plate.

Covered with pasta and sauce, Petey was unable to get himself airborne enough to return to his cage, and he landed with a thud in the middle of the kitchen table. I quickly scooped him up and placed him in the sink under warm running water until he was cleaned of his supper.

You can be sure I never again left Petey's cage open during meals.
—*Doris Danner East Boston, Massachusetts*

Running Board Goat

ON A camping trip in 1929, before I was born, my father had to borrow a goat to take

SIT. STAY. " When Grandma Gross held up her finger (note shadow in the foreground), I stood at attention and my dog, 'Mickey', sat at attention," says Dona Beath Moss of Summerfield, Florida. "The photo was taken in Akron, Ohio in 1933. Obeying one's elders was a must in those days."

along because my sister Sally had to have goat's milk.

My brother Robert said Dad put the goat, "Rosylee", in a crate on the running board of his Essex and faced her forward because he thought she'd like to see where she was going. (That's Robert and Rosylee below.)

"But she bloated up like a balloon," Robert says. "So the next day, Dad faced her in the opposite direction and all was well." —*Janice Dupree Smith Grand Rapids, Michigan*

SWING YOUR PARTNER. "Our parakeet, 'Freddy', could speak at least 50 words and sentences," says Marcella Carter of Liberty, Indiana. "During the '50s, my husband, Paul (above), and I were square dancers and played the guitar and fiddle. Freddy, who could call part of a square dance, also liked to perch on one of our instruments when we practiced. Freddy could open his cage when he wanted to get out, but when it was time for sleep, he'd go back in, pull the door closed and climb on his perch. Freddy was amazing."

Tarzan of New Jersey

By Emil Knab, Cumming, Georgia

This is the story of a German shepherd that was a member of our family in Irvington, New Jersey from 1932 until 1948.

"Tarzan" came to us when he was about 8 weeks old and seemed highly intelligent—almost as if he understood everything we were saying.

He clearly recognized words like "car", "ice cream", "store", "money" and "go". Upon hearing them, he'd run to the door and stand there waiting.

Of course, there were times when we couldn't take him along. On those occasions, Mother would tell us in German, "Close the dog in the kitchen." Fortunately, our *German* shepherd never learned to understand German.

Another sound he recognized was the jingling of coins. To him that meant we were going to the store, where we might buy him an ice cream Dixie Cup.

If we did, he'd take it outside, lie down with the cup between his paws and rotate it until he found the tab on the cover. Then he'd deftly remove the cover with his teeth and lap the ice cream out, leaving barely a tooth mark on the paper.

One day, my brothers, Jack and Carl, and I decided to find out how much Tarzan *really* understood. We jingled some change, and Tarzan immediately jumped up and ran to the door.

We showed him a nickel (the price of a Dixie Cup) and told him to take it to the store. He took the money in his mouth, ran down the stairs and out the door.

When we got to the store, he was waiting outside. We didn't know if he'd lost (or even swallowed) the nickel… however, I asked him to drop the nickel if he wanted ice cream. To our amazement, he dropped the coin at my feet and waited for his reward.

Another time, when I was 24, we tested Tarzan's natural protective instincts. Jack, 15, and Carl, 14, tied my hands behind my back with clothesline and laid me on the floor in the kitchen.

Then they excitedly asked Tarzan to go find me. He did, and when he saw me "struggling" to get free, he whined and licked my face. I showed him my tied wrists and waited to see what he'd do.

Tarzan to the Rescue!

I was more than surprised when the dog carefully laid his head sidewise on my arm, got the rope between his powerful incisors and cut through the rope in three bites!

As time passed, Tarzan learned many more tricks and never failed to amaze us with his intelligence.

Then along came World War II. Jack and Carl enlisted and left home, and Tarzan grieved for days, periodically visiting their bedrooms and resting his head on their beds.

We felt he'd soon forget the boys, as we'd heard a dog's memory lasted only about 6 weeks. The boys were in the service for about 2-1/2 years, and Carl was the first to come home.

Would He Remember?

When Carl arrived in his Army uniform, Tarzan growled as he would at any stranger and shunned Carl's attempt to pet him. He was told to lie in his bed under the sink, which he did, but he still kept up a low-level growl.

About half an hour later, as Carl was telling us about his experiences in the war, Tarzan sprung from his bed and lunged at him! For a moment we were horrified, but when Tarzan started to whine and lick Carl's face, we knew he'd finally remembered Carl. For the next few days, they were inseparable.

Tarzan was 16 when he died—it's said that equates to about 112 in terms of human age. Afterward, my parents adopted other dogs of the same breed… but there never was another Tarzan. ☎

'Welcome to the National Barn Dance!'

By Stella Edwards
Lawrence, Michigan

ON WEEKENDS, my sister Jean took me along to all kinds of interesting places. In 1943, she was 19, out of school and working. I was 13.

Since we lived in Chicago, there was plenty to see. We'd take the streetcar downtown to museums, the aquarium or the beach at Lake Michigan. She'd get tickets for concerts and plays, and once she took me to a "Walkathon" at the Chicago Amphitheater.

My favorite destination was the Eighth Street Theater on a Saturday night for *The National Barn Dance*. Whenever Jean got tickets for that show, the time couldn't pass fast enough for me.

Dressed in our Sunday best, we rode the streetcar down to the theater on the south side, which took almost an hour.

The Curtain Rose

The lobby was filled with couples and families, all excited about the up-coming show. I remember walking down the carpeted aisle looking for our seats. Sometimes we sat in the balcony.

Even before the houselights had been dimmed, a hush fell over the audience. Then the big velvet curtain rose, revealing the stage with a large barn for a backdrop. The entertainers sat on hay bales to play their guitars, banjos and accordions.

The announcer, who always wore a cowboy shirt, boots and a big cowboy hat, would say, "Welcome to *The National Barn Dance!*" Then the music began.

The female performers, many with their hair in pigtails and ponytails, looked so pretty in brightly

DARLING DUO. Talented "Lulu Belle" and "Skyland Scotty" (Myrtle Cooper and Scott Wiseman, pictured at right) were a popular *Barn Dance* pair.

WLS National Barn Dance Cast, October, 1944

WORLD'S LARGEST CAST? The whole cast from *The National Barn Dance* posed for this photo (above) in 1944, when the show was broadcast on WLS (which stood for "World's Largest Store", Sears, Roebuck and Co.). One of Stella Edwards' favorite regulars was Arkie, the Arkansas Woodchopper (far left).

colored gingham dresses and pinafores. Some wore cowboy boots, and others had dancing slippers.

The men wore flannel shirts, jeans and bright bandannas around their necks. Most sported large cowboy hats as well.

Many of the performers were regulars on the show, like Lulu Belle and Skyland Scotty...Arkie, the Arkansas Woodchopper...and Little Genevieve.

I always laughed at the high jinks of Little Genevieve, who wore a baby's

dress and bonnet and carried a bottle. The fact that "she" was a 300-pound man made it all the funnier.

Square Dancers Were Best

But what I enjoyed most was the square dancing. Young men and women would come running onto the stage, form squares and dance to a lively tune while the "caller" yelled out the maneuvers.

The couples dressed in colorful outfits, and often the men's shirts matched their partner's dress. How I envied them

and wished I knew how to square dance.

I got my wish many years later. My husband, Eddy, was a square dancer, and he taught me how. We went to many square dances together.

One night as we were having a cup of coffee and reminiscing about growing up in the '40s, I learned something remarkable.

Eddy told me that he belonged to a group of young people who square danced all over Chicago then. One of the places they danced was on *The National Barn Dance*!

Who knows...one of those square dancers I so envied as a girl might've been my future husband! ☎

177

CHARLIE'S CHUM. That's Gardner Kissack above with one of his prized possessions—a genuine Charlie McCarthy radio.

GREATS FROM THE GOLDEN AGE. The little Art Deco RCA at top pulled in the sounds of the Big Bands back in the early '40s. So did the Crosley and tiny Airline from around 1940 just below it. After World War II, radios—like the Travler seen directly above—became much more portable. Do these bring back memories?

It All Started with a Sonora

By Gardner Kissack, Chicago Heights, Illinois

GROWING UP in the '30s and '40s, I enjoyed radio programs like *Fibber McGee and Molly, The Lone Ranger, The Halls of Ivy, Charlie McCarthy, Ma Perkins* and *Jerry Browning, Private Detective.*

Fibber and Charlie were probably the funniest, but *The Lone Ranger* made the strongest impression. The introduction—"Nowhere in the pages of history can one find a greater champion of justice…"—has always stuck with me.

Despite my early interest in radio programs and the receivers themselves,

1948 Sonora

I didn't start collecting radios until a few years ago…and even then, it came about by accident.

I was moving some furniture when I discovered my old 1948 Sonora (at left). Then I remembered the sedate Minerva I'd won in a photo contest when I was 11…and the Airline portable I received as a birthday present in the late '40s.

Both were tucked away on a shelf in my basement. After that, things got out of hand! Now I have more than 250 different models.

RED ALERT. Above are a plastic Olympic (early '50s), a plaid Firestone (late '50s) and a 1948 Airline portable.

REV 'EM UP! This white '51 Crosley, the '53 Crosley behind it and the '53 CBS Columbia look as if they all belonged on an automobile dashboard or in the cockpit of an airplane.

AHEAD OF ITS TIME? The stylish 1939 General Electric radio at top has push buttons and is actually more "modern" looking than the two plastic Philcos from the mid-'50s shown below it. The Charlie McCarthy radio looks awfully good, too, considering it's about 70 years old.

As you can see from these photographs, old radios have plenty of character and personality. Designs were influenced by automobiles (many look like car dashboards or radiator grilles) or airplanes (there were propellers, swept-back wings and fins—even thrusting jet engine pods!).

Some radios made before World War II reflect Art Deco trends, while other dark and somber models hint at the seriousness of the country's economic situation.

Of course, during the '30s and '40s, there were also whimsical radios featuring Disney characters or famed celebrities, like my Charlie McCarthy radio (above right).

With the advent of plastics in the '50s, color was everywhere—Chinese red, burnt orange, marbles mauve and California avocado, also known as '50 Ford Crestliner chartreuse. Some sets were even clad in plaid or dressed up to look like luggage.

Yes, these old radios certainly have personality. Will the functional black plastic radios of today inspire the same kind of fond memories years from now?

Somehow, I doubt it. ☎

He Knew What The Shadow Knew

By Eric Arthur, Williamsburg, Virginia

CREATED in the 1930s by Walter B. Gibson, *The Shadow* magazine stories and novels became immensely popular and were soon developed into a weekly radio series.

Airing from 1931 to 1954 (and briefly starring the inimitable Orson Welles), the program became one of the longest-running radio shows on record.

With Gibson still turning out stories for publication (he wrote almost 300), the producers brought in freelance writers to help with the growing demand for *Shadow* radio scripts.

In the early '40s, I was writing for a number of mystery radio programs in New York, including *Gangbusters*, *The Molle Mystery Theater* and *Inner Sanctum Mysteries*. A friend suggested I try working for *The Shadow*, which was becoming the most popular drama in radio. I did…and landed a job as a regular staff writer. This photo (left) was taken toward the end of my stint on the staff.

Walter Gibson left us sharply drawn characters and well-developed story patterns to follow. As long as we held to his formula, the plot for each episode was left to our imaginations. With those guidelines, we pitted Lamont Cranston and Margo Lane against a galaxy of vampires, zombies ("walking dead") and other antisocial creatures.

Devising such schemes often resulted in my own unsettling dreams. In one recurrent nightmare, I was chased by a grinning zombie brandishing a machete. Fortunately, I always screamed myself awake before he caught me.

Evidently I wasn't the only victim of such nightmares. On one occasion, the main sponsor of the program, the Blue Coal Company, ordered us to lay off the zombie bit for a while. Mothers all across the country had complained that we were scaring their children with too many scripts about "the walking dead"!

Without zombies to terrorize Lamont and Margo, we had to come up with other creatures. In "Bubbling Death", for example, my leading lady, heiress to a Creole fortune, was drawn to her demise in a Louisiana swamp by the voice of a vengeful ancestor. They had barred the "walking dead", but they didn't say anything about the "talking dead".

Live Shows Were Exciting

I called another script "Dolls of Death". In it, a little toy maker who hated big people acquired the formula used by a tribe of Indians in the Amazon to shrink heads.

The toy maker invited a 6-foot-7 police commissioner to the back of the shop for a cup of coffee. The coffee was laced with knockout drops, and the commissioner soon ended up as a tiny doll on display in the toy shop window.

There was often *real* excitement on the shows that we writers didn't create. Because broadcasts were live, the actors and technicians had to get everything right the first time.

During one broadcast, the sound man's gun jammed. A nervous young director ran into the studio from the control booth and shouted into the microphone, "Bang! Bang!"

Another time, one of Lamont's enemies said, "I'm going to put a bullet through your heart." Again there was gun trouble, but the quick-witted actor ad-libbed, "On second thought, it would give me greater pleasure to choke you with my bare hands." And then the gun went off.

During the 25 years *The Shadow* was on the air, the writing staff turned out over 1,000 episodes. Today the material would probably be called corny. But I like to think that all those programs were a fitting tribute to Walter Gibson's super-sleuth…and to those more innocent times when *The Shadow knew.* ☎

THE Shadow MAGAZINE
A STREET & SMITH PUBLICATION
10 CENTS
MAR. 15 NUMBER
TWICE A MONTH
BELLS OF DOOM
A Shadow Detective Novel

As Queen For a Day, She Rode To Royalty

By Barbara Bashaw Vinciguerra
Blythe, California

WHEN I went to check my mailbox on June 24, 1958, it was a lovely, sunny day in Hermosa Beach, California.

Along with the usual bills and letters was a surprise—two tickets I'd requested to join the studio audience of *Queen for a Day*.

This long-running TV show was my favorite. Host Jack Bailey would invite a few women from the audience on stage, then ask each contestant what she most needed and why. The ladies commonly answered with tear-jerking stories, then the audience voted for a winner by applause. The victor was queen.

My tickets were only good for the following day, so I had to act quickly. I ran to a neighbor's house and asked her to go, but she couldn't.

I couldn't find *anyone* on such short notice, and the trip meant a long complicated bus ride with many transfers. So I decided to go by bike instead.

That evening, I made two egg salad sandwiches for my lunch along the road. The next day, I jumped on my $10 police-auction bike and struck out on a 40-mile adventure.

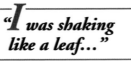

"I was shaking like a leaf..."

Halfway there, I stopped and ate a sandwich under a cluster of palm trees near some houses being torn down to make room for the Santa Monica Freeway. I *carried* my bike across part of that construction area and got my hands pretty greasy doing so.

I arrived at the studio just in time for the show and padlocked my bike behind some bushes.

I rushed to hand the usher my ticket, which was just as greasy as my hands. There had been no time to get cleaned up!

With the other audience members, I filled out a questionnaire asking to tell something unusual about myself.

I wrote that I'd ridden my bike all the way from Hermosa Beach just to be there. That put me in the group of 26 ladies interviewed, and then I became one of the six contestants for the show.

I was shaking like a leaf when Jack Bailey called me up on stage. Someone handed me back my ticket and whispered that I should give it to Mr. Bailey.

He held it up to the camera and gushed, "Now isn't this the dirtiest card you've ever seen in all these many years of *Queen for a Day*?"

He did so with extreme embellishment and then asked me to tell my tale about biking to the show. Next, he asked me about riding a bike on the freeway and what happened when the wind hit my skirt.

"Oh, I was prepared," I said. "I have a bathing suit on under my sundress." I even lifted my skirt to prove it, and by then, everyone was roaring.

At the end of the program, *I* was

BELIEVE IT! Barbara Bashaw Vinciguerra was royally surprised upon being crowned Queen for a Day in '58.

wearing that gorgeous jeweled crown and a long, luxurious (but *heavy*) purple robe. I couldn't believe it!

After the show, they tried putting my bike in the trunk of a golden Cadillac to take me home, but it wouldn't fit. They did get it into the giant backseat, so I rode up front with a very nice chauffeur.

When we reached Hermosa Beach, we rode around town blowing the horn before heading home. I really was *Queen for a Day*—and actually, for even longer than that.

Presents rolled in week after week for nearly a year, including a new Ford from Ben Alexander's car lot (he was Jack Webb's sidekick on *Dragnet*).

I also received a puppy from the *Rin Tin Tin* television show, a sewing machine, clothes, drapes, shoes, appliances, pots and pans, cosmetics and a 16-piece bedroom set!

My Christmas came in June that year, and if I live to be 100, I'll *never* forget it.

My Favorite Radio Program

kind without risers, and grabbed the victim by the ankle as he walked down the stairs.

It was months before I could go down to Grandfather's root cellar without shaking and expecting a hand to grab my ankle and send me head over heels to the bottom.

—Adrian Baylock
Ebensburg,
Pennsylvania

Lunch Ended with a Song

IN 1939, my mother went to work outside the home for the first time.

Since my elementary school was only a block away, I came home every day for lunch. My lunch would be on the kitchen table, along with a cheerful note from Mother saying she loved me and would see me after school.

Also on that table was a small radio. I'd turn on Kate Smith's 15-minute program each day at noon. I enjoyed listening to Kate sing while I ate my lunch. When she finished the show with *God Bless America*, I knew it was time to go back to school.

To this day, hearing *God Bless America* brings back fond memories.

—Lila Barsky, Elizabeth, New Jersey

Pleasant Dreams

MY FAVORITE radio programs when I was a child were the mystery dramas, like *Inner Sanctum Mysteries* and *I Love a Mystery*. What made the tales so frightening was visualizing the events as happening in my own house.

A thud in the basement on the radio was a thud in *our* basement. If the victim was in the bedroom and heard footsteps coming up the stairs, I imagined myself in my own bed hearing the footsteps.

One time there was a story about an incident in a place that I visualized as my grandfather's root cellar. The villain was hiding under the cellar steps, the

Taking a Break with Stella

DURING the Depression, my parents were farmers in southeast Oklahoma and had 10 children. All of us were accustomed to hard work, but if we weren't in the fields hoeing cotton or corn, we could listen to *Stella Dallas*.

If we were in the fields, Mother would send one of us to the house for some fresh drinking water, with permission to listen to *Stella Dallas* so we could all keep up with Stella and her "Lolly-baby".

I really enjoyed the program when it was my turn to sit by the radio, then relay the story to the others when I returned to the fields. Somehow, the work didn't seem so hard when we had *Stella Dallas* to look forward to.

—Myrtle Beavers, Destin, Florida

Pop Used an Alias

POPULAR during the '30s and '40s, *The Quiz Kids* radio show awarded prizes to anyone who could stump a panel of precocious youngsters. My dad once stumped the little geniuses, and he won a big console radio!

I can't remember the brand of that set, but on the front it said, "Clear as a bell". It sure was! We used it to listen to *Amos 'n' Andy*, *Jack Benny* and *Gang Busters*.

Pop was a high school teacher in Chicago, and when he submitted his questions to *The Quiz Kids*, he used the name "Henry Stews". I think he was afraid the program wouldn't take him seriously if they knew his real name was Henry Altyme Swets!

—Jim Hardley Swets, Ada, Michigan

Paid a Premium for Wolf Paw Jacket

THANKS to my father, I am the proud possessor of much of the memorabilia (see photo below) that has survived from a popular children's show of the early '30s, the *Lone Wolf Tribe*.

As fans of "Chief Wolf Paw" will recall, you could send for official "Tribe" items by mailing outer wrappers from Wrigley's gum. And it took a *lot* of wrappers.

The Wolf Paw suede jacket, which I gave to my brother many moons ago, took 160 wrappers. The 100% pure wool saddle blanket required a wampum-whopping 200 wrappers!

I didn't chew gum, as we had been taught that sugar was bad for our teeth. So how did I get all those wrappers?

It was thanks to my beloved father, a 50-year employee with the Chicago and North Western Railroad. He'd comb the passenger cars when they came into the California Avenue coach yards. What treasure those cars yielded!

Bah-nee-ho-nee-nah (I am your friend). *—Virginia Brakrog Wilder*
Arlington Heights, Illinois

Nobody Moved During *Amos 'n' Andy*

I REMEMBER being in a South Carolina restaurant in 1932 when I was on a trip with my parents to Florida. We had just settled down and were scanning the menu when 7 p.m. arrived.

All activity in the restaurant came to a halt. The waiters stopped serving, the cook came out of the kitchen, and the diners put down their knives and forks.

It was time for *Amos 'n' Andy*! The restaurant radio was tuned to the popular program, which on this date was part of a continuing story in which Amos was suspected of having committed a murder. He was, of course, later found innocent.

No one moved, not even during the commercials, until the program was over. I can't imagine that happening today. But, perhaps, it wouldn't be so bad if such innocent diversion still had the power to make us stop, just for a little while.   —*Seabury Lewis*
Hamden, Connecticut

Who's Buried in Grant's Tomb?

PEORIA'S radio station, WMBD, did its own version of the *Whiz Kids* program that was broadcast from Chicago. When I was 14, I was a contestant.

On the first show, I answered all the questions correctly and was invited back the next week. I was doing all right until the emcee, Milton Budd, asked me this question: "What is the name of the wife in the comic strip *Gasoline Alley*, Phyllis?"

Mr. Budd even stressed certain words, but I was unable to give the answer. I knew the husband was Walt, but I couldn't remember his wife's name.

It was, of course, Phyllis. That was my last week on the show.
—*Phyllis Heberling*
Virginia Beach, Virginia

She Cleaned Up on Old Shows

IN THE late '40s, our family's favorite radio shows were *Burns and Allen*, *Fibber McGee and Molly*, *The Shadow*, *The Lone Ranger*, *The Great Gildersleeve* and *The Jack Benny Program*. Several of them were broadcast on Sunday night.

As a special treat on Sundays, Mother let us take our baths in the old tin tub in the kitchen instead of the bathroom so we could listen to the kitchen radio.

I don't recall exactly which of those programs were on Sunday night, but those evenings were very special because of our baths in that old tin tub.
—*Rena Caudle, Redding, California*

She Got Inside Information

A FAVORITE childhood memory is my membership in Captain Midnight's Secret Squadron. My day revolved around the *Captain Midnight* radio show, mainly because a secret coded message was given out at the end of each episode.

The message let squadron members know what would happen to Captain Midnight the next day. Imagine knowing the outcome of a suspenseful situation in advance of the rest of the world!

After the episode, I'd take out my decoder badge and use this treasure to gain access to that valuable information.

Later, the mailman brought me my Captain Midnight Detect-O-Scope. That device allowed me to see behind me without turning around. Every important spy should have one!
—*Lorraine Cripps, Phoenix, Arizona*

Radio a Religious Experience

MY FAVORITE radio show was *The Jack Benny Program*, which was broadcast from 7 to 7:30 on Sunday nights.

Since I was expected to be in church at 7:30, I made a mad dash from the house when the show ended, ran the half block to church and managed to slide into a back pew just as the organist began the prelude.   —*Louise Strayer*
Dallastown, Pennsylvania

Buck Rogers Wore Cardboard?

WAITING for those radio premiums to arrive in the mail built up our expectations way beyond reason. The worst case I remember was the Buck Rogers helmet I ordered for 25¢ plus the inner seal from a can of Cocomalt.

I figured the helmet would go great with the Buck Rogers pistol I already had. I envisioned a streamlined aluminum helmet with a pointed top and built-in earphones.

What I got was several pieces of cardboard with punch-out holes and

JANE BOND? Secret Squadron member Lorraine Cripps peers out from her Captain Midnight decoder badge (top). Detect-O-Scope (above) allowed "behind-the-back" spying.

tabs that bent over. I was shocked and disappointed. Determined to build the helmet of my dreams, I traced the design of the cardboard helmet onto a piece of sheet metal, cut out the pieces and tried to bend them into a smooth oval to fit my head.

I ended up with a metal polygon that barely went on my head and tore out my hair when it did. The space helmet took its final flight into the city dump.
—*Kenneth Roberts*
Riverside, Rhode Island

If the Shoe Squeaks

IN THE MID-'40s, my dad was away on a construction job, leaving Mom, my brother and me at home. My brother was 6 or 7 and slept in a room off the kitchen, in the back of the house.

One night, Mom and I listened to *Inner Sanctum Mysteries* before bed. After the program, Mom was standing in the doorway of my room, when we heard from another part of the house a *drag-clump, drag-clump* sound. We looked at each other, wondering if some horrible character from the inner sanctum was coming to get us.

It turned out my brother had gotten up to go to the bathroom and stuck one foot in a slipper and the other in a shoe.

Once the "mystery" was solved, we couldn't stop laughing.
—*Dorie Peebles, Honeoye, New York*

My Brother Was 'Doctor I.Q.'!

By Madelyn Harris
Las Cruces, New Mexico

BACK IN THE '30s, after homework and chores were done, our family gathered 'round the radio to listen to shows like *Fibber McGee and Molly*, *Amos 'n' Andy* and *One Man's Family*.

Those old shows were great, but another network program was our household favorite. It was called *Dr. I.Q.*, and I remember it well because the star of the show was my big brother, Lew Valentine (right)!

Dr. I.Q., which aired Monday nights on NBC, was one of the first radio quiz shows. Folks all over the country won cash for answering questions from Lew, posing as "Dr. I.Q., The Mental Banker". That was a lofty title for a fellow who never finished high school!

At the time, we lived in San Benito, a small town in the Lower Rio Grande Valley of Texas. Lew was bitten by the radio bug at age 17 and quit high school 6 months before graduation.

The school superintendent consoled Mother by telling her Lew was so intent on a career in radio that he'd probably do okay.
And he did!

Got a Good Start

Lew's first job was at a station in Houston. From there he went to San Antonio, where he worked at WOAI, opening his daily broadcasts with a lusty "Good morning, everyone!" Mother would turn up the radio so my brother's voice boomed throughout the house.

Around 1935, the *Dr. I.Q.* show was born. It was first broadcast nationally in 1939, sponsored by Mars Inc., maker of Mars bars, Snickers, Milky Way and Three Musketeers candy bars.

The show was broadcast live from different movie theaters in large cities across America. After the movie, Lew would take the stage while several assistants with handheld microphones spread out in the audience.

"I Have 10 Silver Dollars…"

An assistant would select a contestant and exclaim, "I have a lady right here in the balcony, Doctor!"

Lew would reply, "I have 10 silver dollars for that lady if she can tell me…", and then he'd ask a question. The amount of prize money would vary with the difficulty of the question.

If the lady in the balcony (or any other contestant) missed the question, she or he would get a box of Mars candy bars and two tickets to a movie.

In addition to the questions, there was an impossible tongue twister that hardly anyone got right. Called "The Monument to Memory", it was spoken only once by Dr. I.Q. and then had to be repeated by the contestant.

One that I recall was, "Jim is slim, said Tim to Kim. Jim *is* slim, Tim, to him said Kim."

Another game was "The Biographical Sketch", which was worth 75 silver dollars—a very generous prize in those days.

The contestant was given a clue about a famous person. If the contestant guessed the name after the first clue, he or she won $75. The amount decreased with each clue.

Made Mom Proud

Whatever the game, residents of San Benito were very proud of their hometown boy. But none was prouder than Mother.

Lew traveled with the show until the start of World War II, when he enlisted and entertained the troops. Family and friends never grew tired of hearing Lew's stories about all of the people he'd met over the years and the fun he had being Dr. I.Q.

Lew passed away in 1976, but I'm sure many listeners out there still remember him…and all those ladies in the balcony! ☎

'47 Blizzard Brought Unexpected Company

By Bea Wolfe Barth
Sun Prairie, Wisconsin

IF WE HADN'T left our yard light on during that blizzard in January 1947, several people might not have made it through a storm that caused snowdrifts up to 14 feet deep.

We were living on a farm near De Forest, Wisconsin when my husband, Clem, heard about the coming storm on the radio. To prepare, he drove into town on the tractor and stocked up on bread, coffee and cookies. We didn't have a car at the time.

The farmhouse we rented sat below a hill, and the wind started blowing massive amounts of snow over us and the nearby state highway late in the afternoon of January 28.

Folks Sought Shelter

After a while, stranded motorists desperate for shelter started rolling in, and some didn't even knock. As they arrived, we offered food and coffee. Luckily, we had an indoor bathroom and plenty of bedrooms upstairs.

Our daughter Jackie was a year old and our son Bruce was about 4. My brother Rodney, 10, was also living with us. They loved all the excitement.

It wasn't easy, but somehow we made space for everybody. A county snowplow had broken down nearby, so four county workers rested with pillows under our big dining room table.

A hospital patient who was being transferred was carried in after the ambulance got stuck in the drifts.

Ambulance crew members sat him in a big chair and called the hospital to report the patient was safe.

I remember one couple from Chicago came in, and the man got down to the floor and kissed it because he was so happy to be there safe and sound.

At the top of the hill, two cattle trucks were stalled. The drivers borrowed pieces of cardboard from our basement to better enclose the trucks and help keep the cattle warm. They also took hay and gasoline to keep the cattle fed and the trucks running.

Then a Greyhound bus en route to Madison stalled, and about a dozen college students and the driver ended up at our home.

We kept that yard light on all night so folks could see their way to the house.

Clem and Rodney helped people reach the house from the road, and our telephone was in constant use. Folks let their fami-lies know they were inside and safe.

In the kitchen, several men played cards all night. I had two pails of eggs in the back hall, so some women fried eggs and kept the coffee going.

One neighbor called and said we could send people over there, but no one could get *out* of the house due to the drifting snow.

After the snowplow cleared the road, Clem took the tractor again and got more groceries.

Who's Sleeping in Her Bed?

Some people went upstairs to sleep. Once when I looked in our bedroom, there were two people in my bed!

As they left, several offered to pay for our hospitality, but I refused. After 2 days, when the 30 to 40 "guests" had left, I found money tucked in drawers and the cookie jar, totaling $50 to $60.

We also received many gifts and letters afterward. For years, we continued to hear from these visitors. The bus driver honked whenever he drove past, and the ambulance driver often stopped by.

All in all, we met a lot of nice friends on those 2 snowy days.

SNOW JOB. The author, shown here later in 1947, was kept busy being a hospitable hostess when her family's farmhouse was invaded by 30 to 40 people during a winter storm.

THE YEAR 1936 will forever stand out in my memory.

I was only 6 years old when I was rushed to the hospital with two crushed feet. My parents were told that I might never walk again.

The accident happened when I was sitting on the curbstone in front of our house in Lowell, Massachusetts.

I was playing in a puddle after a rainstorm and suddenly felt a huge weight on my feet. When I looked up, there was a car tire on them. I cried out, but the motor was running and no one could hear me over the engine.

The driver had run across the street for a newspaper. When he got back to his car, he drove away —never knowing he had parked on my feet.

Just about then, our neighbor's son came home and saw me bent over my feet in pain. He scooped me up and carried me home, and I remember thinking how tall and strong he was.

An ambulance came, and I remained in the hospital for 3 weeks while my feet were "repaired". When I returned home, I couldn't walk.

Three-Wheeled Miracle

I sat in our bay window and watched the children play on the cobblestone street and longed to join them…but I couldn't. I felt so left out.

My parents were told that if I was ever to walk again, I'd need therapy, which in those days meant riding a tricycle to get my feet back into condition for walking.

Our family couldn't afford such an extravagance. Times were tough during the Depression, and there were five mouths to feed, besides buying coal and wood for the stove.

Dad couldn't afford a car and walked 7 miles each way to work every day at Heinz Electric. No, there was no money for a tricycle. I was doomed to be a cripple.

Then one day, while sitting at my usual place in the window, I saw my

Dad's Loving Act Took Cold Courage

By Claire Ignacio
Dracut, Massachusetts

LOVING DAD. Claire Ignacio (at top left and below center with sisters) was saved from a cruel fate after her father (above with Mom in 1935) sacrificed his comfort for his little girl.

father walking up the street carrying two tricycles on his shoulders…one red and the other white.

He looked up at me with the *biggest* smile on his face. As soon as he got in the house, he picked me up and put me on one of the tricycles and taught me to ride it.

The other tricycle was for my younger sister, Alice, so she could keep me company on our rides up and down the long hallway that separated the bed-

rooms in our house. My mother made sure we rode our bikes for hours every day. She didn't mind that we banged into the walls and put gouges in the door jambs. She wanted to see me walk…and finally I did.

It took time to learn how to walk all over again. Gradually, I was able to put my whole foot down without pain and then began to take my first steps.

Warmhearted Trade

But the first steps toward my recovery were really taken by Dad. It was many years later before I learned where and how he had gotten his hands on those trikes.

Dad had approached Jack Hanger, the owner of a secondhand store in our neighborhood, and told him about my injuries…and how I watched the children playing with such a sad face. Jack took my father's warm winter coat in exchange for those tricycles.

All these years later, I can still see the scars, but I walk 3 miles a day and can ski on both water and snow. I'll be forever thankful to my father.

I shudder every time I think of those cold New England winter days when he had to walk 7 miles to work without his warm coat.

But I can still picture his smile the day he carried home those tricycles on his shoulders, knowing that he would make me walk again. ☎

Encounter at the Candy Counter

By Ann Champeau, Norman, Oklahoma

MOTHER BELIEVED in the old saying "Idle hands are the devil's workshop". She was ever alert for ways to keep me, my sister and brother busy in our Oklahoma City neighborhood.

One day in 1947, she heard Kress' Five-and-Dime was hiring and decided it was time for me to take my first real job. She accompanied me on the streetcar to the store, then left me standing in front of the floor manager's desk.

"Can you make change?" the tall, imposing woman asked. "And do you know your fractions?"

"Yes, ma'am," I answered.

She looked at me for a long minute while I stood at attention. Turning with a shrug, she picked up some papers and asked if I could start immediately. I stammered another "Yes, ma'am."

Minutes later, I was behind the candy counter weighing coconut haystacks, bonbons, Boston baked beans and gumdrops under her watchful eye.

By 11:30, I'd made no mistakes and was left to work the counter alone. Confidence in my business acumen soared. All was quiet, so I cleaned the case fronts and took a moment to look around the store.

Customers and Creaks

Neatly filled segmented counters displayed a wide variety of items—tablets, pens, screwdrivers, hammers, dolls, toy cars, cups and saucers, needles, thread, combs and hair nets.

The wooden floors creaked as customers walked through the aisles and salesgirls climbed rolling ladders to retrieve bolts of cloth and bed linens.

Suddenly the floor creaked right in front of me. I looked up into the eyes of an elderly man.

"May I help you?" I asked, as I'd been taught.

"Hmmm…" he replied, looking from the bonbons to the macaroons. He pushed his glasses up his nose and gently stroked his nostrils, pouting his lips in decision.

Three children swarmed to the counter, placing their hands on the newly polished glass and pressing their faces close to the candy.

The old gentleman pointed at the coconut haystacks and asked how much three of those would cost him.

I weighed three of them and said, "15¢."

"Hmmm…" was his response.

"I'll be with you in a minute," I told a child impatiently pointing at gumdrops. Then I nervously smiled at a woman removing her white gloves near the chocolate-covered creams.

My elderly customer asked, "How many of those Boston baked beans does a dime buy?"

I weighed the brick-colored candies and showed him. "Hmmm…"

The Pressure Mounted

"Young lady," the white-gloved customer beckoned, "can you please help me?"

The boldest of the young children spoke up, "But we were here first!"

"Don't be sassy, little fellow," the impatient lady snapped. "Now, clerk—I can't wait all day!" she fumed at me.

I didn't know what to do. I looked from the angry woman to the restless children to my picky customer. "Sir," I asked, "may I weigh something else for you?"

"Well…see how much three pink bonbons will cost me."

Trembling with anxiety, I picked them up to weigh them. That's when I saw the manager stalking across the aisles toward me. I didn't know what to do—I was sure she thought I couldn't handle my job.

Marching behind the counter, she asked who was first to be waited on. The white-gloved lady smiled, graciously pointing to the youngsters.

Meanwhile, my elderly customer finally made his selection. "Please give me three of the yellow bonbons," he said, looking over at the manager with a nod. She smiled and nodded back.

The man dug out two dimes from a worn leather change purse. Having satisfied the others, the manager walked over, pointed to my elderly customer and introduced us. "Ann, I'd like you to meet Mr. Kress."

To this day, I don't know whether his actions were a test or whether he was just eccentric…I suspect a bit of both. I *do* know that it was an experience I could never forget. ☎

SUGAR SHAKES. Ann Champeau (left in 1945) thought her new job was sweet as chocolate, until a customer turned the day into lemon drops.

My Favorite Old-Time Poem

"I MEMORIZED this poem in the third grade after our teacher read it to us," writes William Prigge of St. Paul, Minnesota. "That was back in 1918 at a one-room school and I still enjoy it today."

Which Loved Her Best?

"I love you, Mother," said little John;
Then forgetting his work, his cap went on,
And he was off to the garden swing,
Leaving his mother the wood to bring.

"I love you, Mother," said Rosy-nel,
"I love you better than tongue can tell;"
Then she teased and pouted full half the day,
Till her mother rejoiced when she went to play.

"I love you, Mother," said little Fan,
"Today I'll help you all I can;
How glad I am that school doesn't keep!"
So she rocked the baby till it fell asleep.

Then, stepping softly, she took the broom,
And swept the floor and dusted the room;
Busy and happy all day was she,
Helpful and cheerful as child can be.

"I love you, Mother," again they said—
Three little children going to bed;
How do you think that Mother guessed
Which of them really loved her best?

Photo: H. Armstrong Roberts

Grandmother's House Was a Kid's Haven

By Carol Johnson, Sellersburg, Indiana

SPRING OF 1945 was a tough time for my mother. With a 5-year-old daughter and a baby on the way, she faced difficulties common to many women in times of war.

Dad had joined the Navy and was serving in the Philippines in the Seabees, a construction battalion. Mother, meanwhile, was struggling alone with morning sickness, shaky finances and the inability to find tires and gas for our monster-sized Cord.

Mom finally sold our new home, put the car on blocks and moved us in with Dad's mother in Jeffersonville, Indiana. (I then remained with Grandmother after my father returned in 1946, to finish out the school year.)

Not only did *we* land on Grandmother's doorstep, so did Aunt Ruthie when Uncle Ernie left college to enter the service.

Times Were Tough

This could not have been easy. They were sisters-in-law attempting to get along, fearing the war and trying to pool their resources of servicemen's pay plus whatever Grandmother made working at the A&P store.

However, for a 5-year-old, carefully sheltered from the harsh realities of life, this was an exciting time.

Grandmother's house was a child's dream with lots of small rooms to prowl around in. The big U-shaped porch had a cushioned glider and wooden table for magazines and lemonade.

There was even space for an orange crate to use as a desk or dressing table when my friends and I played dress-up with Aunt Ruthie's clothes.

Days Filled with Fun

I'm certain few mothers would have allowed this mess on *their* front porch. We got away with it because Grandmother and Aunt Ruthie worked, and Mother was sick during most of her pregnancy and no doubt glad I'd found something to do.

Our days were filled with fun—flattening cans to give to the rag and tin man, mushing color into bags of oleomargarine, peeling tinfoil off gum wrappers to save in a ball, saving string and watching Mother or Grandmother try to fix something.

Aiding the war effort was like a game to little kids and created lifetime habits of resourcefulness and saving things for a "second life".

Although several people lived in that house, I had my own little bedroom with a white iron bed, nightstand, radio and a chifforobe with a long, glamorous mirror. In a box under my bed were beautifully hand-tailored doll clothes Aunt Ruthie had made for me.

A screened window next to my bed allowed me to eavesdrop on Grandmother and her friends when they played cards every Saturday night.

My favorite room for playing was the bathroom. Grandmother always had talcum powder, lotions and pretty things Mother didn't have. It had a corner sink with a chain that fascinated me.

The claw-foot tub was so tall, I had to use a foot-

MUSICAL FAMILY. The author was 5 (below, in 1945) when she lived at her grandmother's. Today (left) music is still part of her life.

stool to get in. But oh, when you did, it was heavenly. That tub was so deep, you could fill it nearly to the top and pretend it was a swimming pool.

I still remember the feeling of my hair floating in the water and the softness of those threadbare washcloths Grandmother had.

Behind the tub was a laundry chute where you dropped dirty clothes. They landed in a pile in the basement, where a wicked wringer washing machine continually challenged Mother.

Grandmother's living room was so elegant with its Duncan Phyfe sofa. A fancy little mirror hung over a bookcase that had a crocheted lace piece on it. And her piano was different from any I had seen. The top, when closed, looked like a buffet table. It was rarely closed, though, as Mother, Grandmother and I all played.

Music Soothed Them

Mother was quite a musician and could play by ear. Many nights I fell asleep listening to her play the melancholy music of the war years, or Grandmother playing her favorites.

As I think back on what a hard time that was for adults, I realize what a thoroughly annoying child I must have been—rooting through Aunt Ruthie's clothes, using Grandmother's powder and making the front porch a mess.

But I never heard a word of reprimand or experienced a feeling of sadness or fear. For a 5-year-old, it was only a time of discovery, imagination and pleasure that lingers still in my memories. ☎

Our Figures Came From Sears

By Donna Wachter, White City, Oregon

MY GRANDMA was about 5-foot-2, and after giving birth to seven children, she'd long ago lost her girlish figure. Still, she always held her head up and her shoulders back.

She would tell us constantly: "Posture is very important. It shows people you respect yourself."

That information has helped me many times over the years, at job interviews or social gatherings.

It was obvious Grandma wore some type of foundation, but I had never been able to ask her about it.

Then one day in the mid-1950s, she took my sister and me to the Sears store in downtown St. Louis. We had no idea what we were doing there until she introduced us to the saleslady as *the two to be fitted for a foundation*.

Solid Foundation

My sister and I gave each other that "If only I had known, I wouldn't have come" look. And when the lady started taking our measurements, we yelled out how we were only 12 and 10.

That argument didn't wash, though, as Grandma said *she'd* worn a foundation since age 16. Then I asked her if that was why she sometimes smelled like rubber. This didn't go over very well either.

We were finally given girdles to try

> ## *"I couldn't hurt Grandma's feelings by refusing to wear it..."*

---

on and went into the dressing room. Once inside, we couldn't stop laughing as we tried to squeeze ourselves into what felt like rubber bands.

Grandma lost her temper, stormed into the dressing room and warned, "Stop playing around and finish putting on those foundations! Be out here in 2 minutes to show us."

FIT TO BE TIED. Author (above left) and sister Sharon were no match for Grandma, Ethna Wayland (left), when it came time to turn their figures into the so-called ideal (right), made possible by an old-fashioned corset.

When we stepped out, Grandma was the one who couldn't help laughing. We had the girdles on upside down *and* inside out!

Grandma then went into the dressing room with us and showed us how to put the things on.

So we wore them. We were the only grandchildren who were a bit overweight, and Grandma felt we needed a little help.

I hated it, but Grandma had very little money, and she paid for the girdles. It must have been very important to her, so I couldn't hurt her feelings by refusing to wear it.

Comfort Not Considered

I later found out Grandma's foundation was one of those full corsets, with hooks and laces, when she stayed overnight at our house.

Grandma was modest, and after she took off her dress, she'd pull her flannel nightgown over her head, not using the

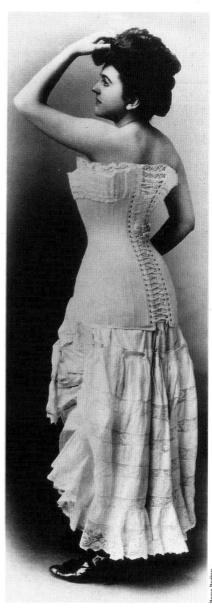

armholes. Then she'd take off her slip and start the struggle to untie and unhook her corset.

I'd have to be careful so she didn't see me laughing. It looked like she was fighting with a wild animal under there.

Then the struggle ended. Grandma would heave a loud sigh of relief as she whipped the corset out from under her nightgown.

I always felt relief for her because she looked so much more comfortable without the corset. Appearance was very important to Grandma, and I guess she felt she looked better with a corset than without.

I wish I could have seen Grandma today as a "free" woman. I think she would have loved the comfy and popular sweat suits and tennis shoes worn by so many women nowadays. ☎

Remember Syrup Squirts and Soda Jerks?

By Julien Tracy
Carmel Valley, California

A FEW WEEKS before the attack on Pearl Harbor, I began working in a drugstore in Los Gatos, California making deliveries, cleaning and clerking. The owner must have made quite an impression on me, since I eventually became a pharmacist myself.

I can still hear Mr. Brown's old oak swivel chair creak as he'd lean back and reminisce about the evolution of the soda fountain: "The drugstore fountain arrived at about the same time as Prohibition. We already had mineral waters, particularly soda water, in our pharmacy stock, and we also carried flavoring oils, extracts and syrups.

"The development of refrigeration, ice cream and Prohibition all conspired to put the druggist in the fountain business. And, as the syrups and flavoring agents moved from the pharmacy to the fountain, their ancient titles were often lost or forgotten.

"*Syrupus Cacao*, for example, became Chocolate Syrup, while *Syrupus Cerasi* became Cherry Syrup. *Syrupus Rubi Idae* was labeled Raspberry Syrup, and *Syrupus Aurantii* turned into Orange Syrup. Only *Syrup of Sarsaparilla* managed to cling to its pharmaceutical title for a few years before it was finally called root beer. By 1929, over half the drugstores in the country had their own fountain."

Drugstore Was a Gathering Place

Mr. Brown's little history lesson may have helped me appreciate the drugstore fountain a little more during the long, hot afternoons when the lines of tar in the pavement became soft and the surrounding hills shimmered in a heat haze.

That's when the local drugstore became a gathering place for our town's schoolkids. Back then, just entering the drugstore held a special gift of magic.

When the large oak doors with their beveled glass panes were swung open, the rays of the afternoon sun were refracted, sending a scattering of colored points across the white hexagonal floor tiles.

As you stepped inside, the fountain was the first thing you noticed—regally elevated on a marble step, it filled up the whole right side of the store. The counter's surface was a huge cool slab of white marble, lightly streaked with gray.

In front of the counter were the stools covered with padded leather cushions secured by a chrome ring, which swiveled on white enameled pedestals. Whenever I treated my girlfriend to an after-school Coke, the stools would creak as we turned from side to side.

After we had ordered our Cokes, the fountain man would remove one of the round, black rubberized covers from the freezer cabinet and crack bits of ice into the glasses with a pick.

He'd pump in three squirts of Coke syrup and carefully add the carbonated water down the side of the tipped glass so as not to create too much foam.

If we'd ordered a lemon Coke or a chocolate Coke,

MAY I HELP YOU? Julien Tracy (today at top left) became a pharmacist (above) after an early introduction to the job.

he'd add a half squirt of the flavoring syrup. The final touch was a delicate swirl with a long-handled spoon.

Along the back bar of the fountain was a long mirror. While lingering over our Cokes, we self-consciously studied each other's reflections between perusals of our comic books—*Wonder Woman, Flash Gordon* or *Mandrake the Magician*. Meanwhile, the nearly constant drone of the compressor was a pleasant accompaniment through the warm afternoon—sweet music from the "Golden Era"…the good old days of the drugstore soda fountain. ☎

thing". She said he was a crook and would either keep the peaches himself or sell them to someone else.

I listened with big ears for a 4-year-old and wondered, myself, if Mom was making a mistake.

But Mom held her ground, and the peaches stayed on the porch. She told everyone who advised her not to do it that she would give the peaches in good faith, and it was up to Earl what he did with them.

"For heaven's sake," she said, "it's just a jar of peaches!" They were finally picked up a few days before Thanksgiving. On Thanksgiving Eve, as we were getting ready for bed, there was a knock on our door and we heard footsteps quickly leaving.

Truth Came as a Shock

When Mom opened the door, she found a box of food on our porch. We were overwhelmed because Mom never really thought of us as being poor. She always stressed how much we *had*, not what we lacked, and taught us to thank the Lord for His blessings. Therefore we didn't expect that anyone would bring *us* a Thanksgiving basket! Excited, we brought it in and began to unpack the goodies.

There was a freshly dressed chicken, some potatoes, dried beans, rice, flour, canned pumpkin and—you guessed it—the jar of peaches Mom had canned herself and given to Earl. She sat on the floor and cried.

I walked with her to the kitchen, where she carefully placed the jar of peaches right back in the empty spot on the top shelf it had left just a few days before. It had come home, bringing all the other good things with it, and we had a scrumptious Thanksgiving dinner the next day.

"You can't outgive God," Mom said as she prepared our meal. "You reap what you sow."

My young mind saw the fruit of Mom's faith, and it made an indelible impression on me. Mother made sure the whole neighborhood knew about the goodness of the Lord, and after that, I never heard anyone call Mom a fool.

'It's Just a Jar Of Peaches'

By Evelyn Smith, Charleston, West Virginia

MOTHER had a lot of faith in God, which she truly needed in 1933. My sister was a baby, and I wasn't old enough to go to school. Dad had left us, and the Great Depression was at its worst. Mom took in washing to make a living.

Around that time, several missions for the poor sprang up in Charleston, West Virginia, where we lived. One was run by Reverend Earl Hissom. He lived in a poor section of town and began preaching in an abandoned storefront, which grew into a church building with a ministry to the needy. Gradually he could afford to air a radio program in the mornings, which Mom would turn on after she got my sister and me up. His message was always one of hope.

On his program a few days before Thanksgiving, Rev. Hissom (everyone called him Earl) asked for food donations to be set out so that his truck could pick them up. Volunteers, he explained, would sort it all out and deliver baskets to the poorer sections of town the night before the holiday.

When Mom heard the request, she went to the kitchen and took a jar of home-canned peaches from the pantry, then set it out on the front porch for the truck to pick up.

The neighbors who saw this told Mom she was too poor to give away that jar of peaches. One, a particularly cynical woman, called Mom a "fool for giving Earl Hissom any-

RP Photo

STILL STANDING. Evelyn (right) recently visited her childhood home (below). "You can see the spot where Mom (that's her at top) left the peaches. I wish she was alive to read this story because she loved *Reminisce.*"